Life² BOOK

WITH LUCAS

DAILY READINGS
THROUGHOUT THE YEAR

JEFF LUCAS

The excerpts in this compilation were taken from issues of *Lucas on Life Every Day*,
previously published as Jan/Feb, Mar/Apr, May/Jun, July/Aug, Sep/Oct, Nov/Dec 2006.
First published in this format 2009 by CWR, Waverley Abbey House, Waverley Lane,
Farnham, Surrey GU9 8EP, UK. Registered Charity No. 294387. Registered Limited
Company No. 1990308.

For full list of National Distributors visit www.cwr.org.uk.

Unless otherwise indicated, all Scripture references are from the Holy Bible: New
International Version (NIV), copyright © 1973, 1978, 1984 by the International Bible
Society.

Concept development, editing, design and production by CWR
Cover image: CWR
Printed in Finland by WS Bookwell
ISBN: 978-1-85345-500-1

Contents

Introduction

Living in Colorado means that every day, when it comes to the weather, comes as a surprise. The locals have a saying: 'If you don't like the weather, just wait 15 minutes.' It really is that changeable. Last week we were sunning ourselves in high temperatures and smiling at gorgeous blue skies; this morning it's cold, rainy and snow is expected. Everything changes so suddenly.

And so it is with life. Personally, I'd like to vote for non-stop sunny days where all is joy, worries don't gather like storm clouds, and the outlook is endlessly summery. But real life brings unexpected downpours and sometimes frightening lightning strikes. The laugh-out-loud birthdays, the tearfully joyful weddings and the days when life seems just as it should be, are punctuated by other times of stress, sickness and sadness. The Lord promises us that we will have joy and trouble both. No one is excluded. Life is seasonal.

That's why it's so vital that those who follow Jesus know His Word and His ways. We must be prepared for the unanticipated seasons of life that all experience. To be caught without an umbrella in a sudden monsoon is foolish, but not tragic. To find ourselves caught in an eclipse-of-the-sun-type tragedy without a torch would be dangerous. Scripture offers us wise counsel and direction on the basic educational necessity required of those who are breathing: how to do life. Through this second compilation of *Life Every Day*, I pray that you'll be informed, challenged, inspired and, yes, amused at times. I've decided that life is far too serious to be taken seriously all the time, and so as I share some of my own follies and foibles along the way (I've got no shortage of material, sadly) I pray that this journey we share together will be one of strength and enjoyment, and that we really will discover that God's Word is a lamp to our feet.

So thanks for joining me. May God's truth strengthen us for the winter times. And if it's summer in your life right now, I'm glad. Just remember the sunscreen.

God bless you

Jeff Lucas

Independence Days?

Independence Days?

As we think about 'Independence Days?' and look at the world of Samuel and Saul, we come to a blockbuster of a story that is loaded with drama, jealousy, corruption, nepotism, swashbuckling bravery, fear and treachery. We have an exciting journey ahead of us. Most of all, we catch a glimpse of a few very real people who tried – with varying degrees of success – to live for God in a confusing time when the trend was for everyone to do their own thing. Sound familiar?

Israel was in a mess. The nation was morally fog bound. Religion had become a pick-n-mix, suit yourself affair. The strict rules for the Levitical priesthood had been relaxed and there were numerous shrines where worshippers paid little heed to the old Mosaic regulations. Even at the Mosaic shrine at Shiloh, standards had slipped badly. Eli the priest was in charge there and despite the fact that he 'judged Israel forty years' (1 Sam. 4:18, AV), his home was in disarray.

Israel was in survival mode, living as she was never designed to live. Independent of God, ignoring His commands, oblivious to their need for His help, the people were headstrong and proud. Four intriguing characters emerge during this troubled time: Hannah, her miracle son Samuel, the tempestuous Saul and his son Jonathan.

As we consider them and their world, let's embrace the invitation to make out own declarations of independence – upon God – each and every day. And as we realise that's it's not just about beginning well, but about continuing on and finishing well too, we will remember Christianity is a marathon, not a sprint.

Thank you so much for joining me.

Yesterday need not dominate today – or tomorrow

1 Samuel 1:1–8
Jeremiah 29:11–12

We Christians are adept at looking as though we are good, respectable and fairly together. But sometimes, behind the veneer, fierce battles rage. Samuel had a home that was a long-term war zone.

> We are all shaped by our past and many of us carry bruises that persist

Weekend

His mother, Hannah, had lived for too long with unfulfilled hope. She was unable to conceive – and spent her days in the bizarre cauldron of tension that is a polygamous marriage. Her husband's other wife, Peninnah, was equipped with a fertile womb (her name means 'prolific'!) and an acid tongue. And Hannah's own marriage was challenging. Elkanah was fairly insensitive and clumsy, dispensing words of 'comfort' to his grieved wife that probably cut her deeply. The simmering rivalry would have stained the atmosphere daily. Samuel didn't remain in this home for long but his early childhood was nevertheless spent in a turbulent relational triangle.

We are all shaped by our past and many of us carry bruises that persist. Without making light of the debilitating power of our history, we do not have to be dominated by it. Hannah was not alone in her struggles and neither are we. Ask God to make this a new year of healing from the hurts of yesterday, coupled with fresh hope for tomorrow.

When your fellow worshippers think you're drunk

BIG PICTURE:
1 Samuel 1:9–18
Matthew 27:11–14

FOCUS:
'How long will you keep on getting drunk? Get rid of your wine.'
(1 Sam. 1:14)

TO BE falsely accused is always hurtful. Hannah's prayerful response to her pain was smeared as Eli called her a mumbling drunk – and suggested that she was often the worse for wear (v.14). As we saw yesterday, the bad news for Samuel was that he was raised in a home that crackled with tension. The good news was that his mother exercised a huge amount of patience and self-control.

I'm not sure that I would have done as well as Hannah. My responses to Eli might have been quite different from hers:

'Your sons are a couple of bullying crooks – who do they take after, Daddy?'

'You're the head man around here – apparently you're accustomed to seeing so-called worshippers who are out of their heads. That's your problem – not mine.'

Of course one could forgo all of the above and simply grab the feckless priest by the ears before leaving in a huff. Hannah resorted to none of these approaches and didn't storm out of the shrine, never to return, bitter and resentful. Instead, she was a model of patience, respect and graciousness (Prov. 15:1). A tricky moment that could have escalated into an ugly fight was diffused by her good character.

We will all be misunderstood; it's part of life and we can't prevent it. But we can control our responses in those testing moments. Have you been trading barbed comments with someone, freezing them out with an arctic silence that is long overdue for a thaw? Think again before you strike out – or storm out.

Prayer: Father, misunderstanding usually flares without warning. Protect my heart – and my lips – in those moments of pressure. Amen.

I SPEND a large part of my life speaking at Christian conferences and weekend retreats. Going home after a spiritual celebration can be a depressing experience. The blessing of God seems to drain away as I ponder the piles of paper waiting back at the office.

For Hannah, the annual visit to Shiloh was over: it was time for the family to return home, back to domesticity – and the probability of renewed conflict with the turbo-tongued Peninnah.

But the blessing of God was going home with Hannah. As normal life resumed, behind the scenes God was at work. Samuel was conceived through the normal sexual relationship between Elkanah and Hannah. No angel appeared, no voice from heaven spoke. Simply, a man and a woman made love. And as Elkanah 'knew' his wife, the Lord 'remembered' her. Of course, God had never forgotten Hannah – but this word is used to describe His response to her cries. The child of promise was conceived within her, not a virgin birth but a miracle baby nonetheless.

God often works His miracles quietly. Gently He breaks into our days with provision and peace, protection and grace – particularly when we ask Him to. His voice is sometimes so small and still, His intervention so subtle, that we forget that today's blessings are the answers to yesterday's prayers and we forget to be thankful. But Hannah knew that her pregnancy was no coincidence and chose a name that celebrated the Answering God. The child was named 'Samuel', meaning 'Name of God' or 'A godly name'.

Prayer: Lord, give me faith when I can't see Your hand at work, and discernment to see it working more. Amen.

God lives at your house

BIG PICTURE:
1 Samuel 1:19–20
Acts 7:44–49

FOCUS:
'Early the next morning they arose and worshipped before the LORD and then went back to their home ... Elkanah lay with Hannah his wife, and the LORD remembered her.'
(1 Sam. 1:19)

.

God often works

His miracles

quietly

Costly worship

BIG PICTURE:
1 Samuel 1:21–28
Mark 14:32–36

FOCUS:
'So now I give him to the
LORD. For his whole life
he shall be given over to
the LORD.'
(1 Sam. 1:28)

LOVE is extravagant. It goes the extra mile, buys flowers when there's no event to 'justify' the purchase and jumps through creative hoops to express itself. Hannah gave her child up for divine adoption, not because God required it but as a free will, over-the-top offering that was truly breathtaking.

After weaning young Samuel, she could have been tempted to wait until the annual sacrifice came around again, particularly as Elkanah had gone ahead. She faced a journey alone with a small child. This decision would have bought her a few more precious months with her son. She could have cited the moral decline at Shiloh as a reason to delay – why should she entrust her child to a man who thought that the fervency of a praying woman was fuelled by alcohol abuse? Instead, she did what she had promised.

And her vow was a response to the love and provision of God. She gave Samuel away, not to earn God's favour but because she realised that the favour of God was already upon her and her boy. That's the difference between the true believer and the religious legalist. The believer, moved by grace, offers their life in response to that amazing love. The legalist, convinced of their ability to 'buy favour' with God, tries to score points. One is performance-based acceptance (I'll be committed so that God will love me') and the other, acceptance-based performance ('God loves me so much, therefore I want to please Him').

Let love move you to extravagance today. That's true worship.

Prayer: I offer myself freely, gladly and gratefully to You, loving God. Help me obey as a delight and not just as duty. Amen.

I HAVE met some staunchly 'committed' Christians who were zealous over every detail but who made discipleship look profoundly unattractive. While I admired their zeal, I don't want to be like them or to sit next to them in heaven ...

As Hannah brought young Samuel to Shiloh, the cost to her as a mother was huge. She offered a carefully prepared sacrifice – new beginnings were always marked by such offerings. A young bull was sacrificed (a very expensive offering), together with wine and flour (v.24); items like these were used because they had been acquired by the sweat of the worshipper's brow. She testified and then burst into a joyful song that celebrated the unique, powerful, holy God who had 'turned things around' for her. She offered the Lord total, unreserved obedience. But Hannah's giving was not begrudging and negative – hers was a joyful, exuberant celebration.

So the farewell scene was no sad goodbye – it was more like a party than a parting. Hannah rejoiced and talked of her 'horn being lifted high'. The concept of 'a horn being exalted' is frequently used throughout Scripture (Psa. 89:17,24; 92:10; 112:9; Lam. 2:17; Dan. 7:8; Luke 1:69). It has been suggested that this is a picture of an animal which holds his head (and thus its horns) high, with pride. Hannah's reference to mocking her enemies (v.1) describes the practice of sticking out the tongue and crying 'Ha!' to your opponents.

Celebrate when you obey, give with hilarity and, dare I say it – have some fun.

Prayer: Let me be glad in my moments of greatest sacrifice. Teach me about hilarious sacrifice. Amen.

Smiling during the offering

BIG PICTURE:
1 Samuel 1:21–2:11
2 Corinthians 9:1–7

FOCUS:
'Hannah ... said: "My heart rejoices in the LORD; in the LORD my horn is lifted high. My mouth boasts over my enemies, for I delight in your deliverance."'
(1 Sam. 2:1)

Celebrate when
you obey

In sharp contrast

BIG PICTURE:
1 Samuel 2:12–17
Matthew 6:2–4

FOCUS:
'Eli's sons were wicked
men; they had no regard
for the LORD.'
(1 Sam. 2:12)

ONE evening I watched as a well-known and widely discredited television evangelist grinned, ranted, whispered and pleaded his way through what amounted to a 60-minute sales pitch for cash. The banner caption that ran across the screen aided the coercion: 'Want a new car? A new home? A new job?' I wanted to turn off the television – and did.

Greed and manipulation among leaders is no modern invention; consider the goings-on at Shiloh. As we have seen, the culprits, Hophni and Phinehas, were sons of the now elderly Eli. These two are described as 'wicked' (v.12). They were violent thugs (v.16).

The law required that the breast and right thigh of each animal offered be given to the priest and the rest eaten by the family bringing the offering. The fat of the animal was to be burned up and offered to God (Lev. 7:28–36). An alternative system had been followed at Shiloh – the priest's attendant would thrust a fork into the pot and whatever stuck to it was kept by the priest – potluck indeed. Apparently this didn't satisfy the selfish brothers – they insisted that uncooked meat be given to them, so that they could pick the best even before any offering was made to God. Not only were they selfish but they also had little concern for the methods that God had specifically ordered for the sacrifices – familiarity had bred contempt.

Be sad and prayerful at the sight of hucksters using the name of God to line their own pockets. But don't be surprised.

Prayer: Lord, save me from sliding into carelessness when I should be careful: guard my heart from the sabotage of selfishness. Amen.

Leadership standards

1 Samuel 2:18–26
Jeremiah 5:20–31

A teachable
attitude is more
valuable than
great talent or
ability

Weekend

Before we leave the wicked pair, notice how stubborn their hearts were. Eli's rebuke fell upon deaf ears – they refused to obey their father (v.25). Beware those who refuse to receive any correction in local church life – especially those who suggest that they are committed to 'God and God alone' (see 1 Cor. 1:12: 'I follow Christ'). A teachable attitude is more valuable than great talent or ability and is a character trait that all of us need to prioritise.

Against this backdrop of corruption young Samuel continued to serve God with patience and integrity – the darker the night, the brighter the light can shine. Dressed in a linen ephod provided annually by his mother, he 'grew up in the presence of the LORD' (v.21) and continued to 'grow in stature and in favour with the LORD and with men' (v.26 – see Luke 2:52 for a similar phrase used to describe the young Jesus). As for Hannah, she continued to enjoy the favour of God too, giving birth to further children, three sons and two daughters.

Samuel spent his early years surrounded by conflict and corruption – but still managed to make great choices for God and serve faithfully.

Out with the old, in with the new

BIG PICTURE:
1 Samuel 2:27–36
Romans 6:16–18

FOCUS:
'I will raise up for myself
a faithful priest, who will
do according to what is
in my heart and mind.'
(1 Sam. 2:35)

AN ANONYMOUS man of God went to Eli to prophesy chilling judgment upon him, his sons and the Eliad family line. It was to be confirmed by a sign – the death of Hophni and Phinehas in one 24-hour period (v.34). Eli was told that he was without excuse, considering all that God had done for him and his family in the past. The reference to Eli's father probably refers to God's historical dealings with the Levites.

But words of judgment are usually married to words of hope. God was preparing to raise up a 'faithful priest', one after His own heart. The old order would be cleared away, leaving an empty stage for new leadership. Surprisingly, this prophetic word probably doesn't refer to Samuel but to Zadok, a priest of David, who came to prominence under Solomon. Zadok's family would fill the position of the Jerusalem high priesthood for some eight centuries.

The prophetic word was fulfilled ultimately in 1 Samuel 22, when the descendants of Eli were massacred by Saul at Nob. As for Hophni and Phinehas, they both died on the same day (1 Sam. 4:11).

Sin is highly contagious. When I think about my life, I wish holiness was as catching. But it can be so easy to fool ourselves that, as the song says, 'a little bit of what you fancy does you good'. Eli's story – a man who apparently gave his sons a mild telling-off and then sat down to fill his stomach with their immoral spoils – shows that the song is misguided.

Prayer: Deliver me, Lord, from beliefs that don't translate into solid actions. Give me a tender heart – even to Your rebuke – today. Amen.

A voice in the night

BIG PICTURE:
1 Samuel 3:1–6
Psalm 29:1–11

FOCUS:
'Then the LORD called
Samuel. Samuel
answered, "Here I am."
And he ran to Eli and
said, "Here I am; you
called me."'
(1 Sam. 3:4–5)

GOD obviously is on speaking terms with us. Whether that voice is heard as we read Scripture, admire creation, listen to wisdom from friends, bump into passing angels, dream strange dreams or sense a whisper in our hearts, there's no doubt we can hear from heaven. The idea may seem strange but God's desire to communicate with us is undiminished.

Yet hearing from God isn't as easy as some make it sound. Discerning His voice from what might just be the passing whispers of imagination can be quite a challenge – as Scripture acknowledges here. Samuel, in an almost amusing episode, tried to tune in to God – and at first, he wasn't clear who was on the line.

It was probably shortly before dawn when it happened – the priests lit the temple lamps from evening until morning (Exod. 27:21) and here we read 'the lamp of God had not yet gone out' (v.3). Samuel was asleep beside the ark and God spoke, calling his name. The confusion that follows illustrates the point – hearing from God isn't always so straightforward.

Becoming familiar with His voice is a learned art, a skill that is sharpened over years; as we continue the lifelong journey that is faith, we can become more attuned to the sound of that voice.

Others can help us with that learning; even Eli, now under judgment, was able to let young Samuel know that a very special messenger was calling. Listening is learned – let others who've 'had ears to hear' help you to learn how.

Prayer: I open my heart and my ears to You today, Lord. If You would like to speak, I'm listening. Amen.

Becoming familiar with His voice is a learned art

More on listening

BIG PICTURE:
1 Samuel 3:7–10
Isaiah 6:6–13

FOCUS:
'Then Samuel said,
"Speak, for your servant
is listening."'
(1 Sam. 3:10)

SOMETIMES we can be intense about hearing from God, as if He will only speak when we're fasting, engaging in hours of passionate intercession or attempting to get our names listed in the *Guinness Book of Records* for attendance at Christian events.

But God's voice can be heard in the midst of the mundane. Samuel was relaxing when God came to him and after the third call, he was told to lie down as usual – no sacrifice to offer, no religious posture to assume. God delights to reveal Himself to ordinary people as they go about their everyday business – so the news of the Messiah's birth came to shepherds on their night shift (Luke 2:8). We should notice, however, that Samuel then made himself specifically available to hear God – the Lord will not shout above the noise of our frantic busyness: we need to learn the art of being still – and then we will know that He is God (Psa. 37:7; 46:10).

God's voice often sounds 'familiar'. The notion that God only speaks with a booming voice should be left in Hollywood. Three times young Samuel confused the voice of the Lord with the voice of his master Eli. Often we fail to hear God because we have preconceived ideas about how His voice should sound.

When God speaks, He looks for an obedient reaction to His word; Samuel heard his name called five times – but no more was said to him until he had made a response of availability as the 'servant' of the Lord (v.10).

Prayer: Lord, meet me in my busyness, in my resting, in noise and in quietness. Wherever, whenever You choose, please meet me. Amen.

When God speaks, He looks for an obedient reaction to His word

REMEMBER the wicked witch who demanded 'Mirror, mirror, on the wall, who's the fairest of them all?' The magic mirror was supposed to come up with the same answer and risked a smashing if it didn't obediently reply, 'You, my queen.'

It's possible for us to only want to hear encouragement, agreement and endorsement from our friends, even when we are making disastrous decisions. Anyone who says what we don't want to hear becomes the enemy and is banished or at least marginalised.

Samuel initially resisted telling his aged mentor about what was to come but finally shared the bad news.

Eli had brought him up, blessed his parents, trained him and taught him how to discern the voice of God. Now Samuel was the bearer of a terrible word from the Lord. Notice the tenderness as Eli described Samuel as 'My son' (vv.6,16). Servants of God should find no joy in proclaiming judgment or in rebuking others, however necessary that painful work might be. Eli, to his credit, realised the boy's dilemma and so commanded him in the strongest possible terms (by putting him under an oath) to hold nothing back – truth, however unpalatable, must be told.

'Niceness' is not always righteousness. Faithfulness to one another will demand that we learn to receive loving rebuke – which can really help us to grow, if we are open and willing to hear (Psa. 141:5). Let's give others permission to say what we don't want to hear. And, when needed and with care, we must say words that we'd prefer not to say to others.

Prayer: Give me grace to hear what I don't want to hear and to speak faithfully to others when it's easier to stay silent. Amen.

Faithful wounds

BIG PICTURE:
**1 Samuel 3:11–21
Proverbs 27:6**

FOCUS:
"'What was it he said to you?" Eli asked. "Do not hide it from me. May God deal with you ... if you hide from me anything he told you.'"
(1 Sam. 3:17)

Pride and presumption

BIG PICTURE:
1 Samuel 4:1–11
Jeremiah 48:29–35

FOCUS:
'Why did the LORD bring defeat upon us today ...? Let us bring the ark of the LORD's covenant ... so that it may ... save us from the hand of our enemies.'
(1 Sam. 4:3)

SOMETIMES faith can descend into mere superstition, where we don't bother with God until an emergency hits and then try to wheel Him out like a good luck charm, a heavenly rabbit's foot. The Israelites treated the ark of the covenant rather like that; a talisman as a last resort.

Judgment day arrived as Philistia mounted a major attack upon Israel. In panic, the Israelite elders called for the ark to be brought to the battlefield, hoping that it would bring victory. Hophni and Phinehas arrived with the ark, greeted by enthusiastic roars. So boisterous was the response that 'the ground shook' (v.5). The battle had now become a 'holy war' – so the Israelites thought. But it was a vain hope. Disaster struck and the unimaginable happened: the Israelites suffered a crushing defeat. Over 30,000 men died, including the infamous Hophni and Phinehas, both slain on the same day as promised. The Philistines captured the ark; the Israelite survivors fled to the safety of home. They had hoped for much. They lost everything.

Israel's defeat was the prophecy fulfilled but it was also due to a national attitude of presumption and pride. Israel asked, 'Why did the LORD bring defeat upon us?' (v.3) but never waited for the answer, leaning instead on their history – symbolised by the ark – rather than a current commitment to God.

Let's check that our friendship with God is current and alive. The Lord wants us to know Him as a lifelong friend – and not just as a lifeguard.

Prayer: Lord, forgive me for only calling upon You when there's an emergency. Give me faithfulness and faith. Amen.

God *is* with us

What is your earliest memory? Mine is of my father waltzing around with me in his arms. I can recall nestling my face into his neck and the warm assurance that came. I was safe because Dad was close. His presence quietened my heart.

Throughout Scripture, God continuously offers the promise that He will always be with us. Eden was paradise because God strolled with Adam and Eve; heaven will be heavenly because we will be with God forever, seeing Him face to face (1 Cor. 13:12). Jesus never said that His followers would escape trouble – on the contrary – but promised He would always be with them.

> Jesus never said that His followers would escape trouble

This is a sombre episode, as Israel is defeated, Eli's sons are killed, he collapses and dies and then a tragic baby – Ichabod – (the name means 'the glory has departed') is born. The scene is laden with darkness and there's little hope. Israel mourns, not just as a defeated nation but because the ark – the symbol of God's presence – is lost.

But another baby has now been born – and that nativity means that we are not alone. He is Jesus, Immanuel, God with us (Matt. 1:23).

Whatever questions loom today, this one is answered. He is with us.

Weekend

The great big God

BIG PICTURE:
1 Samuel 5:1–5
Isaiah 40:9–26

FOCUS:
'The following morning when they rose, there was Dagon, fallen on his face on the ground before the ark of the LORD!' (1 Sam. 5:4)

IT'S a song that's more ancient than modern now: 'He's got the whole world in His hands'. But it's still true. Jesus is not the western God. We need to reaffirm the reality that there is only one God – He is God of all the earth – and the universe with it.

The Philistines returned in triumph to Ashdod (vv.1–2), an important seaport city and a formidable stronghold, which had survived many attacks. But their party wouldn't last long. Trouble began as the captured ark was placed in the temple of Dagon, the chief god of the Philistines.

Perhaps military pride drove them to display their spoils of war – or a hunger for more power, as they tried – in vain – to combine the power of Yahweh and Dagon together. Whatever their motive, it was a bad idea. Early morning worshippers found the Dagon idol, face down before the ark of God (vv.3–4). Yahweh's glory shone bright, even in the mightiest stronghold of the Philistines. The bowing scene was repeated the next day but this time Dagon's head and hands were broken off as well and were found lying on the threshold of the temple (v.4). It was widely believed at this time that demons lived under the thresholds of buildings and that they would punish anyone who stepped on them, so some would jump through entrances in order to avoid demonic wrath. This practice was condemned as pagan superstition in Zephaniah 1:9. The Philistines refused to tread on the threshold from that day on (v.5).

Our God is no local hero: He holds the keys of death and hell (Rev. 1:18). He is Lord; there is no other.

Prayer: Father, in a world of many 'gods', help me to speak about You with clarity, confidence, compassion and kindness. Amen.

YESTERDAY we saw that Jesus is Lord of all the earth. Today we affirm that every inhabitant of our planet is in the same boat – all need saving grace, because 'all have sinned'. That's not to say there aren't some truly wonderful people who are not believers. Goodness is not exclusively Christian. There are some people, who will do marvellous things today, who have no knowledge of God. But the reality of the human condition remains. We weren't designed for independence. We all desperately need God.

The Philistines, with their plethora of 'gods', still needed the real One. A terrible wave of sickness broke out in Ashdod (v.6), possibly a bubonic plague spread by rats. The Ashdodites saw a connection between the curse of sickness and their possession of the ark and, after holding a tribal council, hastily packed it off to Gath (vv.7–8). There the same plague broke out (v.9).

There are a number of parallels between the plight of Israel in chapter 4 and that of the Philistines in chapter 5. The Philistine tribal leaders gathered together in council: it was Israel's tribal council that had tried to use the ark as a quick fix, with tragic results. The battle had been fierce for Israel (1 Sam. 4:2) – now the hand of Yahweh was 'heavy' against the Philistines (v.7).

It had never dawned on the Israelites to ask why God was not blessing them. And the idea of bowing before Yahweh alongside their twice-fallen Dagon never dawned on the Philistines.

Everyone, without exception, needs God. Don't be lulled into thinking that your caring friend can make it without Jesus.

Prayer: Lord, keep before me the reality that everyone, no matter how good, shares the same need – for You. Amen.

The human condition

BIG PICTURE:
1 Samuel 5:6–12
Romans 3:9–31

FOCUS:
'So they called together all the rulers of the Philistines and asked them, "What shall we do with the ark of the god of Israel?"' (1 Sam. 5:8)

Goodness is not exclusively Christian

An unusual offering – and a test

BIG PICTURE:
1 Samuel 6:1–12
Jeremiah 15:19–21

FOCUS:
'What shall we do with the ark of the LORD? Tell us how we should send it back to its place.'
(1 Sam. 6:2)

IT'S not a gift I'd enjoy, so take it off your Christmas list. A golden tumour is an odd present.

Seven long and agonising months of fierce judgment had dragged on for the Philistines, as the plagues continued (v.1). A final solution was needed but where could the desperate Philistines go for answers? They turned to their own magicians and diviners for advice (v.2).

Ten golden gifts – five rats and five tumours – were made and a new cart was used to transport the ark, harnessed to two milk cows that had been separated from their calves.

In the sending there was a test. The Philistines wanted to know conclusively: had the outbreak of the plagues simply coincided with the capture of the ark – or had the hand of God truly been raised against them?

God certainly overruled that day. Two milk cows attached to a cart for the first time are unlikely to produce progress in any direction. Total confusion and an ark thundering around in circles would be more likely. To add to the potential chaos, the cows were milking when their calves were snatched away, so they would have to defy all their maternal instincts to walk away from their young. But the unlikely is likely when God is at work and even though the cows went on their way 'lowing' – grumbling and complaining – they went straight to Beth Shemesh. When God sees genuinely repentant hearts, He responds quickly. Peace that was plundered by bad choices returns; and God, rather than putting us on probation, comes to lovingly take up the reins of our lives again.

Prayer: Lord, teach me to be sensitive to You when I sin; to repent and know Your order in my life afresh. Amen.

REPENT. It sounds like a word from the past, one to be used by a fierce street evangelist. But repentance is a bridge to better days. Yesterday we saw that God responded to the imperfect yet eager repentance of the Philistines. Their response is worth a second look.

An anatomy of repentance

BIG PICTURE:
1 Samuel 6:1–12
2 Corinthians 7:8–13

FOCUS:
'So they did this.'
(1 Sam. 6:10)

The contrite Philistines tried to repair the damage that they had done. Some translators describe the unusual golden items as 'reparation' offerings – they made costly restitution. Repentance that makes no attempt to restore is shallow.

And they climbed down from their high horses of pride. The gold tumours and mice would be a lasting reminder of the humbling of the Philistines at the hand of Yahweh. Repentance is not a moment of emotional response but a lasting humbling of the heart that bears long-term fruit.

They did repentance God's way. Eager not to offend Him, the Philistines were meticulous about the demands and requirements that they thought He might have. It wasn't only the cows that literally went out of their way for Yahweh – so did the Philistines. There was no attitude of presumption that characterised Israel in the earlier battle. The Philistines didn't treat this ceremony as a mechanical means to get Yahweh's blessing but rather hoped that perhaps He would 'lift his hand' from them (v.5). Arrogance and presumption were gone.

And they were keen to know that their apology had been accepted. The milk-cow test would be a final indicator that God had responded to their cries.

Repentance: it's more than a quick 'Sorry' before another excursion into sin. It's a heart change that leads to life change – and one that God always notices.

Prayer: Lord, give me a heart that rushes to repentance and lingers there. Take me beyond 'Sorry'. Amen.

Repentance ...

a heart change

that leads to

life change

Welcoming the Lord

BIG PICTURE:
1 Samuel 6:13–7:1
Psalm 96:1–13

FOCUS:
'But God struck down some of the men of Beth Shemesh, putting seventy of them to death because they had looked into the ark of the LORD.'
(1 Sam. 6:19)

IT WAS a day of cheers and tears. The Philistines' nervous, wholehearted acts of repentance worked. The cows towing the ark-cart suddenly stopped in the field of Joshua in Beth Shemesh, a border town on the edge of Philistine and Israelite influence. Many of the Israelites welcomed the ark with a celebration of reverent joy. It was a great day – but with a tragic postscript.

The sons of Jeconiah (a family of 70) were struck dead by the Lord. The Greek manuscript of this text says that they were put to death 'because they refused to join in with the celebrations'. This seems harsh to us but we need to remember that the town was witnessing a major miracle of God – and yet there were still those who were indifferent. Yet again a cry went up because of the ark of God: 'Who can stand in the presence of the LORD, this holy God?' (v.20).

We need to be reverent when we come to God – but some suggest that this means always bowing down and being quiet. I have frequently heard people criticise noisier worship as 'irreverent'. 'You wouldn't enter the presence of an earthly monarch while clapping and dancing' – so the argument goes. But to revere someone is to show that person respect and obedience. The King of kings has decreed that silence, bowing, clapping, dancing, shouting with a loud voice and a host of other expressions of worship all please Him; therefore we can do all of these things – and revere God as we do so. Reverence is a matter of heart, not style.

Prayer: Lord, when You move, may I notice Your work; teach me to truly cherish and revere You. Amen.

It's been a long time

1 Samuel 7:2
Luke 18:1–8

Some Christians give the impression that their spiritual life is loaded with hourly breathtaking encounters with God. While I don't want to discount the reality that God certainly *is* actively at work in our lives, there are times when we feel not much is happening. Samuel must have felt that way. Following the return of the ark, the celebration was shortlived. Israel fell into a spiritual slumber for 20 years. The writer sums up this sad season: 'It was a long time ...'

Prayer
demands
perseverance

I love it when my feelings match my faith and when I can point to a major, current answer to prayer that cheers me. But there are times when we just have to hang on – perseverance is vital in the Christian life.

Weekend

Prayer demands perseverance (Luke 18:1–8), suffering takes on a positive role, in that it teaches us endurance (Rom. 5:3; James 1:3) which in turn produces true character (Rom. 5:4; 2 Pet. 1:6) and maturity (James 1:4).

A pictorial illustration of the word 'persevere' is to be found in Mark 3:9 where it describes a small boat that was 'kept waiting ready' for Jesus – the word here in the Greek is 'persevere'. Has it been a long time? Stay moored in faith.

27

Rediscovering clarity

BIG PICTURE:
1 Samuel 7:3–10
Romans 6:1–14

FOCUS:
'We have sinned against
the LORD.' (1 Sam. 7:6)

I'VE come to the conclusion that sin is like a drug that attacks our critical faculties, like a powerful hallucinogenic. It ushers in a madness where all the familiar moral landmarks that have guided us, perhaps for years, become lost in a fog of desire. Temptation invites us to throw ourselves headlong into choices that we know will offend God, damage us, destroy our credibility and hurt those who are dearest to us. We know in advance that ultimately sin will not satisfy us: the Bible says it and our experience confirms it. The nudge towards sin is the invitation to be banished from Eden for the sake of a piece of fruit; a very bad deal. Yet still we can mess up our lives, suckered by sin's wiles.

True repentance reverses that madness, recovering clarity. Called together at Mizpah, the site of earlier religious gatherings (Judg. 20:1,3; 21:1,5,8), Israel benefits from the directive leadership of Samuel, now an adult. He prays for the nation (v.5) and then leads the people through a public U-turn that includes pouring out water, fasting and confession (v.6). It's difficult to define the exact reason for the ritual but pouring and fasting are associated with repentance in the Old Testament (Lam. 2:19). Perhaps this was a prophetic drama symbolising the flow of tears from a nation of rebels.

The Israelites made no attempt to excuse their rebel years, declaring, 'We have sinned against the LORD.' Repentance names sin as sin and banishes the rationalising with a newfound focus. Been living for a while in madness? Name it for what it is.

Prayer: Save me, Lord, from the mind-altering madness that wilful sin brings. Give me a heart of clarity and purity. Amen.

We know in
advance that
ultimately sin will
not satisfy us

THE circus clown is fun to watch, because he never learns. His bumps and scrapes are predictable – and he keeps going back for more.

Yesterday we saw that sin can mentally mug us, creating confusion in our minds and behaviour. But we can get revenge. When we use failure to teach us rather than just shame us and our darker moments become stepping-stones to greater maturity, then we redeem something from our stumbling. Yet, if sin creates madness, it also engenders amnesia, where we forget how painful yesterday's foolishness was and so march headlong into trouble today. Some of us spend our whole lives in that stupor of moral forgetfulness and go to the grave having never 'got wise' to sin.

Ebenezer had previously been a location associated with tragedy and defeat. It was there that the pride and presumption of Israel had brought about the loss of the ark to the Philistines (1 Sam. 4). Now Samuel erects a stone and names it 'Ebenezer', meaning 'stone of help'. Erecting a permanent marker to remind subsequent generations of the works of God is a practice recorded in Genesis 28:18 and Joshua 4:6. Building a pile of stones was also a sign of covenant (Gen. 31:45; Josh. 24:26).

The stone was probably named as a reminder of two very contrasting days of battle; one of disaster (1 Sam. 4) and one of dependency (1 Sam. 7).

Don't wallow around in the mire of failure. Get up and learn from the experience. That way you're less likely to make the same mistake repeatedly. The alternative is truly to play the clown – or fool.

Prayer: Lord, redeem my failures as I learn from them. Give me a wise heart, avoiding the pathway of the fool. Amen.

Getting your own back on sin

BIG PICTURE:
1 Samuel 7:11–17
Proverbs 10:10–23

FOCUS:
'Thus far has the LORD helped us.' (1 Sam. 7:12)

What's your blind spot?

BIG PICTURE:
**1 Samuel 8:1–4
Matthew 23:16–26**

FOCUS:
'Samuel … appointed his sons as judges for Israel.'
(1 Sam. 8:1)

IT SEEMS a little extreme but a friend has a car which has a television camera installed in the rear bumper. Whenever the somewhat large 4x4 is put into reverse, a black and white image of whatever is behind appears on a screen. The reason for this costly piece of technology is the blind spot. The design of the car means that there's a small area that's impossible to see without the aid of a camera. Too many bumpers have been mashed and tragically, people have been killed – because of the blind spot.

It's possible to motor through life without ever identifying your blind spots. We've all seen parents who are blinded to reality when it comes to their children. Junior is loud, rude and has the destructive skills of a hurricane, yet his doting parents make no attempt to restrain him and seem to be thrilled about his budding career in demolition.

Samuel apparently had such a blind spot, as he appointed his sons as judges (v.1). They had noble names (Joel means 'Yahweh is God' and Abijah 'Yahweh is Father') but nobility of character is developed, not bequeathed, and bribery and corruption became the norm (v.3). We saw yesterday that we must learn from our histories; this situation was a tragic rerun of the disaster where Eli was blinded to the corrupt hearts of his sons.

Samuel couldn't see what was happening – and the elders of Israel had to sound the alarm bells. Let's ask God to show us some blind spots, where our decisions are blighted by prejudice, ignorance, emotion, pride or nepotism. Alternatively, we can crunch and collide our way through life.

Prayer: Lord, where am I blind? Open the eyes of my heart to see You and then see more of myself. Amen.

WE HUMANS like to herd.

Fashion dresses us in uniforms, as we discover what this year's 'in' colours are. Advertising screams that we *must* have this product in order to appear successful, clever or attractive. Someone has noted that we are the first generation to experience shame about our choice of mobile phone. Not to have the latest gizmo that can apparently text, surf the Internet *and* cook us a bacon sandwich is a cardinal sin. We feel the urge to fit in.

Today we are pausing to take a look at just one verse in 1 Samuel – but it describes a pivotal moment in Israel's history, as they placed their order for a king with Samuel.

Their concerns about his sons were legitimate – but the solution they proposed was not. Israel was unique in the history of the nations. No other people could boast that the God of gods was their King. But now panic and political expediency suggested a 'logical' way forward that seemed right – after all, didn't all the other nations use this method of government? Surely a human king would provide both stability and centralised efficiency, a figurehead for unity. It was time to remove Yahweh's throne – and put a human at the helm as sovereign instead (v.5).

As we mentioned yesterday, Samuel's blind spot was his nepotism – and the elders experienced the myopia that comes when you decide that something must be right because everybody else is doing it. But the logic of conformity is often flawed. Don't just get caught up in the stampede today. Sometimes the herd is heading over a cliff.

Prayer: Father, I pray today for the youth of this nation, targeted by market forces and peer pressure. Strengthen them to choose rightly. Amen.

Lemmings

BIG PICTURE:
1 Samuel 8:5
1 Peter 1:13–25

FOCUS:
'... now appoint a king to lead us, such as all the other nations have.'
(1 Sam. 8:5)

We humans like to herd

Never learning

BIG PICTURE:
1 Samuel 8:6–8
Isaiah 26:1–10

FOCUS:
'As they have done from
the day I brought them
up out of Egypt until this
day, forsaking me and
serving other gods, so
they are doing to you.'
(1 Sam. 8:8)

WE'VE seen this week just how vital it is that we learn from our mistakes, rather than going round in circles repeating them, stumbling on with the same blind spots and allowing ourselves to be seduced by the madness that sin creates in our minds.

But some of us never seem to 'get it'. George Bernard Shaw says, 'We learn from experience that men never learn anything from experience.' Take another look at the Israelite elders' demand for a king. Israel had suffered hugely because of hereditary power. Eli's sons were a disaster and now even Samuel's sons were abusing their inherited authority for personal gain. So what bright idea do the elders come up with? The answer is incredible: they asked for the establishment of a long-term monarchy, which was not only a rejection of God Himself but would also expose them to the perils of power handovers from father to potentially wayward sons. They pleaded for the long-term establishment of the very thing that had been destroying them – inherited power – a tragic example of the madness that we've been considering over these last few days.

God had seen it all before and so spoke to weary Samuel and reminded him that this pattern of rejection was nothing new. Israel had been going through the rejection/repentance/rejection cycle for years, ever since they were delivered from Egypt (v.8).

Some of us have been treading the same pathways for too long. It's time to graduate, learn the lessons from that particular regular excursion and move on.

Prayer: Lord, break any chains that bind me and break unhelpful patterns in my life. Free me by Your power. Amen.

Health warning

1 Samuel 8:9–18
Ezekiel 23:32–49

The television commercial spells out in graphic detail the awful deaths often suffered by those with lung cancer. Then we're treated to an image of a lung blackened by tar. The surprise is that the sponsor of these shock tactic ads is the largest manufacturer of cigarettes in the nation. The law requires that those who make money from nicotine addiction must spend millions warning people of the consequences of smoking.

God insists that we know what the habit of rebellion will do to our hearts and lives and so Samuel was told to warn the people about the consequences of their foolish choices (v.9). God wanted His people to go into their new governmental system with their eyes wide open; the crowning of a king would give them little – and cost them dearly. It was time to cut through their romantic notions and present them with some hard facts (vv.11–17). The elders' theme was 'Give us a king and he will give much to us.' Samuel totally contradicted this: 'If I give you a king he will take, take and take more from you.'

Planning – or drifting – into what you know is wrong? Stop. Think. Take a health warning.

> God insists that we know what the habit of rebellion will do

Weekend

Stubborn to the core

BIG PICTURE:
1 Samuel 8:19–21
Hosea 4:16–19

FOCUS:
'But the people refused to listen to Samuel. "No!" they said.'
(1 Sam. 8:19)

THERE was panic in Washington DC recently, as the pilot of a single engine Cessna plane insisted on steering his aircraft into restricted airspace around the White House, which was evacuated for fear of a terrorist attack. Apparently the hapless aviator also ignored commands to turn around, even when he found himself shadowed by menacing F-15 fighter jets, whose pilots could have been ordered to shoot him out of the sky at any moment. He just kept on going. Refusing to listen can be perilous.

The picture that Samuel painted of what a king would do was dark but it got darker still because he prophesied that there would be no hope of deliverance. The people would cry out to Yahweh but He would refuse to hear them in their hour of agony. They had chosen their own destiny despite clear and specific warnings; they had 'made their bed' – now they would have to lie in it (v.18). The language used here describes a situation that was even worse than the oppression of Israel when they lived in Egypt. There too they were in bondage but when they cried out to God, He heard them (Exod. 2:23). Now, the heavens would be as brass. God would not respond. No hope or help would be in sight.

The stony hardness of the human heart can resist even God's best efforts to help us avert disaster. The elders, undeterred by Samuel's prophetic warnings, insisted on their demand for a king. No wonder the Bible describes human beings as having a sheeplike ability to go astray. Let's listen, learn and live.

Prayer: Lord, I ask for a softened heart, ready and willing to hear and obey You. Amen.

Enter King Saul

BIG PICTURE:
1 Samuel 9:1–2
Galatians 5:1–15

FOCUS:
'... Saul, an impressive young man without equal among the Israelites – a head taller than any of the others.'
(1 Sam. 9:2)

SAUL is usually painted in dark colours, as a totally tragic figure and villain. Certainly his ending was anything but happy. But it didn't have to be that way – even though the request for a king was not what God perfectly intended, Saul was a fine man who could have made a tremendous success of the monarchy. Far from being predestined to disaster, he came from a good family, being the son of Kish, 'a man of standing' (v.1). Saul's father was wealthy and influential, or as one translator puts it, 'a powerful man' or 'a mighty warrior'.

Saul's outstanding features are emphasised as he is introduced. He was physically distinctive, being exceptionally tall and is described in glowing terms as being 'without equal among the Israelites' (v.2). The asses that were lost (donkeys were ridden only by nobility) and the servant sent to help Saul find them (v.3) also suggest a high ranking family. The mention of Saul's Benjamite background (v.1) also made him an ideal candidate for the throne, as this small tribe would never have attempted to dominate the larger tribes and therefore Saul would have been a unifying rather than a threatening figure for the nation. Saul had a great deal going for him.

It's not just how we begin our spiritual life that counts but also how we finish. Paul echoes this in his letter to the Galatians: 'You were running a good race. Who cut in on you and kept you from obeying the truth?' (Gal. 5:7). Saul's bad ending was entirely due to his own mistakes. Let's take responsibility for our own lives. God is for us as we do so.

Prayer: Lord, thank You that 'God is for me' today. Help me to choose wisely and continue today towards a good, strong finish. Amen.

It's not just how we begin our spiritual life that counts but also how we finish

Coincidences

BIG PICTURE:
1 Samuel 9:3–14
Genesis 29:2–12

FOCUS:
'They went up to the town, and as they were entering it, there was Samuel, coming towards them on his way up to the high place.'
(1 Sam. 9:14)

FOR Saul, the day had started out as a wild goose chase – or more accurately, a stray donkey chase. It must have been a hot, frustrating hunt, lasting for some three days (vv.4,20). But here begins a series of 'just happened' events.

Saul just happened to be in the area looking for donkeys and Samuel just happened to be in town that day. Saul's servant had some money, the women knew Samuel's exact whereabouts and finally, Saul and his servant just happened to walk into town and bumped into Samuel as he was walking up to the high place (v.14). A series of divinely choreographed appointments led Saul to his appointment with destiny.

The Bible contains many examples of so-called coincidental meetings that were actually carefully but quietly engineered by the hand of God. The chance encounter between Abraham's servant and Rebekah and the circumstantial sign that followed provided Isaac with a bride (Gen. 24:15–20). The meeting between Jacob and Rachel was similarly organised (Gen. 29:2–12). Other divinely appointed connections include Philip and the Ethiopian eunuch (Acts 8:27ff) and Jesus and the woman at the well (John 4:7ff). We don't need to be concerned about the steps that we take in our daily lives ('Lord, is it Your will that I visit the butcher before the grocer?') but we can be assured that as we make ourselves available for God's use and ask Him to direct our steps, some divine appointments will be set up for us. Are we up for that? Today, you might well find yourself in the right place at the right time.

Prayer: Direct my path today Lord, that I might serve, speak, or strengthen as I go. I am available for Your purposes. Amen.

AS I write this morning, I am marooned in my own house. There's a work crew outside, tarmacking the road, which is good. What isn't so wonderful is that they showed up without warning and the wet surface means that we can't drive the car off of our driveway for a few hours. Any plans we had to go somewhere are on hold – the presence of the work team, with their steam rollers and smoking trucks, is very obvious indeed.

Sometimes I wish that God's daily plans for my life were as obvious. I'd like to know what His current hopes for me are, where He's leading me next, what He would like me to avoid, what issue requires the most attention and what He'd like me to do tomorrow – in precise detail. But no such report is available and it's been noted that most of what God does, He does behind our backs. Every now and again we notice but most of His daily work in us is unannounced.

So it is with the budding king to-be, Saul; he has been 'sent by God' to Samuel. But look again. As far as Saul knew, he was just hunting for errant donkeys. No angel had ushered him towards the district of Zuph, no burning bush had flared to announce the big, widescreen plans of God for his life.

But he was sent, even though he was unaware of the sending. And God had been quietly preparing things, speaking to Samuel (literally 'uncovering his ear') giving him 24 hours' advance notice that he was about to anoint the man destined for the throne (v.15). God *is* at work, even when we don't notice.

Prayer: Prepare the way for me, Lord. Open and close doors and give me a hint of Your heart for me today. Amen.

Sent by God

BIG PICTURE:
1 Samuel 9:15–16
Philippians 1:1–11

FOCUS:
'... I will send you a man from the land of Benjamin.' (1 Sam. 9:16)

God *is* at work even when we don't notice

Disabled by insecurity

BIG PICTURE:
1 Samuel 9:17–27
Judges 6:1–16

FOCUS:
'But am I not a Benjamite, from the smallest tribe of Israel, and is not my clan the least of all the clans of the tribe of Benjamin?'
(1 Sam. 9:21)

HANNAH'S song (1 Sam. 2:1–10) was more than a catchy tune. God really does seat the weak with princes and give them thrones. But that's always a surprise. The suggestion that God knows us, loves us and wants to use us in His great kingdom agenda is one that can be difficult to accept. Most of us don't believe that God wants to have us on His team; on the contrary, we wonder why on earth He would consider using us in the first place.

Perhaps that's what Saul felt as he stammered out his protest at the suggestion that he could rule Israel. Like Gideon's similar speech (Judg. 6:15), his complaint was motivated by genuine humility. But perhaps there's a trace of something else here; Saul never managed to break free from a crushing sense of worthlessness, and the seeds of his own downfall were sown early. Whatever his motives, his comments about his own tribe were strange. The men of Benjamin enjoyed a fine reputation as brave warriors. The ancient blessing of Jacob over Benjamin was that he would be a 'ravenous wolf' (Gen. 49:27) and the tribe was famed for its special 'crack' troop of seven hundred sling shooters who could 'sling a stone at a hair and not miss' (Judg. 20:16).

Insecurity can mean that every day is yet another occasion to prove ourselves. Blinded to our own gifts and abilities, we crave approval, are devastated by small failures, endlessly compare ourselves with others and never relax into what God calls us to. Know the difference between humility and insecurity.

Prayer: Lord, set me free from a driven need to prove myself today. Help me rest secure in the knowledge of Your gracious approval. Amen.

More assurance

1 Samuel 10:1–12
Titus 3:1–7

We know that God is great, loving and powerful. But He is also kind. Paul speaks of the 'riches' of God's kindness (Rom. 2:4). It will take forever for God to show us just how stunningly kind He is (Eph. 2:7). One of the most beautiful concepts of the Old Testament is that of the 'loving kindness' of God. The original word, *hesed*, is hard to translate fully, it's so rich in meaning but it speaks of loyalty, devotion and covenant faithfulness. And it's beautifully portrayed here.

> God is great, loving and powerful ... He is also kind

An early 'wake up call' from Samuel catapulted Saul into another day of breathless excitement, a day bursting with God's words, works – and kindness.

It was time for the anointing – and then, perhaps sensing that Saul found it difficult to accept that he was God's man for the throne, Samuel prophesied a number of specific events that would unfold before Saul's eyes as the day went on. Again, God was heaping confirmation and assurance upon His nervous servant. God was shouting at Saul, like a sports coach urging his team forward with words of encouragement.

Saul was so deeply impacted by God's care that he experienced a massive change of heart even before the signs were fulfilled (v.9). God *is* kind; grace transforms us.

Weekend

Keep some things to yourself

BIG PICTURE:
1 Samuel 10:13–16
2 Corinthians 12:1–6

FOCUS:
'But [Saul] did not tell his uncle what Samuel had said about the kingship.' (1 Sam. 10:16)

PERHAPS it's my capacity to talk too much (common among preachers) but I tend to tell everybody everything – including a few things that they probably don't need to hear. Being an open book is not always wise – particularly if we are processing our thoughts and therefore make definitive statements about issues that we are still working through.

Saul's epic day ended with a visit to the place of worship (v.13) and there he met his uncle, who was eager to hear all that had happened over the last few days (vv.14–15). Saul was careful in his reply and told of how he had visited Samuel and of how the prophet had spoken of the safety of the donkeys but kept the bombshell news of his kingship to himself: no mean feat. He has just received the most epic, cataclysmic news of his life – but keeps his mouth shut. It's not always a good idea to blurt out everything that God has revealed to us – there are times to be silent (Matt. 8:4; 17:9) and there are some moments of intimacy that are really just between us and God and not for public consumption. Paul testified to the Corinthians that he was 'caught up to paradise', where he 'heard inexpressible things, things that man is not permitted to tell' (2 Cor. 12:4). Personal revolution is inevitable when either the call or anointing of God touches a human life; Saul was kissed by both on the same day – but remained silent. Know when to speak – and when to be quiet and just ponder what God has said (Luke 2:19).

Prayer: Lord, help me to be slow to speak, so that my words won't bruise, or cause me regret after I have spoken them. Amen.

THE press called her the Runaway Bride. She got the jitters the day before her wedding, staged her own abduction – and all America searched for her. When the truth came out, people were not amused – and unlike the fictional film of the same name, this runaway bride was for real.

Here's the Runaway King. It's a bizarre scene, this coronation day for Israel's first human ruler. Samuel gathered the whole of Israel together at Mizpah (v.17). Lots are cast, confirming earlier events and the roar goes up for Saul as the lot falls upon him. But he's missing. The king-to-be is crouching in the area where luggage was stored and has to be extracted from the piles of bags. Most commentators are generous to Saul at this point and feel that he hid because he wasn't anxious to step into the glare of fame. If they're right, then Saul did well. John Dryden, the sixteenth-century poet, said: 'Kings fight for nations, madmen for applause.'

But I'm not so sure. We've already marvelled at the continuous kindness of God that confirmed Saul's calling – over and over again. He knew beyond any reasonable doubt that to lead was his destiny and yet still he hides. We'll see later that Saul had a tendency to react rather than respond when under pressure; his impulsive personality was a major reason for his downfall. Demonically fuelled temper tantrums (1 Sam. 19:9) and impulsive quick fix decisions (1 Sam. 13:5–15) characterise Saul's later life. Perhaps here he allows himself to be driven more by fear than calling and so hides in desperation.

Under extreme pressure? Respond, don't react.

Prayer: Lord, thank You that You have promised to provide all that we need to serve as You require. When I am under pressure help me to respond, not react. Amen.

Fugitive royalty

BIG PICTURE:
1 Samuel 10:17–25
2 Timothy 1:1–7

FOCUS:
'… [Saul] has hidden himself among the baggage.'
(1 Sam. 10:22)

Under extreme pressure? Respond, don't react

Right, yet wrong

BIG PICTURE:
1 Samuel 10:26–27
Ephesians 4:14–16

FOCUS:
'But some troublemakers said, "How can this fellow save us?" They despised him and brought him no gifts.'
(1 Sam. 10:27)

... there are times

when it's wise

just to keep quiet

and let God

vindicate us

SOMETIMES we are right and wrong both at the same time. We hold an opinion that is valid, even biblically correct but the attitude that we have as we express that orthodox view makes us wrong. History is littered with stories of Bible-waving belligerents who were correct in their conviction but caused untold hurt and damage because of the way that they did life. It's possible to be theologically correct and still function independently of God – as the Pharisees sometimes demonstrated in Jesus' day.

Not everyone was happy with the new king. Some 'valiant' men, 'whose hearts God had touched' (v.26), volunteered to accompany their new monarch to his home. But others, described as 'troublemakers', grumbled loudly and refused to pay homage to the young Saul. These so-called troublemakers were partly right in their choice of words, 'How can this fellow save us?' At first hearing, their complaint sounded like a confession of loyalty to the saving power of Yahweh alone. But although their theology was half right, their attitude was very wrong. They were, to quote Mark Twain, 'right in the worst possible way'.

If we don't speak the truth in love (Eph. 4:15), then we don't speak the truth at all because the heart behind the words corrupts them. It's a credit to the young Saul that he kept his own mouth shut in the face of his critics (v.27). When we come under verbal attack, there are times when it's wise just to keep quiet and let God vindicate us.

Sometimes being 'right' is dangerous. Silence might be the best option.

Prayer: Lord, may I know when You want me to speak out and when You don't – and may I obey. Amen.

The dark agenda

BIG PICTURE:
1 Samuel 11:1–3
2 Corinthians 4:1–4

FOCUS:
'But Nahash the
Ammonite replied,
"I will make a treaty
with you only on the
condition that I gouge
out the right eye of
every one of you ..."'
(1 Sam. 11:2)

JABESH Gilead was an isolated and strategic border town, very vulnerable to attack, both from the Philistines as well as its neighbours, the Ammonites. Nahash, the Ammonite leader, put the city under siege and demanded that all the inhabitants enter into a covenant of servitude (vv.1–2). It was designed to ridicule Israel, as every citizen would have their right eye poked out as a sign of the new agreement. The Jewish historian Josephus has suggested that this ritual blinding was to render men unable to fight, as a soldier would cover his left eye with his shield and view the enemy with his right eye – no right eye, no fighting! But eyes were also gouged out in biblical times as a sign of complete humiliation, as in the tragic case of Samson (Judg. 16:21).

Nahash was obviously over-confident. He was so convinced of his own victory that he even gave the Gileadites seven days to consider the deal and call for help! (v.3). Here is a picture of Satan's strategy against humanity – humiliation, blindness and grief. As the accuser (Rev. 12:10) he comes to shame us, stealing the grace and peace of God from our hearts. He wants to blind us (2 Cor. 4:4), permanently destroying our vision of God and of hope. He wants to pluck joy from us, which is our strength (Neh. 8:10) and ultimately drive us into a siege of sadness.

Sin sometimes carries the offer of enlightenment and growth in maturity. The opposite is actually true. The people of Jabesh Gilead desperately needed a saviour. How much more do we.

Prayer: Lord, please give me that 20/20 vision needed to see myself as You see me. Amen.

Passion

BIG PICTURE:
1 Samuel 11:4–11
Mark 3:1–6

FOCUS:
'When Saul heard their words, the Spirit of God came upon him in power, and he burned with anger.'
(1 Sam. 11:6)

IN A big city, a woman recently gave birth – on the pavement. Bystanders hurried on, a taxi driver glanced and then drove away and a nearby hotel refused to offer a blanket. No one cared enough to help. George Bernard Shaw affirmed: 'The worst sin towards our fellow creatures is not to hate them but to be indifferent to them.' We live in a 'couldn't care less' culture, where elections often produce such a low voting turnout that no one political party has a genuine majority of the population deciding in their favour. It's been said that an appropriate epitaph for our culture could be, 'This civilisation died because it didn't want to be bothered.' The story of Israel shows that apathy is highly dangerous; often it leads to apostasy and then to anarchy.

The people of Gilead were in deep trouble and Saul, the farmer-king coming home at the end of a hard day's work in the fields, experienced an immediate and fiery ignition of anointing and anger: 'the Spirit ... came upon him ... and he burned with anger' (v.6). Righteous anger is not a passive simmering that leads to cynicism and bitterness but a desire to rise up and take action that will bring change. Samson (Judg. 14:19), Ezekiel (Ezek. 3:14), Nehemiah (Neh. 5:6) and Jesus (Mark 3:5) all experienced appropriate anger.

But notice that it is not irrational, undirected passion that changes the world, as we can see from Saul's experience. His rage at injustice was connected with the anointing of the Spirit. When we allow God to stir our hearts and direct our hands, useful things happen. Independent passion produces little but steam.

Prayer: Lord, may the anger that stirs You stir me also, that Your heart may be imprinted upon mine. Amen.

Danger: success

When Kay and I began in ministry many years ago, trusting God was easier because we had nothing. Our faith levels were high. God always took care of us – but I've noticed that as life has become easier and we don't have to hold a prayer meeting every time a bill arrives, we can drift away from that vital trust that was ours in the early days.

Success can be highly dangerous. God loves us all, but knows that some of us might not cope with great blessing, knowing that sometimes, newfound strength would cause us to drift away from Him. Saul, soaring high on the thermals of victory, could have seized the heady moment and crushed his critics. But he shows restraint.

Winston Churchill, lauded by some as Britain's saviour during the Second World War, was said to be generous in victory. Saul demonstrates that quality here, showing grace and offering an amnesty while others are calling for a mass execution. The day ends with a huge party at Gilgal. Mercy always leads to joy. But as we will see, this magnanimous character doesn't last very long in Saul; he began so well and ended so tragically.

Let's finish well.

Let's finish well

Weekend

Phone a friend

BIG PICTURE:
1 Samuel 12:1–5
John 8:42–47

FOCUS:
'Here I stand. Testify against me in the presence of the LORD and his anointed. Whose ox have I taken? Whose donkey have I taken? Whom have I cheated?'
(1 Sam. 12:3)

OVER the weekend we saw the importance of finishing well – and Samuel surely embodies that virtue. He was able to stand before the people of Israel and challenge them in a way that few of us would dare to: 'Testify against me.' He was old and grey at this stage and had spent a lifetime serving as a leader but most important of all, his integrity was intact. The New King James Version says that Samuel had 'walked before' the people (v.2), as a consistent model of living. The word 'example' (1 Tim. 4:12; Titus 2:7) means to 'strike a blow on wax' – which literally means 'make an impression'.

Samuel's words give us a few hints about potential pitfalls that might conspire to trip us up. Covetousness and greed (sins which, as we saw, Samuel's own sons slipped into) are up there at the top of the list, as Samuel is able to say that he was no thief or cheat. The abuse of power is another tripwire ('Whom have I oppressed?') together with making poor or biased choices and judgments ('From whose hand have I accepted a bribe to make me shut my eyes?') Samuel was clean. It's possible to 'succeed' in life by spinning a few yarns here and there, bullying our way to the top and shoving others out of the way as we do. But what price success – and just how real is that success when we have to lose our character in order to gain it?

Samuel was bold enough to ask a nation, 'How did I do?' Perhaps we could muster the courage to phone a friend and ask 'How am I doing?'

Prayer: Lord, may I have the courage both to ask how I am doing and then to change as a result. Amen.

Long-term love

BIG PICTURE:
1 Samuel 12:6–25
Luke 13:31–34

FOCUS:
'But they forgot the
LORD their God.'
(1 Sam. 12:9)

VALENTINE'S Day often reminds us of unrequited love. Hearts brimming with hope, we compose dreadful poems and scribble them on greeting cards. Perhaps we wreck our bank balance buying a breathtaking bouquet. We wait for a response, which never comes. Finally we face the hard fact: our love is not returned.

Throughout Israel's history, God was the long-term lover who repeatedly tried to turn the heads of His stubborn people. Samuel took the nation 'back to the future' and painted a sad portrait of love generously given but not returned. Israel had rejected God's best efforts to woo them into faithfulness.

The atmosphere and language here resembles a court case. The preacher prophet draws a striking comparison between the faithful righteousness of the Lord (faithfulness is the heart of righteousness), and the people who would occasionally come to their senses and determine to live for God again. Fervent vows and promises would be made. But soon the familiar pattern of rebellion would be resumed, an empty cycle.

In the middle of the sermon, Samuel paused to allow the Lord Himself to make a point – the onset of a terrifying thunderstorm and driving rain when Samuel called for it (v.17). This was the time of harvest – the season when such bad weather was unheard of.

The people were exhorted to ponder the faithfulness of God to them. Surely, they would never forget this day of reckoning. Or would they?

Sin seeks to establish a pattern in our lives, deep ruts that we follow for years. Let's respond to love.

Prayer: Lord, thank You for Your unfailing love and faithfulness to me and all those You love. Show me ways in which I can respond to love. Amen.

Let's respond

to love

Reaction

BIG PICTURE:
1 Samuel 13:1–9
2 Corinthians
11:16–28

FOCUS:
'So he said, "Bring me
the burnt offering and
the fellowship offerings."
And Saul offered up the
burnt offering.'
(1 Sam. 13:9)

PRESSURE reveals the true us. It is in the cauldron of pressure that true character is revealed, whether we are in the heat of opposition, temptation or some panic-inducing circumstances. There we are faced with the question: will we live dependently according to God's plans and purposes or 'do our own thing'?

Sadly, the creeping rot of headstrong self-dependency starts to show in Saul's life now. Under threat of attack from the mighty Philistine army and terrified by the dwindling morale and numbers of his troops, Saul decided to take matters into his own hands – with disastrous results.

The gathering Philistine army was an awesome sight and Saul's soldiers panicked. Many of them ran for their lives, scattering to the nearest caves and tombs. Only 600 remained with Saul – and they were terrified too.

It was time to cry out to God. Saul arranged for Samuel to come to Gilgal to preside over the sacrifices and word came that the old man would arrive in seven days – perhaps a prophetic reminder of the seven-day waiting period at Gilgal that had been part of the process of anointing Saul in the first place (1 Sam. 10:8). But when Samuel didn't arrive on time, Saul decided to offer the sacrifices himself. And then, just as the ceremony ended, Samuel arrived – and was outraged by what he saw. God had decreed that king and prophet should lead the nation together. In offering the sacrifice himself and taking on whatever role he chose, Saul violated that arrangement.

Are you under huge pressure? Stop. Wait. Think. Pray.

Repeat those four steps. And then and only then, think about action.

Prayer: Lord, may I always have time to wait on You and hear Your word before acting. Amen.

GOD loves you.

The statement seems obvious, even hackneyed, because we use language like that so much. But while Christians believe passionately that God is love and that He loves His world, there's often a disconnection when it comes to accepting that He loves *us*. Perhaps we are all too familiar with the murky shadows that linger within our souls; the good news of His love seems too good to be true. But a failure to settle the issue – that we are greatly loved – will create a long-term insecurity that will weaken our faith when we are under pressure.

A closer look at the showdown between Samuel and Saul reveals a man who was still deeply insecure about God's attitude towards him. A literal translation of his spluttering defence to Samuel reveals that Saul offered the sacrifice 'to put God in a gentle mood'. Then he tries to diminish his own responsibility by saying 'I forced myself to do it.' Finally, Saul tries to shift the blame onto Samuel himself, suggesting that his lateness was the reason for the debacle. Samuel promised that Saul's throne would not endure and that another king, a man after God's heart, would be raised up to take his place – an indirect but clear reference to David. The prophet and king then abruptly separated.

If our daily impression of God is that He is trembling with anticipation, just waiting to smite us, then we won't be motivated to much obedience. After all, if He is consistently angry with us anyway, then what's the point?

God loves you. Ask Him to help you believe it and know it.

Prayer: Lord, grant me a much greater understanding of Your love for me – and for others. Amen.

Excuses

BIG PICTURE:
1 Samuel 13:10–22
1 John 4:7–21

FOCUS:
'I thought, "Now the Philistines will come down against me at Gilgal, and I have not sought the LORD's favour." So I felt compelled to offer the burnt offering.'
(1 Sam. 13:12)

God loves you

Tokenism

BIG PICTURE:
1 Samuel 13:23–14:3
Exodus 28:6–30

FOCUS:
'Saul was staying on the
outskirts of Gibeah ...
With him ... was Ahijah,
who was wearing an
ephod.' (1 Sam. 14:2–3)

WHEN I was a relatively new Christian, I'm sad to admit
that not only did I want to *be* a spiritual young man – I
was also rather keen to *look like* a godly teenager.
Everyone that I respected in our church seemed to 'look'
so holy; they smiled a lot, carried gigantic Bibles and
peppered their speech with exclamations such as 'Praise
the Lord' and 'Hallelujah!' I believe that they were totally
genuine and I wanted to be like them – so I practised
'looking right', I stood in front of my bedroom mirror
and rehearsed saying 'Praise God!' over and over again.
The following Sunday morning, my performance was
impeccable. I looked the part. Sadly, one of the snares
about being preoccupied with appearances is that we
can start to believe that we are really are what we are
projecting. The Pharisees in Jesus' time demonstrated
that profound self-deception.

Saul looked the part too. He has included Ahijah from
Shiloh as part of his camp; Scripture notes that this man
was wearing an ephod. This was the priestly robe that
was used to discern the will of God (Exod. 28:6–30).
But beneath the veneer, Saul is becoming a man who
was out of touch with reality. His son goes off on military
manoeuvres and Saul was unaware that he'd left. Then,
as we'll see tomorrow, when the battle began in earnest,
no mention is made of Saul 'consulting the oracle'.

It's not enough to have the look – and the apparatus
needed to know what God wants. What really counts is
doing it, not looking the part.

**Prayer: Lord, I need to know myself more – grant me
that understanding, to serve You better. Amen.**

Waiting and moving

We've seen that Saul was guilty of taking action when he should have waited, when Samuel was delayed in coming to the battlefield. Now, he's waiting around when he should be stirring himself to action and it's left to his eldest son Jonathan to get out and initiate something. There are times when God has to stir His people to get moving (Deut. 1:6). But notice that Jonathan becomes action man only when he's convinced that God is with him.

Jonathan is a wonderful contrast to his father, as he looks for signs of God's favour – and once that sign is forthcoming, he climbs what was thought to be an impassable rocky mount. The difficulty of the terrain and being vastly outnumbered by the Philistines (who also had the weaponry franchise) was not the issue – once Jonathan knew that God was on his side, nothing else mattered. Sometimes God answers what could potentially be a thousand questions with just one answer: 'I am with you' (Matt. 28:20).

Perhaps that's a good definition of what it means to be dependent upon God: someone who waits when it's time to wait and moves when it's moving time. Now that's what I'd love to be like. How about you?

There are times when God has to stir His people

Weekend

Unfinished business

BIG PICTURE:
1 Samuel 14:15–23
Isaiah 48:12–22

FOCUS:
'So Saul said to the priest, "Withdraw your hand."' (1 Sam. 14:19)

I HATE to confess it but I'm not terribly successful with those Bible-reading plans that take you through all 66 books in a year. I kick off on January 1st with tremendous enthusiasm, determined to imbibe the whole book by December. Initially things go well but somewhere around the third week of January (when we are deep in the thickets of Leviticus) I stumble and fall. I then get behind by four or five days, requiring me to read about 75 chapters to catch up. Does this sound familiar to anyone? I've done better with exercise lately; I started running about 15 months ago and the habit is now well and truly established. I wish I could be as consistent in every area of my life.

News comes from Saul's sentries and lookouts that the Philistines are on the run; something big is happening. Saul once again makes a move to consult God, in calling for the ark of God (although the Hebrew is confusing – this may have been the ephod) and the priest (v.19) but then it becomes obvious that the God-sent panic in the Philistine ranks was increasing. Saul decides there's no time to lose and so tells the priest to 'withdraw his hand', most likely from the Urim and Thummim, the stones that were used to cast lots and so determine God's will. Most commentators castigate Saul for not waiting a few seconds to hear from God before rushing off to battle. He seems to be not really leading but stumbling around in the dark, calling out to God and then running off before an answer comes.

Prayer: Lord, thank You that You wish to talk to us so much – may I always listen. Amen.

Legalism

BIG PICTURE:
1 Samuel 14:24–26
Matthew 23:1–4

FOCUS:
'... Saul had bound the
people under an oath,
saying, "Cursed be any
man who eats food
before evening comes,
before I have avenged
myself on my enemies!"'
(1 Sam. 14:24)

ISRAEL wins a great victory and Saul continues to stagger along, making extremely unwise decisions. He has already claimed his son Jonathan's victory as his own (1 Sam. 13:4). Insecure people are desperate to claim credit even for other people's victories. But then it gets even worse ...

Perhaps Saul felt guilty about fighting before he had finished consulting with God and so he now puts his exhausted army on a fast – something God hadn't asked him to do. The text might not be too kind to the now eager Saul: one translation of the words 'Saul had bound the people under an oath' is 'He played the fool'.

We human beings are odd. Some of us drift our way through life with little care for God and His ways. Others become so zealous that they go to huge extremes to try to please God, often placing themselves under regulations that He never initiated in the first place, apparently trying to outdo God in the pursuit of holiness. It's an old habit, once again demonstrated by the Pharisees, whose complex system of holiness angered Jesus, mainly because it placed such obstacles between ordinary people and their Maker. Just today I saw a group of ladies who were all dressed in the same drab clothing that membership in their denomination demands. I don't doubt their sincerity for a moment; but I'm sad for them because the Bible makes no such demands. Legalistic tradition (which, incidentally, often seems to target women) is a harsh taskmaster.

Is it possible to be too zealous for God? Certainly it is.

Prayer: Lord, may I know You in such a way that I know what pleases You – and what doesn't – in all things. Amen.

Is it possible to be too zealous for God?

Common sense and mutiny

BIG PICTURE:
1 Samuel 14:27–45
Matthew 11:25–30

FOCUS:
'But the men said to Saul, "Should Jonathan die – he who has brought about this great deliverance in Israel? Never!"' (1 Sam. 14:45)

OUR friend was a man of 'faith', his youngest child was very ill and he refused to call the doctor, believing that to do so was an act of doubt. Eventually, thankfully, he was persuaded; but his zeal was dangerous. Other reckless 'faith steps' followed and his wife could finally stand it no longer. That lovely family has now been shattered by divorce.

Have you met a Christian who was so spiritual that they seemed to have abandoned basic common sense? As we saw yesterday, some people are over-zealous and abandon all logic in what can only be described as a reckless pursuit of God. The exhausted person who insists on getting out of bed at 5am to pray; the person with no money in their bank account who feels compelled to write a large (and bouncy) cheque for the offering: some acts of faith, motivated by a genuine heart, are irresponsible.

Tired warriors need food and Jonathan, unaware of his father's command to fast, dips his staff in an abandoned beehive. He didn't stop and indulge himself but just found nourishment as he passed by and his eyes brightened. Angered by his father's foolishness, Jonathan roundly criticised the vow and insisted that Saul 'had made trouble for the country': a strong accusation (Josh. 7:25).

The day ends with yet another portrait of a man out of control, as his own men effectively mutiny against his decision to have his own son Jonathan executed. Saul seems to be a man who was forever trying to appease God, rather than walk with Him.

Prayer: Lord, may I know Your commitment to me so deeply that I can walk with You free from fear. Amen.

A vow undone

BEFORE we leave this episode, it's worth pausing for a moment and considering this issue of vow making. A lot of Christians get tangled up over this, especially as they make rash promises in the earlier days of faith. The story of Jepthah doesn't help. He was the man who put his own daughter to death in fulfilment of a hasty vow.

Certainly the Bible makes it clear that we should be people who keep our promises; one of the tragedies of our day is the ease with which some seem to discard their wedding vows. But Saul, having made a foolish vow, now goes ahead and compounds his sin and error by insisting that his warrior son be executed – because he ate honey, a notion that Jonathan finds incredible. Saul would have drawn a finger across his throat, symbolising a willingness to die himself if he did not follow through on the vow: 'May God deal with me, be it ever so severely …'

Thankfully, others 'help' Saul out of his misguided zeal and save Jonathan's life – with their own oath and vow (v.45)! They simply insist that the planned execution should not take place. There's no suggestion that this displeased God; on the contrary, we then immediately read of Saul's valour and victories over the Philistines. Don't use these words to wriggle out of promises that have been made and must be kept but if you have entered into vows to God that you now know were hasty and perhaps over zealous, then ask Him to forgive you and then move on. Don't add foolishness to foolishness.

Prayer: Lord, may I know what things I should promise to You – and deliver on – and what things I should not. Amen.

BIG PICTURE:
1 Samuel 14:38–52
Judges 11:29-39

FOCUS:
'Saul said, "May God deal with me, be it ever so severely, if you do not die, Jonathan."'
(1 Sam. 14:44)

… we should be people who keep our promises

Independence Day

BIG PICTURE:
1 Samuel 15:1–9
Hebrews 2:1–4

FOCUS:
'But Saul and the army spared Agag and the best of the sheep and cattle, the fat calves and lambs – everything that was good.' (1 Sam. 15:9)

WE'VE watched and wondered as Saul has run amok, bouncing from moments when he desperately wanted to know God's plan to times when he completely ignored it or started to look for guidance and then did his own thing. Now God speaks through Samuel and gives precise and detailed instructions about a battle against the Amalekites – long-standing enemies of Israel who pop up all through Israel's history. Despite the prescriptive directions, Saul now blatantly disobeys what he knew was the direct command of God. Gradual compromise ultimately leads to deterioration and outright rebellion. Independence Day has now fully come for Saul.

So why did he do it – and for that matter, why do any of us deliberately flout what we know is God's way for us?

Perhaps we cling to the bizarre notion that we really do know better than God. Some think that Saul may have taken Agag into custody as a potential bargaining chip, a hostage to make a deal with. But God's command had been emphatic. Others trace Saul's hunger for acclaim as the source of his downfall; perhaps the Amalekite king was held as a trophy of war. Still others point to simple greed as the reason for the sparing of the 'best' livestock; Samuel accused Saul of 'pouncing on the plunder' (1 Sam. 15:19). Whatever the reason, it all comes down to one issue: self versus God.

But notice that this is a story of gradual erosion rather than cataclysmic fall. Most of us don't wake up one morning and decide to desert God; we drift, rather than march away from Him.

Prayer: Lord, forgive me for those times when I believe I know better than You – and may I serve You first and self last. Amen.

Independence Day examined

1 Samuel 15:10–12
John 15:9–17

> The Christian
> life is a walk of
> daily friendship
> with God

Weekend

Over the last couple of months we've been looking at what happens when nations and individuals declare themselves independent of God. Now, Saul is digging his heels in and consolidating his separation from the Lord. Notice three vital realities about independence in his story. First, it involves turning away from God – the loss of intimacy ('he has turned away from me' – v.10). We might think that disobedience would be the first on the list but in the life of faith, loss of relationship always comes before the breakdown of morality. The Christian life is a walk of daily friendship with God and facing life with His power, rather than a distant conformity to a set of commands.

Secondly, disobedience follows ('and has not carried out my instructions' – v.10).

Then, an ugly preoccupation with self follows quickly – Saul heads to Carmel to build a monument (literally, 'a hand') to himself (v.12). In ancient near eastern culture, it was common to build pillars and then place a sculpture of a hand – the symbol of power – on the top. But Saul was about to lose his power, because he had turned away from God and not carried out His instructions. Let's avoid the steps down to independence at all costs.

Lies and blame

BIG PICTURE:
1 Samuel 15:13–21
Genesis 3:1–13

FOCUS:
'What then is this bleating of sheep in my ears?' (1 Sam. 15:14)

SOME habitual liars are so fogged in by deception that they start to believe their own tales. Now seriously sliding downhill, Saul is in that dingy place of self-deception. He was caught red-handed with king and cattle by Samuel's visit. But instead of confessing his guilt, he moved into religious overdrive, greeting Samuel loudly and piously. It's a sickening sight, as Saul insists, without even being asked, that he has carried out the Lord's instructions. He's so emphatic and insistent, it seems that he believes his own lie.

But old Samuel could hear the cattle lowing, tacit evidence for the prosecution. Even then Saul wriggles, pointing the finger of blame at his men. Passing the buck is an old habit that goes back to the Garden of Eden. Even when Samuel speaks a word from the Lord, Saul digs in more, protesting once again that his soldiers are the guilty ones. But the blame game is a waste of time. Some of us *are* bruised by our past. But when we insist that every mistake we make is because of our upbringing, our education, our misfortune, we slam the brakes on personal growth, frustrate God's purposes and whine our way through our days.

J. Michael Straczynski, the American television producer and director remarked, 'People spend too much time finding other people to blame, too much energy finding excuses for not being what they are capable of being and not enough energy putting themselves on the line, growing out of the past and getting on with their lives.'

When we fail, let's bow the knee rather than point the finger.

When we fail, let's bow the knee rather than point the finger

Prayer: Lord, may I take responsibility for those things I can change and rest in You for those things I cannot. Amen.

SAUL now has to live with the consequences of his poor choices: he would continue to be king but would gradually descend into an abyss of paranoia, unaided by either God or God's prophet. The ominous symbolism is obvious, as it is announced that Samuel would not ever see Saul again this side of death.

And in what is almost a poetic litany, Samuel sums up for all of us just what really matters to God, as he laments, 'To obey is better than sacrifice'.

God is looking for people who do more than sing to Him, pray their prayers in His direction and give even their hard earned resources into offerings: He is looking for and longing for relationship with us, so that He can speak and we will not only hear but heed His voice. We realise that our God does not come to us as an advisor or consultant but as absolute monarch and Lord. He is not to be ignored, negotiated with or appeased by tokenism. Obedience is called for: anything less is as bad as witchcraft.

It's not a happy ending. Samuel was sad, God was grieved and Saul was desperate. But there is a glimmer of hope in this dark episode, as we read that God's delight is in those who obey Him.

Let's choose to follow in the footsteps of Samuel, Hannah and Jonathan, who lived dependently, rather than wandering independently as the tragic Saul did. He could have lived so differently and finished well.

Our road stretches before us. How will we end?

Prayer: Lord, may I finish well – having done well in Your eyes in the meantime. Amen.

Sad ending

BIG PICTURE:
1 Samuel 15:22–35
2 Timothy 4:1–18

FOCUS:
'But Samuel replied: "Does the LORD delight in burnt offerings and sacrifices as much as in obeying the voice of the LORD?"' (1 Sam. 15:22)

Friendly Fire

Friendly Fire

FRIENDLY fire hurts! Perhaps it's more wounding to be bruised by those who say they love you than to be shot by strangers; it can be a bewildering experience to see Christians in conflict. But it happens none the less, and to the best of people. The Bible is the truth, and so reveals for us, warts and all, some of the ugliness that always appears whenever humans fall out.

In our world of 'smart' weapons, huge casualties result from soldiers inadvertently killing their compatriots – so-called 'friendly fire'. During the Gulf War Campaign (1990–91) 367 Americans lost their lives. Of those dead, 165 American casualties, or 45 per cent, were because of 'friendly fire'. According to the United Nations, friendly fire caused 51 per cent of all Allied deaths during the Gulf campaign. Killing is not a precise science: innocent people get hurt or die. And the pain is the same, from wherever the bullet originates. No matter that your fellow soldier didn't mean to press the button when he did. The damage has been done.

Sometimes our churches and homes are battlegrounds. Sniping, spiteful words find their targets and leave horrifying long-term wounds. Misunderstandings lead to blame landing where it doesn't belong. Let's not deny that conflict can happen to us, in our friendships, marriages and churches – rather, let's face the facts and consider what we can do when the cloud of conflict appears. We'd all prefer the clear blue sky of perfect harmony, but until that day comes – when Jesus returns – let's navigate our way through tense times with faith, hope and humility.

So come with me as we consider this uncomfortable subject of conflict. Edward Rowell said wisely, 'Wherever two or three are gathered, conflict is in the midst of them.' Fasten your seatbelts – it might be a bumpy ride as we tour some of the killing grounds of biblical history but we'll learn some vital lessons along the way.

And perhaps – please God – the 'casualty' statistics might be reduced as a result of our trip.

God bless you!

IT'S called fratricide – the act of killing your brother. And Cain is the most famous fratricidal murderer in history. Driven mad with jealous rage by the 'better' sacrifice that his brother Abel offered (Heb. 11:4), Cain struck out at one of the people he should have treasured and protected, in this first, horrifying family tragedy. It's a shocking sight. And it's all over the issue of worship.

Conflict happens …

Unfortunately, it can be all too easy for us to take 'the way of Cain' too (Jude 11). While actual murder may not be involved, we are liable to bruise and cut each other when we don't handle conflict well. We assassinate each other's characters, trading accusations and insults back and forth. There's nothing more depressing than the sight of God's people acting like frenzied piranhas, 'biting and devouring each other' as Paul describes it (Gal. 5:15).

BIG PICTURE:
Genesis 4:1–16
1 John 3:11–12

FOCUS:
'We should love one another. Do not be like Cain, who belonged to the evil one and murdered his brother.'
(1 John 3:11–12)

But while we should be grieved when Christians squabble, we shouldn't be totally surprised. From Cain's story onwards, the Bible catalogues dozens of fall-outs. Jesus anticipated conflict being a reality among His people before the Church was ever born. The list of apostolic churches where conflict broke out is long. The Christian communities in Antioch, Jerusalem, Rome, Corinth, Philippi and Thessalonica all experienced tension of one sort or another.

The Bible is a gritty, down-to-earth manual for everyday living. God is willing to walk with us through those times when war breaks out among those who call themselves brothers and sisters. Hopping mad? God can help. He's seen it all before.

Prayer: Father, we Your children seem to fight easily. Help me, when conflict comes, to behave so Your name is honoured. Amen.

Hopping mad?

God can help

Conflict happens in the strangest places …

BIG PICTURE:
Mark 9:33–37
Luke 22:24–27

FOCUS:
'Jesus said to them, "The kings of the Gentiles lord it over them … But you are not to be like that."'
(Luke 22:25–26)

IT'S called the ceremony of the Holy Fire. It takes place on the Saturday before Easter, in the darkened tomb in the Church of the Holy Sepulchre in Jerusalem, where tradition insists that Jesus was buried. The event is so-called because it's believed that fire descends from heaven to the tomb during the ceremony. But recently another kind of fire broke out. As the Greek Orthodox Patriarch Irineos and the Armenian Archbishop Pakrad Bourjekian made their way towards the tomb, fights broke out between the priests of the two communities – with police attempting to separate them. The two senior church leaders, who had entered the tomb alone, faced off inside. During the argument between the irate primates, Irineos opened the tomb doors and called for the assistance of the local police commander, who refused to intervene.

And it's not the first time that there's been trouble in the holy place. Back in 2002, a huge brawl broke out involving hundreds of the faithful. So now more than a thousand police are required to be on hand for each year's ceremony. Another fight broke out over whether a chapel door should remain open or closed. A valuable Oriental carpet extended a few inches into the Franciscans' space, so a friar cut it off with scissors. And a ladder has been parked against a wall for decades because the various denominational custodians can't agree about who should move it; an enduring monument to territorialism.

So why this scandalous behaviour? It's all about power, self-interest and who calls the shots. And it's the opposite of the servant heart that Jesus calls us to embrace daily.

Prayer: Lord, save me from immaturity that makes me insist on everything being done my way. Your will be done, today. Amen.

IT DOESN'T take much to start a war. Today conflict will flare over a parking space ('I got there first') and violent road rage will erupt ('He overtook me and cut me up'). Sadly, Christian churches will also fracture over minutiae – we believers can be quite good at pursuing trivia while a lost world looks on amazed and stays lost. We get picky about gnats and swallow camels in the process. Sometimes we try and make our fights nobler than they are: immaturity, not principle, is the driving force behind a lot of church fights.

One church had voted unanimously on an expensive building programme but found itself in strong disagreement over the £20 purchase of used choir robes.

And I've heard of a minister being dismissed without notice for the 'crimes' of asking people to respond at the end of a sermon, having a missionary speak in the Sunday morning service and using too many illustrations during preaching.

After a distinguished 100-year history, a Baptist church in the USA split into quarters – over the position of a piano stool. Apparently the four different factions in the church can't agree about where the seat should be placed, so now they are holding separate services, each led by a different minister. None of the clergy are speaking to each other and people are afraid that violence could break out.

Of course, it's a known fact that church furniture is a good reason for a fight: one of the best ways to fuel a feud is to change the seating arrangements in church. We can get rather passionate and possessive about seating, as we'll see next week …

Prayer: Lord, give me the gift of perspective, to see what really matters and what does not. Amen.

Conflict happens over the oddest issues …

BIG PICTURE:
Matthew 23:23–24
James 3:14–18

FOCUS:
'You strain out a gnat but swallow a camel.'
(Matt. 23:24)

It doesn't

take much to

start a war

It's not fair, Jesus

John 21:15–25
**2 Corinthians
12:20–21**

One of the first falsehoods that we believe about life is that everything should be fair. If I suffer, I'm tempted to scream, 'Why me?', appealing to some money-back guarantee of a pain-free life which no one – God included – ever gave me. Jealousy, the root cause of so many problems (Gen. 37:11; Acts 17:5–9; 1 Cor. 3:3) lingers in all our hearts and makes its vile appearance when someone seems to be getting a better deal than we are.

Are you green with envy?

Weekend

So it was with Peter. Having been forgiven and restored from the shameful shadows of denial, he was prophetically warned by Jesus about trouble up ahead. And then suddenly the beloved John shows up and joins Jesus and Peter in their stroll on the beach. Peter, smarting and perhaps nervous of the dark horizon ahead, asks, 'What about him?' Jesus' response is a firm but kindly, 'Mind your own business.' Envy has no right to answers.

This week we'll take a look at a dispute that was sparked by jealousy. Are you green with envy? Ask God to help you change colour.

WE HUMANS can be breathtakingly brilliant and spectacularly stupid in turn. Today, witness one of the more dubious aspects of being human: the ability to experience group rage ('they became indignant' – v.41), in the actual presence of the Son of God, the Prince of Peace Himself (Isa. 9:6)! As a woman (her name was probably Salome), the mother of James and John, puts her bid in for the best seats for her boys, the other disciples explode with anger. Salome was somewhat out of order with her request. One commentator remarks, 'Her asking was in the manner of a business transaction.'

But the disciples' irate reaction was not so-called 'righteous' indignation – often we Christians like to use that term to give unmerited dignity to our petty squabbles – rather this was the blatant jealousy that surfaces when someone else gets a better deal than we've got. And this was no mild-mannered spat with a few chaps muttering quietly – quite a fuss broke out. The Greek word that is translated 'indignant' means 'much grief and reproach'.

Stop and wonder. You'd think that an awareness that Jesus was watching them and listening to their words would have created a more measured and reasonable response to Salome's request. But Jesus' disciples were not an endlessly happy and harmonious group, ever grinning, always agreeing: they fought in His presence. The fact that Jesus was in the midst didn't prevent the crisis from happening. Struggles happen. Yet as Ezra pointed out in his reference to the 'eye of God', the Lord *is* watching (Psa. 33:18). We do what we do before Him.

Prayer: Father, nothing is hidden from Your view. Let an awareness of Your presence with me affect my behaviour today. Amen.

Let's make a deal

BIG PICTURE:
**Mark 10:35–45
Ezra 5:5**

FOCUS:
'When the ten heard about this, they became indignant with James and John. Jesus called them together ...'
(Mark 10:41–42)

Speaking through others

BIG PICTURE:
Matthew 20:20–28
Mark 10:35

FOCUS:
'Then the mother of Zebedee's sons came to Jesus with her sons and, kneeling down, asked a favour of him.'
(Matt. 20:20)

Be careful about

using others to

fight your battles

for you

I CAN'T remember exactly what the issue was that had made the church member so angry but enraged she certainly was. I listened, trying to look patient. Then came the guided missile, the statement that I always dreaded as a church leader. 'I've talked to lots of people about this and they all agree with me.' I pressed her for details: who exactly were those who shared her opinion? 'Well, there are one or two – and they are thinking about leaving the church' (the second missile).

This furious lady was falling into the trap of summoning unidentified witnesses, putting words in their mouths, possibly without their permission or even knowledge. And I've seen another version of this, when someone, unwilling to engage in conflict, goes around the church quietly sowing their ideas, subtly nudging others that 'something needs to be done' – in the hope that the others will take action. I recently heard an internationally respected Christian leader boast about how he 'primes' deacons in his church so that they end up speaking on his behalf and making decisions that he approves of. I fear that he acts more like a puppeteer than a pastor.

Take a careful look at Matthew's version of this 'How about the best seats for my lads?' incident. Salome makes the original request but Jesus responds to James and John (v.22). He saw past Salome to who was really behind the request. And Mark gets right to the point in his description, clearly identifying James and John as the architects of the proposal (Mark 10:35). Be careful about using others to fight your battles for you – especially your Mum.

Prayer: Father, expose any tendencies I have towards manipulation. Help me see when I am driven to control others – or You. Amen.

TAKE a look at exactly *when* this spat broke out among the disciples; Matthew gives us the detailed chronology. It all ignites as Jesus, after three years of epic ministry, now figuratively sets His compass towards Jerusalem to do the great redemptive work. At last, His 'hour' had come – and *then* the fight begins. Scripture regularly uses this idea of 'hours' or 'open door moments' to describe seasons of opportunity (1 Cor. 16:9; Rev. 3:8). And often that is when conflict breaks out among God's people. They don't realise that they are right on the brink of their 'hour' – their church is seeing a real harvest evangelistically, their programmes and activities are being especially effective in the local community – and then everything is ruined by the exhausting and distracting arrival of conflict.

The down side of the hour/open door is that heaven rarely announces these epic destiny days of our lives with an email. When David walked into his 'hour' and ended up giving Goliath a radical and effective haircut – starting at the neck – he didn't stir that morning and ask his father what chapter of 1 Samuel he was walking in. Rather, he just strolled faithfully into another day – and nothing was ever the same again for David by the time that darkness fell (1 Sam. 17).

Are we too busy squabbling to notice that we might well be spoiling the best and most opportune moment that our church has ever had?

Now … is that fight really worth continuing?

Prayer: God, grant Your people the wisdom to make the most of their every opportunity. Amen.

His hour had come

BIG PICTURE:
Matthew 20:17–19
Colossians 4:2–6

FOCUS:
'Now as Jesus was going up to Jerusalem, he took the twelve disciples aside and said to them, "We are going up to Jerusalem …"'
(Matt. 20:17–18)

Losing sight of our humanity

BIG PICTURE:
Matthew 20:22–23
Romans 12:1–3

FOCUS:
'"You don't know what you are asking," Jesus said to them. "Can you drink the cup I am going to drink?" "We can," they answered.'
(Matt. 20:22)

Conflict is

often fuelled

by unrealistic

expectations

CONFLICT is often fuelled by unrealistic expectations. We feel disappointed in our fellow believers, expecting so much of them but forgetting that we were never promised that everyone would always get it right. Mistakes are made, misunderstandings spread and the failure of human 'flesh' is everywhere in evidence in the church. Sometimes, we lose sight of our own humanity and of our own propensity to fail – we forget that we are all sinners saved by grace.

James and John were temporarily blinded to their own fragility as they fantasised about thrones with Jesus. In God's economy, thrones are only reached by the way of the cross. Challenging them about their ability to walk such a path, Jesus asks if they would be prepared to drink the cup that He was about to lift. In Jewish thinking, the 'cup' represented a brimming portion of suffering – and one that He would gulp down to the last dregs (Matt. 26:39). With the haste of the deluded, the pair said yes. And indeed they would: John would taste the exile of Patmos (Rev. 1:9) and James would be executed on a whim by King Herod (Acts 12:2) – but all of that would come only after they deserted Jesus in the garden and fled (Matt. 26:56).

Like Peter, who nursed totally unrealistic notions about his strengths and weaknesses (Luke 22:33), we can rush to assume that we are strong and be equally quick to condemn others in what we perceive as their weaknesses. Next time we are tempted to strike out, perhaps we should take a long look in the mirror.

Prayer: Show me myself, Lord, and grant me grace when I see the weaknesses of those around me. Amen.

SALOME'S request for special seating 'pre-arrangements' for her boys might have been founded on a popular (but erroneous) belief that a Messiah figure would come, head for Jerusalem (Luke 19:11), overthrow the Roman authorities and then set up an earthly throne. The idea lingered in the minds of the disciples, even after the resurrection of Jesus (Acts 1:6). But Jesus was working towards a vision that dwarfed the tiny idea of a localised revolution. God is usually at work on something far greater than our minds can grasp. The Early Church initially thought that the gospel was only for the Jews – but God, once again, was doing something much bigger (Acts 11:1–18).

Conflict is often sparked, quite simply, because life with God is such an epic adventure. Being around such a pioneer who carries such world-changing hopes for His Church can be uncomfortable at times. Like those little people who tried to pin down the giant in *Gulliver's Travels*, we cling to our small agendas, park in our comfort zones and hope for a quieter life. Perhaps we even long for a throne to recline on and a waiter to serve us a long, cool drink as we bask in the sun.

But the church is not a holiday resort: it is called to be an active, flexible, enduring group of people who are willing to sacrifice their small notions so that God's plans and purposes can become reality. In that sense, the church is no place for a quiet life and we'd do well to remember that she is called to be an agent *of* change, not a refuge *from* change.

Prayer: Lord, save me from my small, perhaps selfish thinking. Help me to see and participate in Your agenda. Amen.

A narrow view

BIG PICTURE:
Matthew 20:20–21
Acts 11:1–18

FOCUS:
'She said, "Grant that one of these two sons of mine may sit at your right and the other at your left in your kingdom."'
(Matt. 20:21)

Continuing the journey

**Matthew
20:25–28
Acts 15:1–22**

I can only imagine what might have happened if the disciples, called together for a peace summit with Jesus (v.25), had not decided to resolve their differences and continue the trek towards the Holy City with Him. And where would we be today if the Early Church meeting that we considered yesterday (Acts 11:1–18) had been characterised by unwillingness to consider that God was working to a surprising, mind-stretching plan? We are all beneficiaries of their willingness to accept that they might be wrong.

None of us should enjoy conflict

This summit meeting shows us that sometimes we have to go through the awkward business of facing up to our tensions – and then submitting to the teachings and commands of Christ. None of us should enjoy conflict but sometimes tensions deepen when we are unwilling to admit that they exist and try to smile our way through. Jesus 'called them together' for what would not have been an easy event. Sometimes there's no other way to break some stalemate situations, as the Council in Jerusalem demonstrates (Acts 15:1–22). Has your journey ground to a halt because you don't want to face facts? Perhaps it's time to take the initiative today.

Weekend

'WHAT'S happening in our church can't possibly be of God. If it is, why is it so difficult at times? Surely only good fruit comes from a real move of God?' It's an argument that I've heard many times and at first hearing, it sounds plausible. But think again.

We saw last week that God's blessing upon a church can bring about what Charles Dickens called 'The best of times and the worst of times'. The suggestion that God's activity in the life of a church will automatically lead to peace and unity is a false notion that we should demolish. Following the spectacular and obviously genuine work of the Holy Spirit on the Day of Pentecost, many were converted and now Acts 6 numbers around five thousand people as part of the blossoming Christian family in Jerusalem. A cursory study of Scripture will reveal that most of the fights that broke out among God's people were *because* He was very much at work.

Putting it crudely, when churches grow, new people show up, and instead of greeting them with open arms, we get irritated by them, because they are not what we hoped for. So it was in the Early Church.

Sometimes I wonder if we know what we are praying for when we ask God to make our churches more effective. We can develop romantic notions of lovely, sorted-out people coming to join us – what sheer joy it will be. But we forget that many of them will come bruised and broken and in some cases, they'll be angry – and very immature. Let's be realistic – and be ready to pay the price that comes with growth.

Prayer: Take away my misconceptions about what Your blessings look like, Lord, and help me face the pain that they bring. Amen.

Blessing and conflict

BIG PICTURE:
Acts 6:1–7; 2:41–47

FOCUS:
'In those days when the number of disciples was increasing, the Grecian Jews among them complained …'
(Acts 6:1)

Old prejudices surface

BIG PICTURE:
Acts 6:1
**2 Corinthians
3:17–4:7**

FOCUS:
'… the Grecian Jews among them complained against the Hebraic Jews because their widows were being overlooked in the daily distribution of food.' (Acts 6:1)

IN CHURCHES in Belfast, Northern Ireland, you will find former paramilitary terrorists from both sides of the Protestant/Catholic divide, who would once have killed each other, now sharing fellowship as new creations in Christ. It's a miracle to behold – but one that has taken years to come into fruition.

Yesterday we saw that tension often crackles in growing churches for the simple reason that growth means yet more human beings around the place. Whenever we, 'in-the-process, saved by grace yet still prone to sin', people are around, there's always potential for problems. Racists who come to Christ may have to wrestle for years with their prejudices: those struggling with bad habits may struggle for a long time. Sanctification, the biblical word that describes the change that God takes us through, is a lifelong project. We've got treasure but it really is in 'jars of clay' (2 Cor. 4:7).

Look again at this squabble over food distribution. At first glance it looks like little more than an immature selfish tiff. But it's just possible that there was something behind it and that racial prejudice was simmering in the background. The Grecian Jews were Greek-speaking Jews, mostly born in the provinces. The Hebrew Jews were those actually born in Palestine; they spoke in their native tongue and tended to look down on the Grecians as an inferior class – hence some disparity surfacing in the food distribution programme. Old rivalries and hurts are reappearing. Are some long-term sinful attitudes fuelling conflict in your life?

Sanctification …

is a lifelong

project

Prayer: Father, change my heart. Root out long-term sin. Please strengthen me and help me grow up. Amen.

WHATEVER the reason for the 'food fight' in Jerusalem, the apostles demonstrated one of the most admirable qualities that leaders – and indeed all of us who follow Christ – should show. They listened. When conflict breaks out, our first response is often defensive; we fail to hear others because we're too busy talking. No wonder we're commanded to be 'quick to listen, slow to speak' (James 1:19). Ever been frustrated by those people who try to finish off your sentences for you? Listening means more than pausing before speaking again.

A church in Wales experienced a feud while searching for a new pastor. A local newspaper printed the details, which would almost be funny if they were not so tragic. 'Yesterday, the two opposition groups both sent ministers to the pulpit. Both spoke simultaneously, each trying to shout above the other. Both called for hymns and the congregation sang two – each side trying to drown the other. Then the groups began shouting at each other. Bibles were raised in anger. The Sunday morning service turned into bedlam. Through it all, the two preachers continued trying to out-shout each other with their sermons. Eventually a deacon called a policeman. Two came in and began shouting for the congregation to be quiet. They advised the 40 people in the church to return home. The rivals filed out, still arguing. Last night one of the group called a "let's-be-friends" meeting. It broke up in an argument.'

Conflict often drives us to ask the question, 'What should I say?' But perhaps that's not the first query to pose. Let's check our listening skills first.

Prayer: Give me grace to listen and wisdom to think before I speak. Amen.

The listening church

BIG PICTURE:
Acts 6:2
Ecclesiastes 5:1–3

FOCUS:
'The Twelve gathered … the disciples together and said, "It would not be right for us to neglect the ministry of the word of God in order to wait on tables."' (Acts 6:2)

Action stations

BIG PICTURE:
Acts 6:3
James 1:19–27

FOCUS:
'Brothers, choose seven men from among you who are known to be full of the Spirit and wisdom.' (Acts 6:3)

IT'S an uncomfortable and frustrating feeling. Someone has asked for your advice, has seemed eager to listen, is nodding with apparent attentiveness – but you know that they won't be taking a single step to implement anything that you say. They thank you, tell you that the chat has been so very helpful – and then carry on regardless.

Many marriages collapse with the complaint, 'I've had it with words. We've talked about change – but it never comes. It's over.' And the same complaint is sometimes heard about church leaders. Apparent 'listening' that never leads to any action makes people feel patronised and adds fuel to the fire of conflict. James shows us that it's an attitude that we can bring into our relationship with God, which is as bizarre as seeing something in the mirror that needs correcting in our appearance but then going away without making a change.

The apostles heard the complaints from the Greek quarter and responded with radical action, allowing the people to appoint responsible stewards 'from among them'. There's no hyper-defensiveness or determination to control events. The apostles face the fact that they have a problem and are willing for steps to be taken to resolve it before further damage and neglect result.

Interestingly, every one of the seven chosen came from a Greek background – all have Grecian names and so real confidence is restored in that section of the church family.

Let's not just nod in apparent agreement when we're challenged. Actions really do speak louder than words.

Prayer: Lord, help me to *do* as well as to *hear*. Amen.

A happy ending here

BIG PICTURE:
Acts 6:3–7
Ephesians 4:1–3

FOCUS:
'This proposal pleased
the whole group.'
(Acts 6:5)

IT WAS a bad year for church fights. In 1987, America's popular *Nightline* television show, hosted by Ted Koppel, devoted no less than eleven nights of coverage to church/Christian conflicts. And in the spring of the same year, *Time* magazine devoted its cover to the rash of church and Christian media scandals. The headline was depressing: 'TV's Unholy Row – Sex-and-money scandal tarnishes electronic evangelism'.

I've visited literally hundreds of churches and seen many of them at their best and their worst. There are times when I'm tempted to despair when I hear of another raging conflict. Hope in me dies as I wonder if there are any churches that can stay together long enough to be effective in the long term. A sense of inevitability tires my soul and I settle sadly into the jaundiced conclusion that conflict will always end in tears and division. But it is not so.

This week we've considered a major church conflict that *was* resolved in peace and *everyone* was content with the solution. But more than happiness all round, the apostles were free to continue to preach and pray and many priests came to know Christ as a result of the church's ministry. Not all problems have to remain problems. Resolutions can be found when all are willing to change. The conflict paved the way for greater effectiveness and the church grew all the more because the apostles were now relieved from the daily details of the food distribution. And the tension created a situation in which Stephen emerged, who would serve with great power and effect before his martyrdom (Acts 6:8–7:60). Good endings happen.

Prayer: Lord, grant me hope when I am tempted to be overwhelmed with disappointment. You can bring light out of darkness. Amen.

Not all problems
have to remain
problems

A theological crisis and crossroads

Old habits die hard – especially when they originate from a direct command from God. In Old Testament times, circumcision was far more than hygienically inspired surgery practised by clean-living Jews. The act of male circumcision was a covenant ceremony, reminding every male Jew that he was profoundly different and distinct – he was part of a nation that was in a unique relationship with the living God. So it is that we have the somewhat odd scene of Joshua circumcising his troops just days before they went into battle at Jericho – a strange military strategy (Josh. 5:2–8)!

Now another battle was brewing for the Early Church, as they wrestled with the key question of whether circumcision was necessary any longer for those who would follow Christ. It's little wonder that there was such a lot of heat around the subject – traditionalists would have found it unthinkable to lay aside the practice that had characterised God's people for centuries. This week, as two of the church's heavyweights – Peter and then Paul – come under fire over the issue, we'll see how well the Church did as they negotiated this vital question.

Old habits
die hard

Weekend

Freedom is worth fighting for

BIG PICTURE:
Acts 11:2–3; 15:1–2

FOCUS:
'Some men ... were teaching the brothers: "Unless you are circumcised ... you cannot be saved." This brought Paul and Barnabas into sharp dispute and debate with them.' (Acts 15:1–2)

IN SOME churches, conflict – and indeed any kind of dissent – is simply not allowed. Anyone who raises an awkward question is quickly dubbed 'divisive' – and the modern equivalent of burning at the stake soon follows, as the non-conformist loses his or her reputation and is often either thrown out or marginalised. Sadly, churches exist where anybody who disturbs the millpond of unity by making even a ripple (never mind a wave) is seen to be doing the devil's work – and should be shunned. We'll look at the issue of spiritual abuse in more detail later in our study.

But some issues are worth fighting for – and freedom in Christ, being liberated to live His way – is one of them. Peter, Paul and Barnabas refused to comply when they were challenged about spending time with uncircumcised believers. They shrugged off any false guilt about 'offending' the staunch circumcision fundamentalists. Another controlling mechanism that has been hugely overused is the suggestion that I must never say or do anything that will 'cause a weaker brother to stumble' – a comment that is often used by brothers who are anything but weak!

Martin Luther's great reforming work brought division – and horrified the religious hierarchy of the day – but the cause was freedom in Christ, biblical obedience to Him. Luther could not back off. In the case of the Early Church, disputes flared. The Christian way is *not* that we should avoid all conflict at all costs.

Let's check our attitudes; monitor the way that we speak, put our questions and face that we might be wrong. But if your church doesn't allow questions, here's a suggestion – leave.

Prayer: Lord, help me to walk in Your freedom today. May we help others to enjoy liberation in You. Amen.

It's good to talk

BIG PICTURE:
Acts 11:4–18,
15:3–12

FOCUS:
'Peter began and explained everything to them precisely as it had happened.' (Acts 11:4)

HOW do we hear from God? In the case of these two crisis moments, revelation came through discussion. The decision to bless what was happening among the Gentiles came because it really is good to talk. There was no casting of lots (as when Matthias was chosen as an apostle – Acts 1:26). And the prophets were not called upon to prophesy about the specifics of the decision, despite their strong influence in the church at this time (Acts 15:32).

The church business meeting has become an object of scorn for many. It has often degenerated into either an annual exercise in tedium (where many are healed of insomnia) or an opportunity for people who don't attend the church very often to show up and stick their oar in. But this episode demonstrates how a group of gracious, listening, godly people can experience a download of divine wisdom as they discuss issues together. The Quakers have used this method of decision-making for years, assuming that groups, searching together, can reach a better decision than one person alone.

Peter did well in this incident. Sometimes those who hear from God can start believing they don't need to be accountable, they have heard from heaven – as Peter had (Acts 10:9–23). But God hates pride and they risk losing His voice. Peter, having been such a key leader until this time, could have pulled rank and taken an 'I'm the boss, don't question me' approach. Instead, he explains his actions. Others listen. They discuss back and forth. And God's mind and will are revealed in the process.

... revelation came through discussion

Prayer: Give me humility and patience to explain when I need to, and grace to listen and learn today. Amen.

SOME people live by the 'If you give an inch, they'll take a mile' principle – and spend most of their lives fighting unnecessary wars as a result. A Canadian church has put up a divider down the centre of its pews to keep apart two warring families, who display very little generosity of spirit towards each other.

Thankfully, the conflict that ignited around the Gentile Christian issue was resolved with a magnanimous attitude. Absolutely affirming that circumcision was unnecessary and wanting to 'not make it difficult' for the Gentiles, the gathering at Jerusalem tried to help oil the wheels of fellowship between Jewish and Gentile Christians and so avoid future tensions. And so a request was made that they make certain ethical choices about eating food that had been offered to idols, sexual morality and eating meat with blood in it. Why pick on these three and not include instructions about stealing or lying? Commentators agree that the Council was wanting to call the Gentile converts away from 'typical' Gentile living and avoid potential flashpoints with their Jewish brothers and sisters.

James and the Council repeatedly spoke in terms of a burden placed upon the Gentile believers (vv.19,24,28) but it was a request inviting the Gentiles to thoughtfulness and love. This was a call away from the tub-thumping 'I want my rights' attitude where we refuse ever to give ground, towards pleasing and blessing others. According to Paul (writing to the Corinthians), while everything may be 'permissible', not everything is 'beneficial' (1 Cor. 10:23). Have you demonstrated generosity of spirit lately?

Prayer: Father, let generosity characterise my life. Save me from being dominated by what I see as my rights. Amen.

Free but generous – rights

BIG PICTURE:
Acts 15:12–21
1 Corinthians 10:23–11:1

FOCUS:
'... we should not make it difficult for the Gentiles who are turning to God. Instead we should write to them ...'
(Acts 15:19–20)

Communication and misunderstanding

BIG PICTURE:
Acts 15:22–30

FOCUS:
'... the whole church, decided to choose some of their own men ... With them they sent the following letter ...'
(Acts 15:22–23)

ARRIVING to speak at a conference recently, I was confronted – kindly – by a leader who was concerned about me and my ministry, as he'd heard that I was a supporter of some teaching which has proved to be destructive. The irony is that I have been an extremely vocal opponent of the ideas that he thought I'd been championing. It was good to be able to iron out the misunderstanding.

Misunderstandings often start church wildfires. Truth is twisted by gossip (of course, some Christians don't gossip – they share); little wonder the Bible repeatedly commands us not to allow careless whispers to destroy our fellowship (Prov. 11:13; 18:8; Eph. 4:29).

Then we have an innate capacity to hear what we want to hear, which thickens the fog of misunderstanding even more. Too many times I've been thanked for mentioning something in a sermon – and then realised that I had made absolutely no reference to the subject whatsoever. Somehow, the listener, preoccupied with their own thoughts, read their needs into my words.

Poor communication creates misunderstanding. In some churches, decisions are reached behind closed doors but only the conclusions are shared – the process that led to those conclusions is not discussed with the congregation. Confusion results – and resentment, if people are never consulted.

James wisely determined that the conclusions of the Jerusalem Council should be written down and properly communicated by special envoy – that way, the potential for misunderstanding would be reduced.

Upset about something? Make sure you haven't got the wrong end of the stick.

Prayer: Help me to hear what others are really saying and to say well what needs to be said. Amen.

Misunderstandings often start church wildfires

EVERY church probably has one or two people within it who are never quite happy. If the dead were raised on Sunday morning, these folks would complain that the service went over time while all the empty coffins were cleared away. For them, the building is always too hot, too cold, the music too loud, too soft, the translation of the Bible used is not to their preference and one definitely gets the impression that if and when they arrive at the marriage supper of the Lamb, then even there their sense of irritation won't cease: they probably won't like what's on the menu …

If you think I'm exaggerating, consider the stubborn obstinacy of the Pharisees who witnessed Lazarus emerge from the tomb – and then went away to a committee meeting to frame a plot to get rid of Jesus (John 11:47). Some people's capacity for bristling unhappiness is nothing short of epic. Even if an issue is resolved well, they tend to move on to another one; they aren't happy when others are happy. And I often hear people like this complain, 'I haven't been heard.' They *have* been heard – it's just that others don't agree with them.

The result of the Jerusalem conference was a sense of gladness among the people – but the Judaizers were only silenced for a while. Obviously unconvinced and angry, they quietened down, waiting for a better day to start their complaining all over again and they would seek to unsettle Paul's work in Antioch, Corinth, Galatia, Jerusalem and in Rome. Beware those who are always on a crusade of complaint.

Prayer: Reveal Yourself to those who are never content and go to the roots of their discontent, I pray. Amen.

Never happy

BIG PICTURE:
**Acts 15:31–35
John 11:17–47**

FOCUS:
'The people read it and were glad for its encouraging message.'
(Acts 15:31)

Conflict and growth

Conflict is not only part of life but also a vital element of real living. Education produces conflict, as learning clashes with ignorance. The process of shedding opinions that are flawed is usually painful but is the only way to real understanding. Conflict can be an unwelcome bridge that we need to cross in order to become more effective. In times of conflict, issues are explored; healthy questions are asked and better decisions result. Those of us who are leaders need to take the bold step in our preaching and teaching to encourage disagreement and foster an atmosphere where conflict is safe.

Conflict is …
a vital element
of real living

Weekend

Without conflict, our corporate and personal growth will be stunted. And so this week, we'll explore a standoff between the Early Church's greatest heavyweights – Peter and Paul. Paul refused to back away from the true faithfulness (and brotherly love – Luke 17:3) that is willing to confront because of genuine concern. This was the first of three conflicts that occurred in this same region in just a few years. Let's see what we can glean. Confrontation helps us to grow. But it must be done in the right way – and in my view, Paul didn't get it completely right …

Confrontation: face to face

BIG PICTURE:
**Galatians 2:11
James 5:19–20**

FOCUS:
'When Peter came to Antioch, I opposed him to his face, because he was clearly in the wrong.'
(Gal. 2:11)

PETER and Paul's conflict was not a theological fight: they both shared the conviction and revelation that the gospel was for the Gentiles. But Paul was convinced that Peter was not 'walking the talk' – living daily life according to that revelation. Scholars disagree as to whether this event took place before or after the Jerusalem Council but it seems most likely that it occurred before that decision. Otherwise, Paul would simply have referred to the Council's verdict, which as a written decree had been sent to all the churches in Antioch and vicinity (Acts 15:23).

The issue here was not whether Gentiles could be saved but whether Jewish Christians should associate with them! Apparently Peter was happy to eat and drink with his Gentile friends, until ultra-conservative Jewish Christians arrived and he backed off, probably leaving the Gentile converts feeling rejected.

Paul does well, at least initially, in that he takes up his complaint with Peter personally, 'face to face'. That description doesn't necessarily imply hostility but a direct encounter (Acts 25:16; 2 Cor. 10:1). But no punches were pulled and, as we'll see later, Paul's methods may have been a little harsh. 'I withstood him' is the same verb used by James when he said to 'Resist the devil'!

Confrontation by rumour, where people are tried, judged and condemned behind their backs, is no confrontation at all – it's cowardly gossip. When we fall out, let's talk *to* each other – not talk *about* each other (see Matt. 18:15). Chuck Swindoll wisely counsels, 'If we have areas of disagreement and we will, let's work them out face to face, courteously and confidentially.'

Prayer: Lord, it's easier to talk about others than talk to them. Grant me courage mingled with kindness. Amen.

Confrontation: exhibit 'A'

BIG PICTURE:
Galatians 2:11–12
Amos 5:7–15

FOCUS:
'… he was clearly in the wrong.' (Gal. 2:11)

MISCARRIAGES of justice are always a tragedy. It's a terrible crime to take years of an accused person's life – or even their life itself – for a crime that evidence later proves they didn't do. But churches can be guilty of allowing and even perpetuating, 'kangaroo court' justice.

Sometimes we make judgments about each other and our conclusions are based more on our subjective feelings rather than hard evidence. When Christian leaders are told that their preaching isn't 'deep enough', how is any response possible? How deep should deep be? Who is to judge what 'depth' is enough?

Another destructive weapon is the accusation that someone is not sufficiently 'spiritual'. No defence can be offered: the prosecutor always wins. Kevin Miller sums up the dilemma of one so accused: 'How do you answer a charge that you're not godly?' And church members with genuine concerns are too quickly dubbed as 'divisive'. But God hates *all* injustice (Amos 5:12) and 'dishonest scales' (Prov. 11:1) and commands us to back up our accusations with the hard evidence of witnesses (1 Tim. 5:19).

When Paul challenged Peter, at least he was confident that there was a case to answer. 'He was clearly in the wrong' actually means 'condemned before God'. In fact some early writers used this term to describe someone worthy of the death penalty: Paul was very confident that Peter had sinned. And notice that Paul's words infer that Peter had done something to displease God – not just him. Let's confront because of real sin – and not because someone irritates *us*.

Before we rush to a conclusion, let's get our facts straight.

Prayer: Lord, let me see, speak and be one who exemplifies truth, mingled with love. Amen.

I WAS recently asked to be involved in a fairly difficult meeting called to resolve a few sensitive issues between some high profile Christian leaders – and the reason given for my invitation was that 'Jeff is willing to engage in plain speaking'. Horrors – it sounds as though I know how to 'call a spade a spade' – a saying that makes me feel that my verbal skills have the finesse of a slap over the head with a shovel …

We had better face up to the uncomfortable fact that confrontation is always difficult, requiring courage from the confronter. I can think of some Christian leaders whose blind spots are known (and sometimes sniggered about) by many – but no one has the guts to confront *them*.

It was courageous of Paul to take Peter to task. Peter was the man generally recognised as the number one among Jesus' disciples – he is named first on every list of disciples. He was their spokesman and was in charge of the election for a successor to Judas. He was the fervent preacher on the Day of Pentecost. Peter was involved in almost every significant action in the first twelve chapters of Acts, except a few involving Stephen and Philip.

And here, Paul, who was not even an original disciple, confronts Peter face to face and accuses him of hypocrisy: brave indeed but vital bravery, because a virus was spreading that had infected even the astute Barnabas (v.13).

It hurts to be confronted but it's painful to confront too. Faithful friends are willing to face that pain …

Prayer: Lord, I want to be a friend in the truest sense today. And give me faithful friends too. Amen.

Confrontation: it takes boldness

BIG PICTURE:
Galatians 2:13
Proverbs 27:2–6

FOCUS:
'… even Barnabas was led astray. (Gal. 2:13)

… confrontation

is always

difficult, requiring

courage from

the confronter

Confrontation: softly, softly

BIG PICTURE:
Galatians 2:14–21;
6:1–10

FOCUS:
'When I saw that they were not acting in line with the truth of the gospel, I said to Peter in front of them all …'
(Gal. 2:14)

DONALD Burna speaks for us all: 'I want to treat others the way I'd want to be treated when needing reproof.' And I know that if I was in the dock and found guilty, I'd like to be handled with care and love.

'If someone is caught in a sin … restore him gently.' So Paul wrote to his friends in Galatia. The word translated here as 'restore' is also used to describe the delicate work involved in mending fishing nets. The gentle touch is needed. But here's a tough question: did single-minded, passionate Paul, who knew how to be blunt, practise what he preached in Galatians 6 when he rebuked Peter, described in Galatians 2? Commentators have struggled with this incident and some wonder if Paul's 'tough love' was just a little too tough.

Paul stood on the moral high ground – but did he have to be so very public, so quarrelsome and perhaps even vitriolic? What happened to the private discussion that Jesus encouraged when believers disagree, to allow one to win the other over without a public bruising (Matt 18:15ff)? Perhaps Peter's hypocrisy had caused such damage in the church that a public encounter was the only way forward. Peter had acted publicly and his actions would influence others – he needed to be put right publicly as well (1 Tim. 5:20).

Whether Paul was right in his approach is a matter of debate and there is not a 'one size fits all' approach to confrontation that covers every situation. Marshall Shelley says: 'How much firepower is appropriate in a church fight? No Geneva Convention has established rules.' One principle is sure: gently does it.

Prayer: Lord, in all I do, may I bless rather than bruise, even when the words spoken are difficult. Amen.

IN CONFRONTING errant Peter, Paul spoke up, loud and clear. But Peter's response isn't recorded. Just how did the senior Peter respond to the stinging rebuke of Paul? This was a dangerous moment – the church in Antioch could have easily divided into warring factions, each one supporting their favoured heavyweight. All the other churches could have followed suit.

Perhaps the answer is found in the way that Peter wrote about his faithful friend Paul years after this incident, describing him as 'our dear brother Paul'. Peter, who had tasted the bitterness of serious failure before (Luke 22:60–62), surely realised that the painful encounter in Antioch had saved him from a serious blind spot. And he was right to be grateful and to speak of Paul's God-given wisdom with gratitude. It's one thing to sin – but to be oblivious to our errors is to live in great darkness. 'The way of a fool seems right to him, but a wise man listens to advice' (Prov. 12:15).

Loving confrontation saves us from smug self-deception. Perhaps we've made our minds up – prematurely and unjustly – about someone who has been brave and faithful enough to show us our faults. We've categorised them as the enemy rather than counted them as a true friend. Stinging from the wound that is inevitable when we're shown something ugly in us, we shoot the messenger because we're unhappy with the message. Think again: just as the unwelcome intrusion of the surgeon's scalpel wounds and saves us at the same time, so honest confrontation can save us from all kinds of deadly traps.

Prayer: Save me from believing that I am right when I am wrong. Fill my heart with light and truth. Amen.

Confrontation: thank you very much

BIG PICTURE:
2 Peter 3:11–18
2 Timothy 3:1–17

FOCUS:
'Bear in mind that our Lord's patience means salvation, just as our dear brother Paul also wrote to you with the wisdom that God gave him.' (2 Pet. 3:15)

Loving confrontation saves us from smug self-deception

April Fools?

This week, we visit Corinth, a divided church where some folks, convinced that they were wise, needed to realise that their puffed-up wisdom was 'foolishness in God's sight' (1 Cor. 3:19). Each needed to humble themselves and 'become a "fool"' in order to be truly wise (1 Cor. 3:18).

It had all began so well in Corinth. Paul visited the city during his second missionary journey and spent eighteen months winning both Jews and Gentiles to Christ (Acts 18:11). But now five years had passed and Paul discovered that conflict was raging. Radical action was needed, prompting him not only to write but also to make three visits, one of which was 'painful' (2 Cor. 2:1).

| Radical action
was needed

Weekend

A united church was desperately needed in Corinth. It was an influential city, situated on the main land routes between the East and West and had become the sex capital of the day. The temple of the goddess Aphrodite was housed there and was famous for its vices.

Would the divided Christian family there resolve their differences and become a much-needed light? Let's find out.

WHEN a church descends from conflict into serious division and fractures into factions (Gal. 5:20), suddenly people start taking on what I'd like to describe as secondary identities. Once, they were content to be known simply as members of the same local Christian family, be it Baptist, Anglican or whatever. But when the spirit of division wreaks its havoc, suddenly people describe themselves differently. Now they are *Those who love the old hymns* or *The progressive contemporary worshippers*; they are *Those given to deeper intercessory prayer* or *The practical, caring social action group*. We are *Those who love the pews* or the *We need new chairs as our bottoms have become corrugated* group.

The adoption of these newer labels causes us to forget our primary identity; that we are Christians, fellow followers of the same Christ – the description of us as 'brothers' and 'sisters' is not just quaint religious verbiage or a useful device to help us out when we forget each other's names! Paul appeals to the contentious Corinthians to return to that foundational family reality. It's an argument that he frequently uses; those tempted to attack and hurt each other are to remember that the victim is in fact a 'brother for whom Christ died' (Rom. 14:15; 1 Cor. 8:9–13).

It's worth remembering that that irritating person in your church who is the cause of much gnashing of your own teeth is in fact sporting a label: this person is hereby worth dying for. It's a label that's been signed by Jesus. And when I hurt them, I hurt Him (1 Cor. 8:12b).

Prayer: Thank You for my worldwide, wonderful, encouraging, irritating, growing, frustrating family of brothers and sisters. Amen.

Remember who you are

BIG PICTURE:
1 Corinthians 1:10
Romans 14:13–15

FOCUS:
'I appeal to you, brothers, in the name of our Lord Jesus Christ …'
(1 Cor. 1:10)

Want to win?

BIG PICTURE:
1 Corinthians 1:10
Ephesians 5:15–21

FOCUS:
'… that you may be
perfectly united in
mind and thought.'
(1 Cor. 1:10)

IT WAS a beautiful, cut glass vase; it had sadly got in the way of my indoor cricket practice and was now shattered in many pieces. Fearing the parental wrath to come, I wondered how on earth I could stick it back together. But it was just too broken to be fixed.

Paul surely felt something similar when he pondered the fragmented fellowship of the Corinthian Christians, who were divided into at least four rival groups. Where do you start when trying to fix such a mess?

He began with a call to unity – and used a word that describes the adjustment of the parts of a musical instrument, the setting of bones by a physician, the mending of nets or the outfitting of a ship for a voyage. Figuratively speaking, the Corinthians had their backs to each other: they were estranged, hostile and unwilling to listen to or value each other's opinions. Now Paul calls them to realignment, which required humility and the placing of individual desires and opinions on the 'back burner' for the cause of the whole body. An attitude of mutual submission would be needed; Richard Foster defines submission as 'the ability to lay down the terrible burden of always needing to get our own way'.

Paul doesn't announce which group is right – the winner identified over the losers. In a sense, everyone was wrong in the way that they were handling their differences, whatever their specific opinions. We can be very wrong in our rightness. Togetherness – not personal triumph – was the goal. Are you hungry to win, to be proved right after all? There is yet a better, bigger prize.

Prayer: Set me free from turning today into another opportunity to be proved right. Amen.

We can be very

wrong in our

rightness

I NEVER saw the attack coming and even though it happened over thirty years ago, I still shudder as I remember it. He had a reputation as the school bully, he was three times my size and he jumped me from behind. Before I knew what had hit me, I was on the ground, being kicked repeatedly with his Doc Marten boots.

Sign your name

Tragically, similar tactics are sometimes employed in churches. I fear anonymous, unsigned letters almost as much as that playground bully – and for similar reasons. Being hit while blindfolded, so that you can't see where the blow comes from, is torture. When I get a spiteful, critical letter that doesn't include a signature, it's a dart from the dark, a case of hit and run where I have become a target, not a person. I can't respond, ask questions, explain myself or apologise for any wrong I've done. I can do nothing except take the kicking lying down.

BIG PICTURE:
1 Corinthians 1:11
Mark 14:57–65

FOCUS:
'My brothers, some from Chloe's household have informed me that there are quarrels among you.'
(1 Cor. 1:11)

Paul had heard of the war in Corinth because some members of Chloe's household (probably slaves who were in Ephesus on business) had taken the initiative to tell him. This is commendable; often division simmers on because no one will take any constructive action. Peter Robinson, a conflict resolution expert, notes that the preferred option for dealing with church conflict is avoidance. But notice that the source of information was willing to come forward and be identified. The verb translated 'have informed' actually means 'made very evident or clear'. The information came to him personally, so he believed it to be trustworthy. Perhaps it's time to take some action today – or come out of hiding.

Prayer: Help me, Lord, to own my opinions with clarity and grace and to be a person of godly action. Amen.

I follow Jesus, you know

BIG PICTURE:
1 Corinthians 1:12;
3:1–23

FOCUS:
'What I mean is this:
One of you says,
"I follow Paul"; another,
"I follow Apollos";
another, "I follow
Cephas"; still another,
"I follow Christ."'
(1 Cor. 1:12)

Let's be careful

about what we

insist God puts

His name to

THERE were four warring groups in Corinth – and their fight wasn't just about theology. Sometimes conflict arises because we dislike the style of things (as evidenced by the raging 'worship wars' – the number-one reason for current conflict in the American Church) or because we have aligned ourselves inappropriately with a leader, turning them into an idol to be worshipped rather than a servant who helps to equip us.

In Corinth, there were those who professed to follow Paul, perhaps because he was the founding father of the church: 'Our former minister was so much better.' Then there were the fans of Apollos, the gifted orator from Alexandria – 'The preaching just isn't feeding us like it used to.'

Others claimed to follow Peter (Cephas in the text). These may have been Judaizers or, more likely, they thought that Peter carried more authority, as he was with Christ in His earthly ministry. But perhaps the scariest group was the one that at first glance might have seemed like the purest: they 'followed Christ'. Far from being those who rejected factions, they were perhaps the guiltiest of all, claiming that they alone were truly serving Jesus (2 Cor. 11:23) and belonging to Him (2 Cor. 10:7).

I've met people from that group lately: just about everything they say and do is because God has commanded them to do so. Discussion or disagreement is off limits – after all, they are doing God's will, so who are we to question them? Paul genuinely appealed for unity 'in the name of Jesus'. Let's be careful about what we insist God puts His name to.

Prayer: Lord, please speak to me but help me never to be arrogant when I believe I have heard from You. Amen.

Back to Jesus?

IN TRYING to repair the fractured Corinthian church, Paul calls them back to Jesus. We exist for Him and not for our worship styles or our preferred Bible version or any other secondary issue.

Paul nudges the Corinthians to consider the utter absurdity of the factions, by asking bizarre questions. Has Christ been broken into parts so that each of the groups has a quarter of Him? He is one. Was Paul crucified for them? None of the Corinthian preachers or favoured leaders had died on a cross – and so none were worth so much attention! And not one of the Corinthian Christians went through a baptism in the name of Paul – or, for that matter, Peter or Apollos.

So did the arguments stop? Probably not. The division there ran deep; perhaps there's something dangerously delicious about a fight. We find ourselves relishing the rumours, the intrigue and finding out who is with us and who is against us. Christians in Corinth hauled each other into court (1 Cor. 6:1–11), fought about eating meat (1 Cor. 8–10) and indulged selfishly at the Lord's Table (1 Cor. 11:17–22). The famous thirteenth chapter of 1 Corinthians was written, not as a piece of beautiful poetry to be attached to 'Christian' refrigerators (!) but as a desperate call for some maturity instead of the Corinthian cat fight. And later, the condition of the Corinthian church led to Paul's closing plea in his second letter: 'live in peace' (2 Cor. 13:11–14). It appears that the Corinthian Christians, despite Paul's best efforts, didn't refocus on Jesus. How about us?

Prayer: Save me from walking the same endless, repetitive circles of conflict. May I hear and heed Your voice today. Amen.

BIG PICTURE:
1 Corinthians
1:13–31; 2:1–16

FOCUS:
'Is Christ divided? Was Paul crucified for you? Were you baptised into the name of Paul?'
(1 Cor. 1:13)

**Philippians 4:1–5;
2:1–11**

Women at war

They'd been real team players with Paul in the past. Their names, Euodia and Syntyche, mean 'prosperous journey' and 'pleasant acquaintance'. But when Paul writes to the church in Philippi, there wasn't much pleasant acquaintance going on between these two women, whose conflict was serious enough to merit a mention from Paul.

Some commentators believe that they were deaconesses in the church: certainly they had enough influence to make a real difference in the local Christian community, hence Paul's words. Perhaps there was a power play between the two. Whatever the root cause, Paul, who had written so extensively in his letter about the need for servant heartedness, with the attitude of Christ as the ultimate example, was looking for an end to their fight.

In recent years I've watched too many close knitted teams unravel. Without exception, all of them were made up of people I was convinced would be friends forever. Now the heady hopes and shared dreams of their youth have been dashed for good. I'd like to grow old – perhaps older is the best term – with my friends and whatever investment is needed to make that a reality, I think it's worth it. How about you?

Paul ... was looking for an end to their fight

Weekend

EUODIA and Syntyche were good, respectable people who were behaving badly. Let's get rid of the myth that churches are torn apart by rampantly evil-looking monsters. It only takes the presence of ordinary human beings – like you and me – for wrong things to happen.

Soviet dissident and prison survivor Alexandr Solzhenitsyn observes:

'If only there were evil people somewhere, insidiously committing evil deeds, and it were necessary only to separate them from the rest of us and destroy them. But the line dividing good and evil cuts through the heart of every human being.'

An extreme example of this is Yahiel Dinur, an Auschwitz survivor who was called to testify against Adolf Eichmann at his trial in 1961. When Dinur saw his oppressor in the courtroom, he fainted. He later said that his shock was caused by the realisation that the Eichmann before him at the trial was not the godlike army officer who had sent millions to their death. This Eichmann, he said, was an ordinary, unremarkable man. And if this Eichmann was so ordinary, then what Eichmann had done, any man could do – even Yahiel Dinur. He was capable of acting in exactly the same way. Solzhenitsyn said: 'One and the same human being is, at various ages, under various circumstances, a totally different human being. At times he is close to being a devil, at times to sainthood.'

You and I are capable of great evil – or great good. Doing the right thing doesn't come naturally – but because we know ourselves, and realise what we are capable of – we submit to Jesus.

Prayer: Lord, within me is the capacity to bless or destroy. May my life bear witness to Your Word today. Amen.

Men – and women – *do* behave badly

**BIG PICTURE:
Philippians 4:2–3
Romans 7:7–25**

FOCUS:
'… these women who have contended at my side in the cause of the gospel …' (Phil. 4:3)

Breaking stalemate

BIG PICTURE:
Philippians 4:2
Matthew 18:15–17

FOCUS:
'I plead with Euodia and I plead with Syntyche to agree with each other ...'
(Phil. 4:2)

BECOME a referee for a boxing match and you stand a good chance of getting slapped around a bit yourself – that's my experience. I was asked to mediate in an unholy row between two Christian leaders who were not good at burying the hatchet, other than in each other's heads. I played the ref and sure enough, one of them didn't like my conclusions and turned on me. Hearing that there was trouble, I telephoned him, told him that I knew he wasn't thrilled with me and asked if we could get together to straighten things out. He refused point blank to meet with me. Scripture tells us to live in 'love and peace with all men' – as far as it is up to us. Sometimes it isn't.

In the case of these two warring women, Paul was desperate that their irritations with one another be sorted out and so he begged them to be reconciled. Notice that he pleaded with each of them, individually, to take their responsibility for the arguments. Sometimes people who have been offended like to play the waiting game: 'When they come to see me to apologise, then we can talk – and not before.' We fold our arms and flatly refuse to budge an inch (Prov. 18:19).

But the Bible calls us to take the initiative if we have been sinned against (Matt. 18:15), or if others have something against us (Matt. 5:23). Either way, stalemate is not recommended. And meanwhile, as the wounded referee, I still believe that there are times when a third party can help us in our disputes – as we'll see tomorrow.

Prayer: Father, save me from stubbornness. Help me to be a person of initiative and responsibility. Amen.

The issue isn't the issue

BIG PICTURE:
Philippians 4:2
Romans 12:9–21

FOCUS:
'… agree with each other in the Lord.' (Phil. 4:2)

THE man's face was crimson red, the veins in his forehead were bulging and I feared that he might have a heart attack at any moment. His voice was raised, his arms were flailing like a windmill and I wondered what on earth could be creating such upset. Had he heard of some tragedy? Was he concerned about the safety of a hospitalised loved one? As it turns out, his irate explosion was due to the presence of drums in the church building. This instrument was loud, worldly, unsuitable and even if God liked them, he didn't. And he failed to see that, even if he had been right, his attitude was so very wrong. His obsession with a relatively trivial issue blinded him to something far more serious in his own heart.

Paul does not bother to mention the issue of contention between Euodia and Syntyche. The specific issue that had divided them wasn't of primary importance; what mattered was how the issue would be resolved. Would peace be restored before more damage was done? What about the testimony of the church to the wider community? Many feuds and fights of duration move away from the root cause of the conflict anyway. The primary issue that launched the divisiveness normally gives way to personal feelings, hurt and pride before too long. Interpersonal conflict often stems from incompatibility between individuals and does not necessarily include facts or values.

It's possible to win a battle but damage God's work in the winning.

Prayer: Father, may what I do and how I do it be right both in Your eyes and those of others. Amen.

It's possible to win a battle but damage God's work in the winning

Yell help

BIG PICTURE:
Philippians 4:3
Exodus 2:13–14

FOCUS:
'Yes and I ask you, loyal yokefellow, help these women …' (Phil. 4:3)

MY LITTLE bruising as a conflict referee fades into nothing compared with Moses' experience as a failed conflict mediator. He had to emigrate because of the trouble that was stirred up by his intervention in a Hebrew fight. Yet despite the risks of being misunderstood, there *are* times when we will be called upon to help those who have got themselves entangled in a messy relationship. So Paul calls upon his friend – perhaps Sygygus (there has been endless speculation about the identity of this person) to step in with the helping hand of mediation. And some commentators believe that Paul was not calling upon just one individual for assistance but was making an appeal to the whole church – a corporate 'loyal yokefellow' – to help get these women back on the same page.

Perhaps the shoe is on the other foot and it's time for you to face up to the difficult reality that you need some outside help if that friendship, that marriage, that family dispute is going to even have a hope of being mended. A mediator can bring perspectives that those in the conflict don't see, make suggestions that would be rejected if either of the warring parties came up with them and can bring a sense of order and calm to the tension created by conflict. Perhaps some pride will need to be swallowed by asking for help: it is a confession that we haven't got all the resources within us to sort out our issues. And that step of humility may be the very best step we take today.

Prayer: Show me, Lord, where I need the wisdom of others. Help me to ask for help. Amen.

Perhaps some pride will need to be swallowed

AS WE conclude our look at these clashing ladies and think again about how there are times when we need outside intervention to help resolve our differences, it's worth noting Paul's gracious manner as he looks for a solution. Christians at war can be frustrating people: we can see them acting foolishly and be tempted to jump in with heavy handed help, which is no help at all. I've seen too many sledgehammers used to crack nuts. But Paul pours soothing oil on troubled waters; he doesn't take sides and he doesn't demean these women because of the impasse in which they found themselves. And he doesn't tar the whole church at Philippi with the same brush, scolding them because of the folly of two of their members.

He uses terms of endearment and kindness ('my brothers'; 'my joy and crown'; 'dear friends'). Genuine mediation should bring calm – not precipitate a further crisis. He honoured the women publicly for their years of faithful service and reminded them of their past teamwork. Paul's words were not a put-down but an invitation for them to step into the dignity of their calling. Of course, we don't know if his kindly strategy worked. It is a little sad that, whatever the sacrifices and achievements of this fighting pair, they go down in biblical history only because of their capacity for a fight. The inscription on their gravestones could read, 'They fell out' – not a noble obituary.

How shall we be remembered?

Prayer: May my legacy on this earth be good and the memory of me point to You, Lord. Amen.

WEEK 15 FRI

Oil poured on wounds

BIG PICTURE:
Philippians 4:1–9
1 Corinthians 4:1–13

FOCUS:
'Therefore, my brothers, you whom I love and long for, my joy and crown …' (Phil. 4:1)

Spiritual abuse

He was mean-spirited, manipulative and he hurt people in many ways. He had a super-sized ego and an undersized capacity to care. And he was the main leader of a local church, where people were more likely to be bruised than blessed. This week, as we look at Diotrephes, we lament that he was not the first and won't be the last leader to abuse his position and throw his weight around in Jesus' name. Diotrephes stands in stark, ugly contrast to the apostle John's 'dear friend', Gaius. According to the fourth century *Apostolic Constitutions*, this Gaius (there are three mentioned in the New Testament) was appointed as the first Bishop of Pergamum by John. Gaius was faithful to the truth, influential, respected and generous. He was a good man.

Before we think this week about abusive leadership, let's pause and thank God for those countless Christian leaders who daily sacrifice, endure, serve and give in so many unseen ways for the sake of God and His people. Why not take time today, perhaps with a note or a phone call, to let them know that their faithfulness is appreciated, not only by God – but also by you?

... let them know that their faithfulness is appreciated ...

Weekend

Who's the boss?

BIG PICTURE:
3 John 9
1 Peter 5:2–4

FOCUS:
'... Diotrephes, who loves
to be first ...' (3 John 9)

DIOTREPHES means 'God-nurtured'. Sadly, the man didn't live up to his name. Far from allowing God to develop and care for him, Diotrephes was more into feathering his own nest. He is one 'who loves to be first'. This description is only used once in the New Testament to refer to a human being. In Colossians 1:18, the idea of 'being first' is used of Jesus Christ: '… that in all things he might be first …' Biblically, there's only room for one ultimate champion and winner in the Church: Jesus alone breasts the tape. This doesn't mean that leaders should not be confident and even strong in their leadership style, or that to be 'in the spotlight' is automatically wrong. But Diotrephes enjoyed power so much that he abused it and he had become a boss rather than a serving shepherd. And you don't have to be a leader to succumb to the sin of bossiness – there's a reverse version of this problem where leaders become the slaves of the people, who will withhold their offerings, boycott meetings and generally make life excruciating for any leader who actually dares to lead.

Lust for power makes our opinion the only one that counts – usually because we say, 'The Lord told me.' Anyone who questions or challenges us is made to feel that they need to get back in line. Those who get worn out with the situation and leave are dismissed as being unspiritual or rebellious. And we become driven always to be 'the top dog'.

Bosses belong in the Mafia – not the church.

Prayer: Father, You are calling for servants. May I be one? And may servant attitudes pervade Your Church. Amen.

No point of reference

BIG PICTURE:
3 John 9
Hebrews 13:17–21

FOCUS:
'I wrote to the church,
but Diotrephes, who
loves to be first, will have
nothing to do with us.'
(3 John 9)

WE DON'T know the contents of John's lost letter – filed in the wastepaper bin by Diotrephes – but who knows what revelation and insight may have been discarded because of the insolence of one man?

I've been to some highly successful churches that have slipped into isolation and, usually, it is a result of their success. Suddenly their leaders don't have time for local ministers' gatherings: 'They're boring, they're not on the same page as us, we're too busy getting on with the business of building for God to waste any time.'

Successful churches can become fractured from their own denominations and networks too. The result of this is that, sooner or later, there's no one overseeing local leaders. Now there's no one to call upon if local leaders go astray and no accountability to anyone. And those leaders who are demanding accountability from everybody else are not living in that harness themselves: a sure recipe for trouble. The command that we 'obey our leaders' is also true for leaders!

Diotrephes refused to submit to those in authority over him. The apostle John was the 'presbyter' of the region. Diotrephes refused even to read John's correspondence to the congregation, perhaps because it incriminated him and showed his actions were wrong.

No one – not even John, author of the Gospel of John and Revelation, disciple and best friend of Jesus – was going to tell Diotrephes what to do in any given situation. When others try to send you an 'awkward' letter of unwelcome advice, do you return the mail unopened – or unheeded – to the sender?

Prayer: Give me a teachable, hearing heart. Save me from surrounding myself only with those who agree with me. Amen.

Attack by gossip

BIG PICTURE:
3 John 10
Proverbs 26:20–28

FOCUS:
'… I will call attention to what he is doing, gossiping maliciously about us.' (3 John 10)

I COULD hardly believe my ears. The minister had been telling me about a recent exodus of people who have decided that the church he led was not for them. There were a variety of issues that had apparently prompted them to walk, but I was already becoming suspicious that perhaps the main cause of their discontent was this minister's aggressive style of leadership.

During our chat he had interrupted virtually every sentence, had maligned a few good people that I knew but now he was about to deliver an Exocet of a comment and one that I hesitate to put in writing here, it's so shocking. But here goes: 'Of course, I'm sad they've left the church but let's face it, Jeff, every healthy body needs a good bowel movement once in a while, now doesn't it?'

I think my mouth fell open so wide my jaw hit the table. How could he describe people – human beings loved by God – in such terms?

I mentioned this week that sometimes abusive leaders habitually demean others and spread gossip about them, especially those who leave the church. That was the fighting strategy employed by Diotrephes, who was a 'prater', to translate the word rendered 'gossip' precisely. The word 'prate', which only occurs here in the New Testament, means 'to boil up hollow bubbles'. Prattling on and peddling nonsensical rumours about the apostle John, Diotrephes disguised his own rebelliousness by smearing the reputations of those he should have honoured and submitted to. Has someone who left your church been swiftly written off or criticised? Don't be too quick to believe what you hear.

Prayer: Help me to treat others with the respect with which You would have them treated, Lord. Amen.

Don't be too quick to believe what you hear

The controlling censor

BIG PICTURE:
3 John 10
Titus 1:5–9

FOCUS:
'Not satisfied with that, he refuses to welcome the brothers.' (3 John 10)

IN THE dysfunctional church led by Diotrephes, not only was the letterbox sealed to any apostolic letters but the door was slammed shut and bolted to outside itinerant teachers who were sent out to strengthen the church. This was a slap in the face for the apostle John who had apparently sent them. Diotrephes also made sure that teaching differing from his own would not be heard by the congregation. Big brother was definitely watching everybody closely.

It's right that leaders be concerned about teaching – especially via tapes, videos and books – that circulates in the congregation. To give appropriate warnings about extreme 'health and wealth' teaching that seems to do the rounds endlessly, or other emphases that are unbiblical, is part of the duty of leadership. Scripture is loaded with instructions to leaders to guard their flocks from false teaching. The leader 'must hold firmly to the trustworthy message as it has been taught, so that he can encourage others by sound doctrine and refute those who oppose it' (Titus 1:9).

But that's different from a controlling attitude that seeks to prevent people from hearing another point of view – simply because it differs from what I am teaching. And sometimes churches become sealed up teaching units where only those who totally go along with the style, strategy and theological bent of the current leadership are ever invited to contribute to the teaching programme.

Healthy churches aren't afraid of dissident voices. If extreme censorship is being practised in your church, be sure to ask why.

Prayer: Give me grace, Father, to be challenged by those who don't see things my way. Amen.

Healthy churches aren't afraid of dissident voices

BEFORE we leave our brief look at the painful subject of spiritual abuse, it's worth pausing again to see an overbearing leader's dark work. Those whom Diotrephes couldn't control, he forcibly ejected from the church. Apparently some were disobeying his command to refuse hospitality to outside visitors but they suffered expulsion from the church as a result.

One leader, asked about how best to deal with people who cause conflict, said simply, 'Get rid of them, pray them out.' But what is left when every dissident is silenced? The answer is chilling: what remains is a cult. The group may be orthodox in its Christology, firm in its approach to Scripture and espouse none of the wackier ideas usually associated with cults; but the controlling mechanisms that dominate these groups turn them into nothing less than a cult.

Abuse of power is always notoriously difficult to confront – being brought to book is a power player's nightmare! Writer A.T. Robertson penned an article about Diotrephes and leadership abuse for a Christian magazine, portraying him as someone who wants to control a church according to his own desires and whims. When the article was released, twenty church leaders from various parts of the country wrote to the editor to cancel their subscription because of this 'personal attack' on them. Confronting any abuser will never be painless. But John refused to allow Diotrephes to continue destroying the name and work of Christ and so, despite his advancing years, assures the church that, if he is able to visit, he will willingly draw attention to the sins of the leader. Bullies must be stopped.

Prayer: Give me wisdom in dealing with those who bully others. Thank You for shepherds who tenderly care for Your people. Amen.

Shape up or get out

BIG PICTURE:
3 John 10–14
Jeremiah 23:1–4

FOCUS:
'He also stops those who want to do so and puts them out of the church.'
(3 John 10)

Exposing some myths

Over the past few weeks, we've taken a long, hard look at conflict in the church – hopefully we're more realistic about conflict and better equipped for it as a result of our daily journey together.

We have considered problems developing because of conflicting personalities, hurt feelings and leadership oversight. We've pondered unjust criticism, doctrinal debate, leadership clashes and one-on-one clashes. We've wondered at our human inclination towards forming cliques, having divisions, making big fights out of small issues. And we've been sobered, as we've considered tyrannical, dictatorial, insecure leadership and the scope that we all have to lean towards manipulation and control.

Now, as we begin to draw our journey to a conclusion, I'd like to sum up over the next few days by exposing a few common myths that can prevent us from handling conflict well when friendly fire breaks out. 'Old wives' tales' (with respect to older married female storytellers everywhere) flourish by the truckload when it comes to relationships. All truth sets us free. Let's take another shot of reality and expose a few untruths about conflict.

Let's ... expose a few untruths about conflict

Weekend

MY DAD helped the Queen of England go up in the world. He spent his whole working life as an elevator maintenance man and, for a while, he took care of the lifts in Buckingham Palace. The thought that Her Majesty might actually have to walk up a flight of stairs because her lift was out of service filled him with an irrational horror – so he worked very hard to keep things running smoothly, often coming home coated in grease and sweat.

God has already given us unity as a work of His Spirit but has given us all responsibility for the maintenance of that unity. Without effort and work, diligence and a sense of ownership and responsibility, the cogs of fellowship will stop turning; one translation of Ephesians 4:3 is '*maintain* the unity of the Spirit'. The Greek text suggests that this maintenance work is a matter of extreme priority: 'Spare no effort, make it a priority for your corporate life to maintain the unity of the Spirit.'

How do we do that? Through pursuing peace, which bonds us together. As we determine to live in peace with each other (1 Thess. 5:13b) or, as Paul would have it elsewhere, 'Live in *harmony* with one another' (Rom. 12:16, my italics), so we become a people who are not all the same in the way that we think and live but are bound together in harmonious, common purpose. Again, peace takes hard work, negotiation, compromise, willingness to listen, talks late into the night, disappointment to wade through and promises to be kept. Unity isn't automatic and self-sustaining; let's be prepared to roll up our sleeves.

Prayer: Sustain me when relationships are hard work. Help me to maintain what You have given. Amen.

Myth 1: I pray for unity – what else do I need to do?

BIG PICTURE:
**Ephesians 4:1–6
James 3:13–18**

FOCUS:
'Make every effort to keep the unity of the Spirit through the bond of peace.' (Eph. 4:3)

Myth 2: I don't suffer fools gladly

BIG PICTURE:
Romans 15:1–7
Colossians 3:12–14

FOCUS:
'We who are strong
ought to bear with the
failings of the weak and
not to please ourselves.'
(Rom. 15:1)

I LOVE being around brand-new Christians. They are often so wonderfully astonished by the good news of the Christian gospel, have a voracious hunger to learn more, are delighted to be part of their new Christian family that is the Church and have real respect and affection for their newly found brothers and sisters in Christ.

Sadly, sometimes the respect and affection wears off quickly. One of the unfortunate by-products that can show up in our lives as we start to mature as Christians is a short-fused intolerance of those who are not, as we perceive them, as far along the Christian road as we are. The problem is compounded when we find out that we don't like everyone in the church, a reality that still astonishes some Christians. Before long, we are writing others off and we form friendship groups – even cliques – with those whom we perceive to be as spiritually strong as us.

But the Bible makes it clear that we can treat those that we don't naturally like with love and that our mission is not to surround ourselves with those that we find agreeable but also to take time to give a helping hand to 'the weak'. I remain grateful to those who nurtured me in my early years of faith. They answered my hundreds of questions, put up with my daft conclusions and smiled warmly at my wildly impractical ideas of how to reach the world by next Wednesday. Over thirty years later, I still have friends who love me despite my weaknesses. They are priceless.

Prayer: Help me, loving Father, to strengthen the weak. Show me my weaknesses and grow and strengthen me. Amen.

OUR wedding day was quite an event. Kay was late (not her fault), my mother couldn't attend as she was hospitalised 150 miles away (our wedding night began with a trip to the hospital to visit her) and, as a young couple starting out in ministry, we were so broke we had to pray that some people would give us cash wedding gifts so that we'd have enough to buy petrol for a few days of honeymoon. But it was also the epic day when we promised ourselves to each other before witnesses. We were no longer two independent units; now I belong to Kay and she to me, for better or for worse.

When healthy conflict goes sour and people get hurt as a result, sometimes the temptation to back away from local church life is strong. Being together seems too painful, too much effort and too intrusive in my already madly busy life. Isolation is easier. Perhaps we forget that, as Christians, we also belong to each other; a commitment to follow Christ is also a promise to be a part of His family of purpose.

Perhaps belonging is for 'better' right now. Your church is going well, you have good friendships and you even enjoy the worship music. Or perhaps it's a struggle; there's sniping on Sundays, the worship is as exciting as watching paint dry and you just don't feel like fellowship. It's for worse.

Even though it will be tough sometimes, we weren't made for desert island living but for one another. T.S. Eliot asks, 'What is life if we have not life together?' For better. Or for worse.

Prayer: Grant me faithfulness when I feel like running and endurance for the tougher seasons in my relationships. Amen.

Myth 3: I don't need anyone else anyway

BIG PICTURE:
Romans 12:1–21
Ephesians 4:17–32

FOCUS:
'... so in Christ we who are many form one body, and each member belongs to all the others.'
(Rom. 12:5)

... we weren't made for desert island living

Myth 4: I'm just called to straighten the people in my church out …

BIG PICTURE:
Hebrews 3:7–13
1 Thessalonians
5:4–11

FOCUS:
'… encourage one
another daily …'
(Heb. 3:13)

THE man looked at me with piercing blue eyes, as if he knew every secret detail of my life; my sins, my struggles and what I had eaten for breakfast that morning.

'I've decided to join your church,' he affirmed, as if telling me that I'd won a million pound prize. 'God has called me to be a watchman. You and I will be talking.' It didn't occur to me to question his appointment as a time and motion specialist in our church.

Talk we did, endlessly and, for the most part, fruitlessly. He spent all his time scrutinising, evaluating, picking and questioning, not in the normal, healthy way that we have discussed over the last few weeks but with an obsessive zeal, a determination to catch us all doing something wrong. And his complaints were always couched in terms of 'this church', 'you' or 'they' – he never used the term 'us' when trumpeting our foibles. And he never noticed that we did anything well. He seemed to relish conflict. Eventually he moved on, eager for fresh pastures to pick at. I wonder what inner sadness made him so keen to endlessly criticise and never encourage? I was always left feeling demotivated and wearied after yet another negative chat with him. Just one word of affirmation could have made all the difference.

Let's not forget the power of encouragement – a daily necessity (Heb. 3:13) that helps spur us on (Heb. 10:24–25). Go ahead and make someone's day. Catch them doing something right. And unless you're willing to work long, unsociable hours, praying into the cold night for your church, avoid the watchman tag.

Prayer: Who can I encourage today? Guide my path, that I might strengthen someone in their walk with You today. Amen.

Let's not forget

the power of

encouragement

SO MANY conflicts could be resolved if the word 'Sorry' was used, in a heartfelt and genuine way. And friendships could be for life if we were willing to humble ourselves and give and receive forgiveness.

Percy and Florence Arrowsmith married on 1 June, 1925 and held the Guinness World Record for the longest marriage and also for the oldest married couple's aggregate age. They said a lot of their success was all down to the word 'Sorry'.

'I think we're very blessed,' Florence (when 100) told the BBC. 'We still love one another, that's the most important part.' Asked for their secret, Florence said you must never be afraid to say 'Sorry'. 'You must never go to sleep bad friends,' she said, while Percy (then 105) said his secret to marital bliss was just two words: 'Yes dear.' The couple had three children, six grandchildren and nine great-grandchildren. 'I'm looking forward very much to my party,' Florence said.

Perhaps the situation of conflict that you're entwined in is very complex and unravelling it feels like unknotting a 'bird's nest' of fishing line – you're not sure where to begin. Often people leave 'Sorry' until the end of a long discussion or argument; perhaps they could have avoided hours, days or even years of sparring and bruising one another if the starting point, rather than the ending, had included 'I'm sorry.'

Prayer: Lord, help me to forgive, to seek forgiveness and to realise the power of apology. Amen.

Myth 5: Don't get mad, get even

BIG PICTURE:
**Matthew 6:9–15;
18:21–35**

FOCUS:
'Forgive us our debts, as we also have forgiven our debtors.' (Matt. 6:12)

Peace at last

Yesterday I saw my first rattlesnake in the wild and it was not a blessing, just yards from my house in Colorado. It was only a baby but junior rattlesnakes can be even more dangerous than their mature relatives: they can't control their venom output when they bite. The rattler took a lunge – and missed. I was glad when it slithered away. Living in the shadow of the Rocky Mountains is beautiful but there are twenty-two different species of snake, brown bears, mountain lions, deer and elk in the vicinity. Removing the snake, a friend offered some wisdom: 'Jeff, watch where you step.'

... let's walk with care and prayer

Watching our step is important in life. As we've seen, conflict is part of growth but unnecessary hurt could be avoided if we would just engage brain before mouth, be a little more patient, think of others before ourselves, generally tiptoe rather than stamping around and be careful about how we live (Eph. 5:15). There will come a time when all will be in harmony, where predators and victims will be no more as the wolf relaxes alongside the lamb. In the meantime, let's walk with care and prayer. God bless you as you do!

Weekend

Rediscovering Jesus

Rediscovering Jesus

I love Mark's Gospel!

Mark's account, which most commentators believe are Peter's recollections of his adventures with Jesus, are written in simple language, with the bustling population of Rome as his target audience. Mark wrote his Gospel to help Roman converts understand the life, ministry, death and resurrection of Jesus – although he shows more interest in Jesus' activities than he does in His teachings. One of Mark's favourite words is 'immediately'. He uses it 41 times. He's interested in the action. Through Mark's pen we will take a long, luxurious look at Jesus – the most compelling person there's ever been. Jesus is surprising, winsome, humorous, tender, forthright and strong. He escapes Houdini-like from the clever traps that the religious set Him; He shows up in the most unusual places – like the crest of the wave in the middle of a terrifying storm.

We'll get a 'behind the scenes' scoop – some of the episodes were only witnessed by Peter, James and John; and we'll also be encouraged as we see the brilliance of Jesus, contrasted with the bungling of His disciples. Peter himself is shown as an impetuous, stumbling, weak man, which is so encouraging when we consider just how massively God used him! Mark writes bluntly, using vivid descriptions: this Gospel is a real page turner.

And Mark wants us to see what a disciple of Jesus is supposed to look like – so there's a wealth of practical encouragement for our everyday living here, as we rediscover Jesus together. He is the centre and reason for our living. I pray that you'll rediscover the reason you decided to follow Him: more than His teaching, His miracles, He is the knowing Guide who invites us to get in step with Him as we make our way through the confusing maze that is life. Perhaps, together we'll see aspects of Him we never noticed before.

I look forward to sharing Mark's Gospel with you.

God bless you!

Radical religion for all

BIG PICTURE:
Mark 1:1–8
Luke 3:1–20

FOCUS:
'... and all the people of
Jerusalem went out to
him.' (Mark 1:5)

FOR some, Christianity has a warm, cosy image. Mention the church, and many think of plummy-voiced parsons, smiling grey-haired ladies, steaming tea pots and Victoria Sponge cake. Faith seems more about comfort than crisis; not so much an invitation to enlist for a cosmic fight, more a call to join the flower rota.

But John the Baptist grabbed the people of Israel by the throat with his revolutionary cry. As God's living exclamation mark, with his shrill preaching and bizarre fashion choices, John turned heads and then hearts. Most of us wouldn't be too comfortable with his sledgehammer 'You're a brood of snakes' sermons (Luke 3:7); seeker-sensitive this man was not. But everyone got the message – even those who clung to the false notion that their nationality and nominal faith made them part of God's in-crowd. John called the Jews to awake from their self-sufficient slumber.

Jews practised ceremonial washings, but only Gentiles converting to Judaism usually went through full baptism. John insisted that *everyone* – regardless of religious background or ethnicity – needed to be ready for a change of heart, mind and behaviour. This 'baptism of repentance' was no vague ceremony. As the crowds flocked out to the desert, and literally shouted their sins out loud before going under water, John was preparing them to open their ears to the message and the radical Messenger who was to come.

Whatever our religious pedigree, we all need Jesus. And true Christianity creates upheaval, life change, and danger. It could even cost you your life – as John himself later found out.

Prayer: Save me from settling into comfortable ideas about being a follower of Christ. Help me embrace the revolution today. Amen.

... we all need Jesus

Sustained by love

BIG PICTURE:
Mark 1:9–13
John 15:9–11

FOCUS:
'And a voice came from heaven: "You are my Son, whom I love; with you I am well pleased."'
(Mark 1:11)

I WAS born a decade after the last World War, and so never experienced the traumas of that terrible time. But as a parent, I have pondered what it would have felt like to hug a soldier son goodbye at the railway station, wondering if I would ever see his face again. What parting words would you choose to sustain someone for such a long, difficult journey: a voyage that might ultimately lead to excruciating pain and even death? Surely the message that you would want left lingering in their hearts would be obvious: 'I love you.'

So it was with God. Mark, typical evangelist that he is, gets right to what he sees as the main point as Jesus, without fanfare, sweeps into the story. No details of His birth or childhood are included: He is, simply, 'from Nazareth' (v.9).

There will be a baptism, and then battle would commence in the wilderness of temptation. And so the heavens are torn open, the Spirit descends, and a voice speaks words that will carry Christ through the awesome and awful days to come. 'With you I am well pleased.' The translation in the Holman Christian Standard Bible is: 'I take delight in you.' And this said before any demons had been scattered, any epic sermons had been preached or any sicknesses healed. The Father's love – a theme that Jesus frequently celebrated – is the *reason for* and not the *result of* what we do (John 5:20).

Perhaps it feels like you're in the Sahara heat right now, and devils seem more real than angels; or worse – it is just eerily quiet, and the spiritual world seems irrelevant. Know this and be strengthened: you are loved.

Know this and be strengthened: you are loved

Prayer: Father, keep the knowledge of Your love for me before me. Help me to accept, enjoy and share that love. Amen.

Destiny's interruption

BIG PICTURE:
Mark 1:16–20
1 Kings 19:20–21

FOCUS:
'"Come, follow me,"
Jesus said, "and I will
make you fishers of
men."' (Mark 1:17)

GOD is a traveller; He's going somewhere, and would like the pleasure of our company and co-operation. As Jesus picks His team, we realise that discipleship is still an invitation to journey with Him. The call to 'invite Jesus into our hearts' doesn't accurately describe the decision to become a Christian. It suggests a God who will come to *us*, a static experience, rather than a loving challenge for us to go with Him: the discovery of our destiny.

The call to Peter, Andrew, James and John came as they were hard at work as professional fisherman. Jesus is wonderfully disruptive and will interrupt our plans without hesitation because He has something far better in mind for us all than survival or even success. Often the best people for a task are the busiest.

Forget the caricature that suggests these were simple, illiterate labourers; most likely these four were the owner-operators and partners (Luke 5:10) in what was often an extremely profitable business in the Graeco-Roman world. Something about Jesus prompted them to turn their backs on security and success, like Elisha running after Elijah: 'at once they left their nets and followed him' (v.18).

With the invitation came the promise: 'I will make you fishers of men'. To live as a Christian on earth is not to just sit around in heaven's waiting room. Peter, James and John would form Jesus' 'inner circle' (Mark 1:29; 5:37; 9:2; 13:3; 14:33). God has unique purposes that He wants to see fulfilled as a result of your being on planet Earth. Let Him interrupt your day and your life.

Prayer: Break into my plans, reshape my hopes and ambitions; surprise me with Your purposes. Only then am I truly alive. Amen.

Jesus is astonishing

BIG PICTURE:
Mark 1:21–39
Luke 8:40–56

FOCUS:
'The people were amazed
…' (Mark 1:22)

JESUS is shocking. One of the most misleading caricatures of Him is the 'gentle Jesus, meek and mild' persona that portrays Him as an insipid chap, who would faint at the thought of rocking any religious boats. Nothing could be farther from the truth.

He launches into ministry with the effectiveness of a stun grenade. Demons shriek in protest and scurry off back to hell. People living under the heel of Roman oppression suddenly meet someone who is in charge of everything; Doberman-like demons are told to shut their mouths. Pain is sent packing and chronically ill patients leap out of bed and cook lunch (v.31). His teaching carries its own incredible authority. Rabbis quoted others extensively to make their words weightier: Jesus speaks as One sent directly from heaven.

Even popularity couldn't pin Him down. Free from the demands of the crowds, He did what few popular leaders would ever do – walking away from their mingled adulation and demands (John 6:15) and playing before the audience of one in solitary prayer.

Little wonder that the people were so shocked: the word 'astonished' means to be struck repeatedly by blows. Jesus came like a repeated slap on the back of the head.

Jesus is no tamed, conventionally nice person who props up the status quo: He is wonderfully alarming and bids us leave our ruts. Being a Christian *does* have its boring bits: when prayer seems ignored, when faith feels like a leap over the Grand Canyon, when Christians fall out, or when we're sneered at for believing. But never let it be said that *Jesus* is boring. Now that is impossible.

He is wonderfully

alarming and

bids us leave

our ruts

Prayer: Give me the gift of astonishment again at You and at Your lavish grace, Jesus. Amen.

I'VE witnessed a few 'dodgy' miracles in my time: healings claimed that at best were unproven; people who fell to the ground (allegedly under the power of the Spirit), but with a little strong arm help from the pushy person praying for them, and 'words of knowledge' that were a little more like words of *general* knowledge. You don't need a hotline to God to know that someone, somewhere in a large crowd suffers from back pain.

But I remain convinced that God is still in the miracle business. Admittedly, we don't see nearly as many stunning healings as we would like, and the issue of why one person is healed while another stays sick is complex. But the Bible commands us to pray for healing (James 5:14–16) and nowhere does Scripture ever hint that the potential for the supernatural has ceased. As a man comes to Jesus and begs Him to cleanse him from the living death of leprosy, we see how a miracle should be performed. Mark wants us to know the motive for the miracle: compassion. Miracles are about people, not mere firework displays for the excitement of the masses.

The miracle is also credible; Jesus touches the man to prove that he was healed: no Jew would touch an 'unclean' leper (Lev. 13–14). And Jesus insists that the healing passes the scrutiny of a priest. To call for medical confirmation to authenticate a miraculous claim is not unbelief, but responsible faith. Finally, far from wanting to hype the event, Jesus insists that the leper keep his stunning story secret – which would have taken an even greater miracle of restraint ...

Prayer: Lord, give me faith to ask for more of Your power, and discernment to know where You are at work. Amen.

How to do a miracle

BIG PICTURE:
Mark 1:40–45
Psalm 77:1–14

FOCUS:
'See that you don't tell this to anyone. But go, show yourself to the priest and offer the sacrifices that Moses commanded for your cleansing, as a testimony to them.' (Mark 1:44)

Authority to forgive sins

Mark 2:1–12
Galatians 5:1–15

Yesterday we considered a man who was cleansed from the living death of leprosy, a consuming, devastating disease that slowly destroyed the limbs of its helpless victim and drove them into the isolation of an unclean outcast. Our modern culture has its own leprosy-like epidemic: guilt and shame. Our hedonistic, 'If it feels good, do it' approach to life carries a terrible psychological price tag. Try as we may to convince ourselves that sin doesn't matter: in most cases, our heart and our conscience just won't agree. Jesus, in speaking forgiveness to another man with cataclysmic disabilities, a stretcher-bound 'paralytic', uses a word that means, 'let the pot drop'.

> Are you circling endlessly ... because you feel so ashamed?

Whatever his history, whatever specific shameful events that punctuated this man's past, Jesus alone is able to tell him: 'Drop the past and pick up your bed.'

Are you circling endlessly because of yesterday's awful failure, or emotionally bed-ridden because you feel so ashamed? Come to Jesus, and hear Him speak words that made the religious people so very mad and the sinners so very glad: 'Drop it.' Of course, such scandalous grace (Gal. 5:11) often sounds like blasphemy to religious ears.

Weekend

Hanging out with sinners

**BIG PICTURE:
Mark 2:13–17
Matthew 11:18–19**

FOCUS:
'It is not the healthy who
need a doctor, but the
sick. I have not come to
call the righteous, but
sinners.' (Mark 2:17)

HE WAS about 6' 6" of solid muscle, he had a dreadful reputation as a violent thug and was considered so nasty that someone had told him that 'he was so bad, he needed to go to church' – an unusual evangelistic strategy but a biblical one. After all, church is for bad people: why would the healthy athlete head for the hospital? He stood at the back, a cold spectator; his facial expression a fixed stare, his every muscle rigid, completely unyielding. Until one of the older ladies of the church, 30 years older and two feet shorter than him, decided to make him feel welcome. She welcomed him with a beaming smile like an old trusted friend. Seconds later he was weeping uncontrollably. Minutes later, he was a Christian.

Why is it that religious people always want to run in pious herds and avoid those that they perceive as sinners? Perhaps we fear guilt by association or the possibility of contamination. Jesus was criticised more for His eating habits than His sermon style: He would insist on socialising with the 'wrong' people. No one would have objected if He had just kept the so-called 'low life' types corralled in a pen and preached at them: sinners make good trophies for 'before' and 'after' stories; we just like them more 'after' than 'before' (Acts 9:26).

Jesus was the guest of honour in the home of a newly converted loan shark and surrounded Himself with a motley crew of failures and low-lifes. What would happen if they showed up in a pack at our churches next Sunday morning?

Prayer: Save me from the narrow confines of my comfort zones, God. Help me to reach out when I dread it. Amen.

Once right, always right?

BIG PICTURE:
Mark 2:18–28
Matthew 22:14

FOCUS:
'Now John's disciples and the Pharisees were fasting. Some people … asked Jesus, "How is it that John's disciples and the disciples of the Pharisees are fasting, but yours are not?"'
(Mark 2:18)

CHRISTIANS aren't usually famous for their parties. But God is. The Bible continually pictures Him as the extravagant banquet host, the persistent party planner who so wants us to learn to celebrate life with Him, He'll even invite total 'strangers' to the bash He is throwing (Matt. 22:9).

But if God is the renowned host, then we humans are rather good at turning His invitations down flat. The elder brother folds his arms and refuses to tap his feet to the music when his kid brother comes home (Luke 15:28). At times we are just too busy, too preoccupied, to enter in (Luke 14:15–20).

Even John the Baptist's followers sniffed at the invite to Jesus' party. Disciplined people have much to teach us about diligent prayer but are often better at fasting than feasting. Some people are so intensely committed to God that they lose their ability to enjoy Him: their Christianity creates a furrowed brow rather than a grateful, celebrating smile. Notice that even those who have been right in the past can slip up today. John the Baptist's team had been pivotal players in the unfolding purposes of God. But just because we have been right in the past doesn't mean that we will automatically be correct today. The possibility that we may be wrong can come as a real surprise to some of us, especially if we have an established record and reputation for being wise. What Jesus came to do was not to patch up the old: only those who were willing to think in an entirely new way could participate in the party He'd planned.

Prayer: Lord, give me wisdom, understanding, and the ability to participate in Your purposes for me today. Amen.

God … wants us

to learn to

celebrate life

with Him …

Irritating God

BIG PICTURE:
Mark 3:1–12
Romans 2:1–8

FOCUS:
'He looked round at
them in anger ... deeply
distressed at their
stubborn hearts ...'
(Mark 3:5)

WHAT is it that upsets Jesus? An angry Jesus is rare in Mark's Gospel, so we should study the picture closely. It's a vital question too; it's possible to waste a lifetime being offended on His behalf, endlessly bristling about issues that probably don't bother Jesus. When we finally get to meet Jesus face to face, I'm convinced that He won't be quizzing us about the layout of our pews, the loudness of our songs, and our preference for the guitar over the organ, or our preferred Bible translation. We Christians famously major on minors, insisting that heaven gets angry with the same issues. Perhaps angels occasionally watch our petty anger, more bemused than bothered.

Nevertheless, God gets angry. Injustice (Ezek. 9:9), oppression (Psa. 10:18), hypocrisy (Matt. 23:13–29), and here, stubbornness of heart (hardness of heart is the literal translation) seem to top the list of things that seemingly frustrate and irritate Him. Stay tender towards God; obey Him quickly.

Jesus' *actions* as well as His *attitude* show that traditionalism and legalism frustrate Him too. Jewish tradition stated that there were 39 acts that were strictly forbidden on the Sabbath. Moses had prohibited work on that day; it was wrong to kindle a fire for cooking (Exod. 35:3), gather fuel (Num. 15:32ff), carry burdens (Jer. 17:21ff), and transact business (Neh. 10:31; 13:15,19). But now that invitation to pause had been turned into a labyrinth of prohibitions, even limiting how far people could travel on the Sabbath. In short, the Sabbath Day had become a prison cell: Jesus' anger over rigid legalism was shown by the way He ignored those rules.

Prayer: Lord, please show me when I'm passionate about things that You are indifferent to, and nonchalant about issues that matter. Amen.

Life's priority

BIG PICTURE:
Mark 3:13–19
John 15:1–8

FOCUS:
'He appointed twelve
– designating them
apostles – that they
might be with him ...'
(Mark 3:14)

YESTERDAY we realised the uncomfortable truth that we can squander too many years crusading passionately about issues that God is indifferent to, while ignoring what stirs Him to righteous anger (Jer. 44:6). Today, as we consider the primary calling of Jesus' team – to be with Him – we realise that Jesus calls us to intimacy with Him that leads to service for Him. Anything less could mean that we expend our energies on activities and projects that God is at best indifferent to. We aren't called to make waves but, like Jesus, to surf the waves the Father makes (John 5:19). It was appropriate that the team later called 'The Twelve' began its life together on a mountain – the place where, biblically, humans experience God, like Moses and Elijah.

Jesus Himself modelled this lifestyle of spirituality that leads to action; we know from Luke's account that Jesus selected His team following a night of prayer (Luke 6:12).

When the 'mountain' of daily communion is no longer our priority, we can be the victims of our own bright ideas. What if God isn't in them? Peter was guilty of this (Luke 9:33). The busier for God we are, the more important it is to check that He still approves today what He sanctioned yesterday. The better the idea, the greater its ability to develop a life of its own.

Throughout his Gospel, as Mark emphasises the failures of the Twelve, we see that the world can be turned right side up by weak people whose daily stumbling along is actually a walk with God.

Prayer: Walk with me today, Jesus. Direct and protect me. I want You, the One who blesses, and not just Your blessing. Amen.

Controlling Jesus

BIG PICTURE:
Mark 3:20–21
John 10:17–18

FOCUS:
'When his family heard about this, they went to take charge of him, for they said, "He is out of his mind."' (Mark 3:21)

JESUS always was and forever is a nightmare for control freaks who'd like to choreograph His moves. He refuses to get in step with their marching orders, or parrot the scripts they've carefully drafted. But that doesn't stop them trying to manoeuvre Him. Satan took Jesus up to the Temple's pinnacle and tried to nudge Him to become the miracle baker from Galilee. He even tried to strike a deal to turn the Son of God into a Satan-worshipper. But Jesus refused to take the bait.

And then there was the lynch mob that pinned His arms and sought to lob Him into oblivion; but He just 'passed right through the crowd'. Devils can't move Him and mobs can't mug Him; He was only finally arrested because He chose to lay His life down (John 10:17–18).

Remarkably, even His kith and kin tried to corral Him. They were concerned about the clamouring crowds that prevented Him and His team from even eating and so they trekked 30 miles, fearful about fanaticism and nervous about His mental health. They tried to take Him into their protective custody – the Greek word here literally means 'to arrest'.

Of course, His family genuinely were doing what they thought was for the best. Some of the world's worst ideas were birthed for the noblest reasons. Perhaps some of us are endeavouring to tell Jesus what to do, deluded by the fantastic notion that we know better than God. We're not the first, and we won't be the last to try it. God made us in His image and ever since we've been trying to return the favour.

Better to let Him be God.

Prayer: Forgive me when I resist or rebel against You; thinking I know best. I choose Your way today. Amen.

Better to let Him be God

Pardon and peace

Thousands of Christians share this fear: have they blasphemed the Holy Spirit? Are they beyond the pale of God's grace? Look at this episode again.

The religious generals were trying to smear Jesus' ministry. His undeniable miracles showed them up; there was only one thing for it. They announced that His power was demonic. As they pumped out their outrageous accusation, they crossed a line. There would be no way back.

Perhaps we've tagged what we didn't understand as evil; we have blasphemed. Is there pardon available for us? Be assured. In a sense, we can never sin as the Pharisees did, because Jesus is no longer on earth as He was. He did His miracles before them and they rejected Him. Paul was a terrible blasphemer and murderer of Christians (Acts 8:1–3) but he found great grace. Our ability to feel guilt is evidence of the ongoing conviction of God – and therefore that forgiveness is available. Thirdly, we *have* turned to Christ. Those Pharisees were drowning men who defiantly rejected God's rescuer. Forgiveness couldn't be theirs: not because it was unavailable but because they rejected and smeared the One who offered a grace embrace (Luke 13:34–35).

Be at peace: pardon is available.

Be at peace

Weekend

128

Kingdom family

BIG PICTURE:
Mark 3:31–35
John 6:35–40

FOCUS:
'Whoever does God's
will is my brother and
sister and mother.'
(Mark 3:35)

IN SOME churches, people still address each other by prefacing their name with 'brother' or 'sister'– I can't tell you how many times I've been called 'brother Jeff'. It all sounds somewhat quaint, and whenever it happens, I feel ever so slightly like a monk. It's also a useful little device for those all too frequent times when I forget people's names. If in doubt, just call them brother – although do make sure that they are male if you do; sisters who are called brothers can get violent …

At first glance, Jesus seems rude to His mother and brothers; they are parked outside, demanding to see Him, while He insists on continuing with His teaching session. He uses the moment of tension to teach about a new family that He is part of – a brotherhood and sisterhood based not on flesh and blood but on radical obedience to the will and purposes of God. Don't forget the reason for the visit of Mary and her boys: they wanted to take Jesus away. But Jesus demonstrates that He answers to the authority of a higher parent; His heavenly Father (John 6:38) – and that all who do the same are now part of a new family order. His brothers and sisters are not those who wait outside, wanting to strong arm Him home, but rather are the ones who don't just believe in the idea of obeying God – but actually submit to Him on Monday mornings as well as Sunday mornings. It's been said that blood is thicker than water; in this case, obedience is thicker than both.

Prayer: Show me Your will, God, and help me to follow it. Help me express my love for You in my obedience. Amen.

Heart attack

BIG PICTURE:
Mark 4:1–20
John 15:1–8

FOCUS:
'Others, like seed sown on good soil, hear the word, accept it, and produce a crop – thirty, sixty or even a hundred times what was sown.'
(Mark 4:20)

IT WAS our first day of Bible college training, our Old Testament lecturer was welcoming us, and his opening words hit us in the face like a bucket of icy water. 'Ten years from now, many of you will have walked or drifted away from faith. The statistics aren't encouraging: stay close to God.'

We looked around the lecture hall, incredulous. Surely this man had fried his brains on too much academia, or he was just plain deluded. We were bright-eyed zealots who collectively aspired to change the world for Jesus by next Thursday. The idea that any of us might end up as casualties was unthinkable. But tragically, he was right. I'm not inspired when I look at my class photograph; too many of those keen young people have changed their mind about Jesus. They burned out, messed up or faded away.

The parable of the seed shows us that while it's always sad and tragic when people fall away from Christianity, it shouldn't surprise us. The deadly cocktail of battle, distraction, persecution, anxiety, and materialism poisons faith, and even those who continue produce fruit with varying success.

It's a sobering warning that should nudge us towards taking more care about what we allow into our hearts and minds. We live surrounded by pollutants that are toxic to faith and life. To open our hearts to junk is to trash our lives: the heart is the 'wellspring of life' (Prov. 4:23–27).

So when someone decides to become a Christian, celebrate – and then pray hard and support them in every way you can.

Prayer: Father, I pray for all of those in this vicinity who are new in faith. Sustain, encourage and protect them. Amen.

To open our hearts to junk is to trash our lives

It's designed for sharing

BIG PICTURE:
Mark 4:21–25
Matthew 5:14–16

FOCUS:
'For whatever is
hidden is meant to be
disclosed, and whatever
is concealed is meant to
be brought out into the
open.' (Mark 4:22)

IT'S a nagging, uncomfortable thought, but one that challenges me almost daily: do I really believe the truths that I say I believe? I affirm my faith on Sunday mornings – but all that talk about people outside of Christ being lost: do I *live* on Mondays as if that were true?

Attending a Sunday morning service can be like going to the cinema. When I'm watching Tom Cruise in action, I temporarily believe that what is before me on screen is real. I participate fully in the fantasy, laughing at the ludicrous and weeping at the tragic.

Then the movie ends, the lights come up, and within seconds I'm amazed at the ludicrous plot, the unsatisfying ending or the terror that pulsed through my nervous system only seconds earlier. Surely something similar happens ten thousand times over in churches every Sunday morning. We wholeheartedly agree with the sermon that calls us to the hard work of mission, to meet the needs of the poor, to roll up our sleeves and help carry the burden of responsibility in the local church. Our heart and brain declare an 'Amen' to the obviously biblical ideas that are being presented. But then the lights come up as the parting blessing or benediction is pronounced and we get back to our real lives in the real world: moved for a moment, unchanged for the long term.

Truth must be shared. It's vital, like a flickering oil lamp that lights a pitch-black house. In a sense, when I stop sharing my faith, I begin to lose it. It doesn't work in secret, hidden under bowls and beneath beds.

Prayer: Let others see Your light as they see me, God. Let Your truth be demonstrated in and through me today. Amen.

The 'X' factor

BIG PICTURE:
Mark 4:26–34
Zechariah 4:6

FOCUS:
'A man scatters seed on the ground. Night and day, whether he sleeps or gets up, the seed sprouts and grows, though he does not know how.'
(Mark 4:26–27)

I'D BE delighted to grow a little more hair, but those miracle potions that promise a Mel Gibson mullet in a few days turn me cold. But within the church there is placed a genuine natural growth ingredient – a divine 'X' factor.

Yesterday we saw that faith unshared won't work. But there's a danger in that conclusion. Our passion to share Jesus can be hijacked and turned into an ugly mania, where we endeavour to win the world by sheer hard work. We decide that if we just pray enough, serve enough, fill every waking hour with activity, then the kingdom of God will come. Life becomes a treadmill; we miss too many moments of joy and burnout beckons us. As the workplace demands that so many people begin work at dawn and vacate their desk long after dusk, the church can add to the already intolerable burden of busyness that has become normal life for so many. If we're not careful, we end up doing what Walter Bruggeman describes as living 'unauthorised lives and unauthorised ministries' – work for God that He never commissioned.

Put simply, God's work will grow, through our work – and while we rest too. No other corporation or organisation on earth enjoys the vital growth ingredient that the kingdom of God has: Jesus has promised to build His Church (Matt. 16:18).

Do what God asks you to do today. And then let Him do what only He can do. Seemingly insignificant moments of kindness revolutionise lives. A sentence or two shared about God becomes a lighthouse to a storm-sick traveller. Small seeds grow into great trees. It's by His Spirit, not by our sweat.

God's work will grow, through our work – and while we rest ...

Prayer: Show me what I am called to, Lord. Help me rest in the knowledge that You are doing what only You can do. Amen.

IT'S easier to accept that God loves the world than to grasp that He loves *me*. Affirming that Jesus is able to heal sickness generally is simple. But then an email from a friend brings news that they are trapped in the grip of a tenacious cancer and I struggle to believe that God's healing power can impact such a close situation. Sullen clouds block out blue skies and banish any possibility of sunshine; faith mocks me, because God's power feels so far beyond my reach. My prayers rage on; and God sleeps on, or so it seems.

Perhaps that's how the disciples felt as they battled a terrifying squall on the Sea of Galilee. They'd seen Jesus at His miracle-working best, but now He naps during a perfect storm. Unbelief washes over them, like the waves that now fill the boat. They shake Jesus awake with a good telling off (in Mark's Gospel, the disciples frequently tell Jesus what to do – see 5:31; 6:37; 8:4,32). The panic-stricken words that spill out of their mouths show why they struggled to believe: 'Don't you care?' They knew His power – they just weren't convinced about His concern. Whatever you don't know today, declare this, even if your mind rebels at the thought: God does care about me (1 Pet. 5:7).

At the end of the day, the disciples get more than a millpond sea. In Jewish tradition, the one who ruled the winds and sea was God Himself (Psa. 107:29). They were sailing with One who mingled awesome authority with unfathomable love. So are we.

Prayer: Lord, You care about me. May the knowledge of Your care steer me peacefully through my storms. Amen.

While you were sleeping

BIG PICTURE:
Mark 4:35–41
Psalm 121:1–8

FOCUS:
'Jesus was in the stern, sleeping on a cushion. The disciples woke him and said to him, "Teacher, don't you care if we drown?"'
(Mark 4:38)

Mark 5:1–15
1 Corinthians
1:26–31

A hopeless case

I know one or two people who would make fantastic Christians – at least by my reckoning. They are caring, kind, engaged in their community and disciplined as well: why, they'd be a serious asset to the kingdom … And there are others whom I could never imagine as Christians. I'm convinced that church would drive them mad, faith would be a step too far and looking beyond their own selfish horizons to a hurting world would probably never happen.

He can do more than we can imagine

But the truth is that there are no great candidates for Christianity – and none who are beyond redemption either. Mark sketches a stark picture of the cave-dwelling demoniac; in every way, he seems a hopeless case. He was human housing for a whole herd of demons. Violent and uncontrollable, madness tormented this tragic man day and night. He seemed to hate everyone, including himself. Hardly Exhibit 1, the man most likely to convert …

Weekend

… which is exactly what he did when Jesus came by. Sanity and dignity restored, his transformation stunned the locals who had viewed him as a totally hopeless case.

Who is it in your life that you just cannot imagine coming to Christ? Perhaps it's time to start praying again, and realise, as you do, that you're talking to the one who bought revolution to a madman in Gerasa. He can do more than we can imagine (Eph. 3:20).

Don't be fooled

BIG PICTURE:
Mark 5:11–17
Romans 6:1–14

FOCUS:
'He gave them
permission, and the
evil spirits … went
into the pigs. The herd,
about two thousand in
number, rushed down
the steep bank into the
lake and … drowned.'
(Mark 5:13)

SOMETIMES sin comes with sugar coating. Darkness disguises itself as light, as the seductive power of temptation works away at our hearts and minds. Can something that feels so good be so bad? Surely everyone else is indulging in what we are desperately trying to refuse? The relentless propaganda campaign rages around us daily, as we switch on the television, walk past advertising billboards, or browse a magazine rack: dive in, and consider the consequences later. And these days the occult is dressed up as a winsome, fascinating and mysteriously beautiful woman, rather than the wizened, destructive crone that she really is. Don't dabble with the powers of darkness: there's real power there, and not the kind of power any of us need. Satan is both an angel of light (2 Cor. 11:14) and a roaring lion (1 Pet. 5:8).

For anyone who doubts the destructive power of sin, consider what must have been a terrifying sight: one to remember for a lifetime. Two thousand squealing pigs charge down the hillside and hurl themselves into a lake. For a while, the waters boil with animals that thrash and fight before they finally drown. It's a hideous picture of destruction – and the creatures that inspire their suicidal stampede had been living inside a man.

Look again and see the truth about sin – and the power of deception too. The locals, distraught at the loss of their livestock and apparently oblivious to the miracle of the former naked madman, now clothed and in his right mind, beg Jesus to go away. It's a bizarre choice – and one that is still made daily.

Prayer: Save me from the power of deception and deliver me from all evil today. Amen.

Go home

BIG PICTURE:
Mark 5:18–20
Ephesians 5:22–6:4

FOCUS:
'Jesus did not let him, but said, "Go home to your family and tell them how much the Lord has done for you, and how he has had mercy on you."'
(Mark 5:19)

AS a new Christian, I used to regularly go out and knock on doors to tell people about Jesus. This was a terrifying experience, sometimes because of the gigantic wolf-like dog that lurked the other side of the door, probably hungry to snack on a passing Christian. Worse still was the possibility that a human being might be behind that door – 'door-to-door work', as we called it, is so much harder when people actually answer the door …

But there was one truly intimidating place where I was called to share my faith – and that was in my own home. Looking back, I was unsubtle ('Hi, Mum and Dad, did you know you're going to hell?'), inconsistent (I wept in prayer for my then pagan parents but I might have made more impression if I'd cleared up my room) and they were confused and bewildered: had their youngest son joined a strange cult?

The home can be a hard place to live out faith. There your weaknesses are most well known, and you can sometimes treat those closest to you with something less than respect; familiarity breeding contempt. But there's not much value in trying to reach the world if we ignore those closest to hand, as the now restored madman discovered. The Gentile area of Decapolis urgently needed to hear the good news and who better to be the newscaster than this former walking tragedy? And he was a successful broadcaster, because people were 'amazed' – literally, they kept on marvelling. Jesus wants us to live for Him indoors as well as door-to-door.

Prayer: God, I pray for those closest to me: help me to love, serve and live for You before them and with them. Amen.

The home can be a hard place to live out faith

JUST the other day I heard a sermon about the 'laws' of sowing and reaping. The preacher told his congregation that God had to respond to a certain type of sacrificial giving – it was a law of blessing. While remaining convinced that God keeps His promises, I'm nervous about this 'six scriptural secrets beginning with Z for a brighter, more prosperous life' approach, because it reduces faith to a set of concrete steps, rather than a daily relationship of intimacy with God. No relationship can be reduced to a set of principles; if it is hereby decreed that I buy my wife flowers on our anniversary and take her to a certain restaurant on her birthday, then spontaneity and joy are lost from our marriage. Israel mistakenly believed that she could twist God's arm with their rituals and routines – which became meaningless and actually irritated God.

Jairus took the huge, risky step of asking Jesus for help; as a synagogue ruler he was a prominent dignitary in the community, and now he is found prostrate before Jesus' feet – his 'little' daughter lay dying. He got a quick response: Jesus headed off directly for the house where the child lay. Jesus could have healed the girl from a distance (John 4:46–54; Matt. 8:5–13), but He chose to go with the worried father – perhaps for no reason other than the fact that traumatised Jairus asked Him to go with him. Perhaps the Lord wanted to encourage Jairus as well as heal his daughter – but, whatever His motives, notice that He doesn't always do the same things the same way. God is dependable – but rarely predictable.

Prayer: Help me to trust You, Lord, when I don't understand Your methods. Amen.

Faith and formulas

BIG PICTURE:
Mark 5:21–24a
Isaiah 1:10–17

FOCUS:
"'My little daughter is dying. Please come and put your hands on her so that she will be healed and live." So Jesus went with him.'"
(Mark 5:23–24a)

No magic here

BIG PICTURE:
Mark 5:24–34
Psalm 33:1–15

FOCUS:
'… she thought, "If I just touch his clothes, I will be healed." Immediately her bleeding stopped and she felt in her body that she was freed from her suffering.'
(Mark 5:28–29)

WE SAW yesterday that it's foolhardy to try to pin God down to a particular formula or methodology – and sometimes He does things in a way that we don't like. But then God will be God …

I've written extensively about my irritation with television preachers who turn the gospel into an emotional circus and bring discredit on the Church with their hallelujah hocus pocus. But one thing frustrates me more – and that is that God apparently does meet some people at these services. What is He thinking? Surely His activity signifies approval of the messenger and the method – so why does He insist on showing up, demonstrating what appears to be an acute lack of divine discernment? And I wish that Paul hadn't done that handkerchief thing in Acts 19:12 – and what was that with Peter's shadow in Acts 5:15?

The truth is that whenever God catches wind of faith, He comes running. That doesn't mean that He endorses the flawed life or methods of the messenger; it just shows how passionately He loves and how eager He is to bless.

A woman, a long-suffering victim of medical quackery (Dr Luke, a physician himself, omits that detail in Luke 8:43) reaches out to touch Jesus' cloak – at best a superstitious and yet desperate act. As one who was considered ritually unclean because of her 12-year long menstrual flow, even touching Jesus' clothing would make Him unclean too. But she ended up healed anyway, and Mark, who loves to celebrate women's faith (7:29; 12:44; 15:40–41) records the moment. Faith is always imperfect and sometimes downright skewed: but God blesses us anyway.

… God blesses us anyway

Prayer: Thank You for Your kindness, Lord, which compels You to run to us; our weaknesses and flaws don't repel You. Amen.

Unfailing kindness

BIG PICTURE:
Mark 5:35–43
Psalm 18:46–50

FOCUS:
'He took her by the hand
and said to her, *"Talitha
koum!"* (which means,
"Little girl, I say to you,
get up!").' (Mark 5:41)

MARK'S eagle eye for detail gives us quite a long gaze at Jesus' beautiful personality. Look at how He deals with Jairus in the synagogue ruler's darkest moment; He offers far more than power, more than the spectacular miracle of bringing life back into a cold corpse. His kindness breathes warmth and compassion into the bleak scene. A friend delivers the hammer blow: too late, Jairus, your daughter is dead. The mourners, their wailing turned to derisive laughter at Jesus, confirm the terrible news. She is gone.

Gently, Jesus encourages the distraught dad to continue in faith. Mark loves to record quotes from Jesus exactly as they were spoken (Mark 7:34; 14:36); the literal translation of Jesus' comforting nudge to faith is 'Be not afraid, go on believing.' And then listen to Him at the girl's bedside. Jesus used a loving phrase in Aramaic, which Mark translates for his non-Jewish readers. The word translated *little girl* has the same affectionate tone to it as calling a child a 'lamb' in English.

The child stirs and, to the astonishment of her parents, gets up. Sometimes 'spiritual' people forget to be practical. Ever concerned for her ongoing welfare, Jesus instructs the stunned parents to give her food. At every step, Jesus shows that His power is far more than an impressive display. He offers genuine concern and comfort as well as the authority to make death itself cower.

Don't relegate God to a power source when you need a breakthrough or demote Him to be your personal GPS system when you need guidance. He wants to be so much more.

Prayer: Give me wisdom to remember what 'spiritual' people sometimes forget, Lord. Thank You for Your interest in the details of my life. Amen.

Familiarity breeding contempt

When you think you have Jesus all figured out, beware!

Weekend

New Christians are usually very flexible. Change the service times, and you won't usually find the less seasoned believers complaining. Relocate the piano and it won't be those fresh to faith that panic. Junior Christians are too new to live in ruts, too thrilled to be bothered about trivial details. It's often those of us who have been around for a while, who think that we know God rather well and therefore can predict His moves – we're the ones who are more likely to struggle with change. Jesus returned to Nazareth where a year before He had been rejected by the people and evicted from the synagogue (Luke 4:16–30). They thought that they really knew Him. After all, He had been their neighbour for nearly 30 years, they had seen Him at work in the carpenter's shop and He appeared to be just another Nazarene. He was a 'commoner' and the people saw no reason to commit themselves to Him.

The people of Nazareth were 'offended at Him', which literally means 'they stumbled over Him'. The Greek word gives us our English word, *scandalise*.

When you think you have Jesus all figured out, beware! Could He surprise you if He tried?

WE CHRISTIANS don't like failure. We prefer prayers that are answered, projects that actually work and statistics that encourage. We get discouraged – and sometimes self-condemning – when all of our hard work produces little fruit. If someone we love decides to become a prodigal and stomps off in the direction of a piggery, some of us assume that it must be our fault; we didn't love, pray or give enough.

But Jesus wasn't a 'success' everywhere He went – if you measure success by how people responded to Him. We've already seen that He was stung by rejection in His home town, booted out by people who chose bacon over deliverance and now as He sends out His two-by-two team, He warns them not everyone will respond to their message or miracles. Paul tasted rejection in Ephesus (Acts 19:9). After spending a whole three months arguing in the synagogue there, he was shunned. It was depressing for the pioneering apostle; he describes his time in the province of Asia (which most commentators believe was Ephesus) as a season when he felt 'the sentence of death' in his heart (2 Cor. 1:9). But there are no breast-beating post mortems. Paul moves to the meeting hall of Tyrannus, where he was to find a more responsive crowd.

Not everything we touch will turn to gold but keep trying anyway and don't let disappointment stifle hope. The act of shaking the dust off of the sandals was not just a petulant, 'You rejected us so we thumb our noses at you and we're out of here' gesture. It was a prophetic action that might show door slammers the error of their ways.

Prayer: Strengthen me when I taste rejection because of You, Jesus. When I apparently fail, give me hope to try again. Amen.

Rejection prepared for

BIG PICTURE:
Mark 6:6–13
Acts 19:1,8–12

FOCUS:
'And if any place will not welcome you or listen to you, shake the dust off your feet when you leave, as a testimony against them.' (Mark 6:11)

Junction moments

BIG PICTURE:
Mark 6:14–29
Proverbs 8:1–10

FOCUS:
'The king was greatly distressed, but because of his oaths and his dinner guests, he did not want to refuse her.'
(Mark 6:26)

IRON Lady Margaret Thatcher famously declared 'This lady's not for turning.' Sometimes we march on a pathway of destruction, to catastrophe. There are moments that change everything. Decades are often determined by what seem to be small decisions; the knock-on effects are felt years after: the chance meeting that leads to a marriage, the conversation over a meal that is the catalyst for a career change, the alcohol-blurred blunder that sparks disaster.

When he raised another glass and drank a toast to the daughter of his wife (and former sister-in-law), Herod couldn't have known that so much hung in the balance in the next few seconds. Seduced by a cunning set-up and eager to appear the extravagant host, he promised her the world: and an innocent man died. Bitter at John the Baptist because of his prophetic finger-pointing, Herodias demands his head on a plate. The life of one of the greatest men in history is snuffed out on a whim, because of the insane oath (the original says 'many oaths') that had tumbled out of Herod's over-active mouth.

The tragedy could easily have been averted. Herod had respected and protected John and knew that he was making a terrible mistake. He was under huge pressure in that hushed banqueting hall as the dancing girl made her demand for an execution – there and then (v.25). But he wouldn't lose face, so the Baptist lost his head.

Have you made a deal, climbed under someone else's expectations, or are heading towards the edge of a moral cliff? Slam the brakes on, and turn – before it's too late.

Slam the brakes on, and turn –
before it's too late

Prayer: Give me understanding, Lord, and an eagerness to turn when I realise that I'm wrong. Teach me Your ways. Amen.

Rest easy …

BIG PICTURE:
Mark 6:30–31
Matthew 11:28–30

FOCUS:
'… he said to them,
"Come with me by
yourselves to a quiet
place and get some rest."'
(Mark 6:31)

I AM currently battling to cut down the busyness of my life – and it's hard. Saying 'No' doesn't come easily to me; when I'm asked to speak at three different events on the same day, I think about self cloning rather than refusing any one of them. I fear that when I die, I'll throw myself headlong into the grave and will twitch there for days, simply because of the accumulated momentum.

But getting away from it all for a while is a great idea, according to Jesus. His exhausted and excited disciples return from their trip, most likely bubbling over with reports of all that had happened. But with dangerous and emotional draining days looming not far ahead, there was a need for some well-earned rest and relaxation.

It's a simple thought, but don't miss it: we need to be able to rest without a sense of guilt. Some of us don't feel right – or religious – unless we're serving, speaking, studying or praying. It takes us days to wind down when we go on vacation, and even then we're agitated because a nagging voice inside us insists that we should be doing something 'useful'. Yet the corny truism sums it up: if we're not willing to come apart for a while, then we'll simply come apart. Laziness is a problem for some (Prov. 24:33–34) but hurry sickness affects more.

Jesus insisted that they go to a quiet – literally 'remote' place. A change of scenery, together with the recognition that there's no sin in feeling 'peopled out', can be exactly what the doctor, or in this case the Saviour, ordered. Relax about relaxation.

Prayer: Show me how to live in an ordered rhythm that leads to peace, rather than a frantic rush that leads to panic. Amen.

A dark, yet lightened day

BIG PICTURE:
Mark 6:32–44
Luke 24:13–35

FOCUS:
'By this time it was late in the day, so his disciples came to him. "This is a remote place," they said, "and it's already very late."'
(Mark 6:35)

KAY and I were eager for some time alone, a quiet dinner, a chance to catch up – I'd been away for a three-week ministry trip. We chose a candlelit corner in the restaurant, and then noticed a couple from our church headed our way. They were good, but difficult people; not our friends, and their social awkwardness had earned them something of a reputation. Now, uninvited, they joined us. Too weary and too embarrassed to protest, we spent the rest of the very long evening grinning through gritted teeth – they ate slowly and talked much.

Plans are scuppered by an unexpected twist in the road, or a long hoped for treat turns out to be anything but. So the disciples must have felt as the sun set in the desert. No one had argued when Jesus issued His warm invitation to some well earned rest; this would be their chance to enjoy the luxury of having Jesus all to themselves, perhaps to share a meal, sip some good wine, and swap a dozen stories from their trip. But the ever-clamouring crowds ruined it. After a few hours, they were probably at the end of their tether – sunset came as what they thought would be a welcome amen to the day. But God is also at work on tiresome days; the disciples are eager to shoo the crowds away, but, as the shadows lengthen and their tired limbs ache more, a miracle of multiplication unfolds, and thousands are fed from a single snack. We all have dull days – and sometimes months. But God can show up in them too.

... God is also at work on tiresome days

Prayer: Father, help me to never write off days, or even months, as times when Your loving care cannot reach me. Amen.

Growing up

BIG PICTURE:
Mark 6:45–46
1 Peter 2:1–2

FOCUS:
'Immediately Jesus
made his disciples get
into the boat and go
on ahead of him …
while he dismissed the
crowd. After leaving
them, he went up on a
mountainside to pray.'
(Mark 6:45–46)

I'VE noticed, after some 32 years as a Christian, that God's dealings with me are different now from the way He acted in my life in those early days. As a brand-new Christian, I felt spoon-fed with His blessing; He shouted rather than whispered, answered some of the most obscure and bizarre prayers, and put up with some of my misguided zeal. I'd throw open the Bible and plonk my finger down randomly on a verse, hoping for guidance in what was little more than a scriptural lucky dip – and strangely, sometimes it worked.

Three decades later, God is unchanging, but He treats me differently. Perhaps His parenting is similar to mine; when my children were small, I expected them to ask me for permission to go outside to play in the street; now, if 22-year-old Richard telephoned to ask me if he could go out, I'd be a little concerned. Surely he can make adult decisions now?

The disciples had been in a storm before – but Jesus had been with them in the boat, albeit asleep. Now, He leads them into a second storm – but without Him present: He leaves to climb the mountain of prayer. They've seen so much since that first event – so have they grown up a little? This was preparation for the time, soon to come, when Jesus would no longer be with them. In the coming months, they would have another mountain-top experience with 5,000 coming to Christ, followed by a storm of persecution (Acts 4:1–22). Would they remember the lessons learned on this day – and would they have grown? God is moving on. Are we?

Prayer: God, help me to hold on to the lessons of life. May what I have learned yesterday equip me for today. Amen.

Cowards can
be brave when
they know
Jesus is around

Weekend

With us

I have recently experienced a milestone day in my
life – Kay and I jumped off a mountain in New
Zealand, and parachuted 3,000 feet down. I had
expected that the sound of my screaming would
scare the entire town far below, but, as it turns out,
there was but one brief moment of fear. Why the
confidence as we leapt into the abyss? It was all
due to the presence of Nick and Rob, our trusty
instructors. They made it all sound so easy, and
promised to be with us all the way. Then the wind
picked up, and we began to spiral down at speed: so I
reminded myself – the instructor is with me, and he
knows what he is doing. Impersonating a gibbering
chimp seemed the right thing to do, but the urge to
scream subsided.

The whole experience was possible only because we
knew we were not alone; there was absolutely no
way that I would have made that jump without Nick
at my side. Jesus doesn't initially calm the raging
storm for His disciples, but shows them that He is
still there – and can walk on the waves that threaten
their progress. Cowards can be brave when they
know Jesus is around.

Used

BIG PICTURE:
Mark 6:53–56
John 6:22–71

FOCUS:
'And wherever he went
… they placed the sick
in the marketplaces.
They begged him to let
them touch even the
edge of his cloak, and all
who touched him were
healed.' (Mark 6:56)

I LIKE to think that I'm a generous person; I enjoy giving and blessing people. But I know myself well enough to admit that I really don't like being used. Whenever I catch a hint that I am being manipulated, I retreat at speed.

But Jesus spent His whole life surrounded by users who clamoured for His attention: not because they wanted Him but because they wanted what He could do for them. In a way, who can blame them? Their lives blighted by incurable diseases, they saw Him as their exit strategy, their one and only hope. Perhaps encouraged by rumours about that woman who was healed simply by touching His cloak (Mark 5:27) they desperately begged to be able to do the same. Everywhere He went now, He was greeted by packed marketplaces (the largest gathering areas in those days) crammed with people all singing the same song: help. And help He did; He allowed Himself to be used.

Within 24 hours Jesus would deliver His famous 'Bread of life' sermon, which would prove to be extremely unpopular. The grabbing crowds would thin and gratitude would be replaced by grumbling. But in the meantime, knowing that He was little more than medicine on legs to many, a mere commodity, Jesus relieved their suffering.

It's been said that you can only find out if you're a servant by noting how you react when people treat you like one. Feeling a little used? It's happened before. You're in good company.

Prayer: Lord, give me generosity to serve when I sense that others' motives aren't pure: help me to spend myself in Your name. Amen.

More grumbling

BIG PICTURE:
Mark 7:1–5
Matthew 11:16–19

FOCUS:
'So the Pharisees and teachers of the law asked Jesus, "Why don't your disciples live according to the tradition of the elders instead of eating their food with 'unclean' hands?"' (Mark 7:5)

ONCE I visited a church that had been hoping for years that local young people would be reached with the gospel. They'd fasted, held lengthy prayer meetings, and at first, had been delighted when the new youth club had proved to be the bridge; those who had only turned up on Friday nights were showing up on Sunday mornings. But there was a snag: cigarette butts littered the car park, some were showing up covered in tattoos and body piercings. And, horror of horrors, instead of saying 'amen' during the worship time, they would cheer and whistle. Some church members started to complain. The wondrous sight of young people praising God had worn thin.

Miracles aren't enough for some people. Let the blind see, and the lame walk again, but if the miracle worker refuses to dance to their tune (Matt. 11:16–19) then they had better look out. There's trouble ahead. The disciples of Jesus were not being cavalier with the Law of Moses and this hand washing that the religious leaders spoke of had nothing to do with hygiene. The real issue here was control: Jesus wasn't doing things their way. Blinded to the stunning miracles, the bigots could only focus on one thing: they were losing their grip as Jesus challenged their rights as sole salvation franchise holders.

Meanwhile, confronted by complaints about the worshipful whistling, the minister made a wise response. 'Two weeks ago those kids were sniffing glue and drinking too much alcohol. They had nothing to live for, nothing to celebrate. Let them whistle.'

Be careful when you pray: it might be answered but not in the way you'd hope for.

Be careful when you pray

Prayer: Lord, give me grace to be thankful when You work in a way that confronts my need to control. Be Lord. Amen.

WE CHRISTIANS like to blame God for what we do or don't do. Rather than refusing to join the cleaning rota at the church, we insist that 'It's just not our ministry.' Challenged about our financial giving, we defend ourselves by announcing that we're making the issue of money a matter of prayer. Strangely, some of us never seem to reach an 'Amen' or write a decent cheque.

Jesus has a marvellous way of cutting through our pious prattle with the efficiency of a chainsaw. We like to blur the issues – but He snaps us back into sharp focus and clarity.

Once again, the religious leaders demonstrate that a little dose of piety can be a dangerous thing. The Pharisees had found a marvellous way to leave their parents destitute, and even managed to blame God for their neglect. Evil could be done, apparently with God's backing. Even when they crucified Jesus, they insisted they were doing God a favour (Matt. 26:65).

'Corban' is the Greek transliteration of a Hebrew term used to refer to a gift devoted to God. A worshipper could declare that a part of their income was dedicated by a vow to God. If a son declared that the resources needed to support his ageing parents were 'Corban' then, according to scribal tradition, he was exempt from his responsibilities to care for them, and they were legally excluded from any claim on him. The scribes emphasised that his vow was unalterable. It was a nifty way of doing nothing – and doing nothing in God's name. Let's be careful about spiritualising and rationalising our reluctance to do what we know is right.

Prayer: Save me from hiding behind clichés or religious slogans, Lord. Help me to do what is right, and not make excuses. Amen.

Corban: it's God's fault

BIG PICTURE:
**Mark 7:6-13
Matthew 26:57–68**

FOCUS:
'But you say that if a man says to his [parents]: "Whatever help you might otherwise have received from me is Corban" … then you no longer let him do anything for [them].'
(Mark 7:11–12)

The patience of Jesus

BIG PICTURE:
Mark 7:14–23
Acts 10:1–23

FOCUS:
'After he had left the crowd and entered the house, his disciples asked him about this parable. "Are you so dull?" he asked.'
(Mark 7:17–18)

Don't give up

on yourself;

after all,

He doesn't

SOMETIMES I really worry about me. I feel like a spiritual tortoise surrounded by Ferrari turtles when it comes to moving ahead with God. Earlier in our journey through Mark, we looked at the importance of learning the lessons of life. Sometimes I think that I've graduated a class or two, only to discover that I have to retake the same course a few years later. Is there any hope for me?

Mark's Gospel reveals to us the brilliance of Jesus, often contrasted with His slow, dull-witted disciples, who often didn't 'get it', despite all His best efforts. At first glance this passage shows us Jesus teaching a revolutionary and vital truth: holiness is not about mere external rules and regulations, it's a matter of the heart. It's possible to tick all the right boxes of the current do's and don'ts of the church, but still have a heart that reeks like a decomposing corpse (Matt. 23:27).

But look again at just who is in the crowd – and also in the private class later where Jesus explains His teaching more fully. Peter is there, with a front row seat to hear that kosher snacking doesn't impress God. And yet years later, the Holy Spirit has to disturb his rooftop nap with a dramatic dream that would make exactly the same point and would release him to preach the gospel to the Gentiles. He had to relearn a principle that Jesus had clearly taught him already. Sound familiar?

Take heart. Dull people, to coin Jesus' phrase, can still change the world. Don't give up on yourself; after all, He doesn't.

Prayer: Lord, sometimes I'm so slow. Help me to understand, to see and to know Your ways. Amen.

EVER meet armchair radicals? They wax eloquent about the ills of the world, and are gifted experts when it comes to identifying the weaknesses of the Church – but they don't actually *do* anything to help things. In their cleverness they imply that they have a faith that will move mountains, but they are unwilling to move a muscle. But true radicalism is about what you do, not what you say you believe.

Jesus, having just dropped a prophetic stun grenade with His teaching about what is clean and unclean, now moves to practice what He preaches as He steps beyond the borders of Palestine and takes His message and miracles to the Gentile populations of Tyre and then to the region of Decapolis. Two miracles occur: one of deliverance, the other of the healing of a man who was deaf and had almost no ability to speak. Jesus seems to deal harshly with the woman whose daughter was tormented by demons, until you realise that He talks of throwing food to 'the little pet puppies' (the literal translation); the Jews called the Gentiles 'scavenger dogs'. Perhaps He was trying to provoke her faith with His words; and perhaps He was attempting to nudge those 'dull' disciples to see what exclusive faith looks like …

Twice in His ministry Jesus commends 'great faith', this Syro-Phoenician woman and the Roman centurion (Matt. 8:5–13). In both cases, it is faith found among Gentiles, a reality that would have stunned the Jews.

Let's walk the talk. Let's not just talk revolution, but live it.

Prayer: Lord, save me from ideas that go nowhere and build nothing. Help me live what I know to be true. Amen.

Radical words, radical actions

BIG PICTURE:
Mark 7:24–37
James 2:14–19

FOCUS:
'Then Jesus left the vicinity of Tyre and went through Sidon, down to the Sea of Galilee and into the region of the Decapolis.' (Mark 7:31)

Déjà vu

We've already seen that the disciples were somewhat thick – 'dull' to be exact. Now they stretch the extent of their stupidity to the limit, and they are placed in a situation that is almost an exact replica of an event we considered a few days ago. They saw and participated in the feeding of the 5,000 in a remote place – now there are 4,000 to be fed, in (you guessed it) a remote place. And they ask the very same question as before: what are the catering arrangements? It's almost unbelievable, as that amnesia that we mentioned earlier kicks in again. The two events are so similar that some commentators suggest that they are the same – which is untenable: Mark records both, Jesus discusses both incidents separately, and there are clear factual distinctions between the two. But it is like déjà vu.

Let's not rush to judge this hapless crew. If we know anything about our human nature, then we have to admit that we too often insist on carrying on asking God questions that He has already answered, as if, somehow, as we keep on He will change His mind.

So are you currently somewhere you've been before?

... are you currently somewhere you've been before?

Weekend

AS A NEW Christian, I felt that I had suddenly had my eyes opened and now life made sense. Unfortunately, it's taken me a few years to understand that there's still much that I don't understand – and that's OK. My quick and somewhat clichéd answers won't work for me anymore. I've had to make friends with the half sight of mystery.

Seven blind people receive their sight miraculously in the Gospels; Jesus used a variety of approaches in healing them. But here we have something strange – a gradual, two-stage healing. Some think that the unbelief of the city of Bethsaida contributed to the battle (see Mark 6:5–6), which might be why Jesus deliberately led the man out of town in order to help him. Others suggest a lack of faith on the part of the blind man himself, although I'm always nervous about rushing to that conclusion.

Many commentators believe that this miracle is in fact a living parable, a working demonstration of the twilight faith and half-vision that Jesus' disciples consistently displayed. Certainly the event follows their unbelieving ineptitude in the feeding of the 4,000, and just before we hear Peter making a profession about who he believed Jesus was.

Perhaps we'd do well to pause and face the fact that we don't see things nearly as clearly as we'd like to believe. Our 20/20 vision is well out of focus and utterly blurred compared to what God knows and sees. Now we see 'but a poor reflection as in a mirror' (1 Cor. 13:12).

Perhaps you're fretting because there's so much that you don't see. Join the crowd.

Prayer: Help me to trust You when I don't see, and stay close to You when I think I see clearly. Amen.

We don't see clearly either

BIG PICTURE:
Mark 8:22–26
1 Corinthians
13:12–13

FOCUS:
'Jesus asked, "Do you see anything?" He looked up and said, "I see people; they look like trees walking around."'
(Mark 8:23–24)

The bottom line

BIG PICTURE:
Mark 8:27–29
1 Corinthians
11:23–26

FOCUS:
"'But what about you?'
he asked. 'Who do
you say I am?' Peter
answered, 'You are the
Christ.'" (Mark 8:29)

I THINK I'd quite like to be an Anglican.

I've come to appreciate the power of creative liturgy, and believe that there is such tremendous strength to be found in being part of a community that weekly makes a profession of faith in Christ. Whatever the weather, whatever is happening in the world, our Anglican friends gather and proclaim: 'We believe.' Critics argue that this can be repetitive and meaningless ritual, which is true of any religious expression or style. But the creeds bring us back to the core foundation of who God is, who we are as a result and how we are called to live.

We saw yesterday that there are times when we can feel lost in the fog, bewildered by what we don't know. But at times like that, we come back to the bare minimums of our faith, the non-negotiables that can get us through the darkest seasons.

So, just six months before the shadow of Calvary would fall over Jesus, He brings His friends back to the central issue and asks them to make a declaration of His identity.

Perhaps you're in a shadowy land yourself right now and your mind is confused and agitated. Your faith is weak, you have more questions than answers and, like the disciples, everything you've seen yesterday isn't helping you to make sense of today.

Affirm, by faith, this truth: He is the Christ. And if you can find a community of others who will join with you in that proclamation, however they express it and whatever style they use, then do it.

Affirm, by faith, this truth: He is the Christ

Prayer: You are the Christ, the Son of the Living God: You are my Saviour and Lord. Amen.

His way

BIG PICTURE:
Mark 8:30
Isaiah 55:8–13

FOCUS:
'Jesus warned them not
to tell anyone about
him.' (Mark 8:30)

'CHRISTIANS' gather at a gay funeral, clutching 'God hates faggots' placards and screaming Bible texts. They think that they are serving God and take the abuse and criticism that they receive as confirmation that they are doing the right thing. An anti-abortion zealot, who also is a believer, bombs a clinic. A sincere, good man with a loud hailer bombards passers by with verbal missiles, informing them that they are on their way to an eternal barbecue. Is he helping or hurting?

History is littered with too many examples of human beings doing God a favour. The Bible has been used to justify slavery, the hanging of a child for stealing a loaf of bread, the injustice of apartheid and the Crusades.

One of the worst things that we can do is to do God's work in our way. Billions are being spent every day, in Jesus' name, on activity that seems good and logical but that God Himself has never sanctioned and that ultimately does more harm than good.

Why did Jesus warn His friends to keep quiet about Him? For one thing, the disciples themselves still had much to learn about Him and what it truly meant to follow Him. The crowds wanted to see His miracles but not to submit to His message. The religious leaders of the nation had already made up their minds about Him, and to proclaim Him as Messiah now would only upset God's plans and might result in a political uprising that would only do harm. Sometimes what seems to be the obvious thing to do is not the best course of action.

Prayer: May what I do in Your name only be those acts that You have called me to do, Lord. Amen.

Out of this world

BIG PICTURE:
Mark 8:31
Philippians 1:12–30

FOCUS:
'He … began to teach them that the Son of Man must … be rejected by the elders … and teachers … and … be killed and after three days rise again.'
(Mark 8:31)

WE SAW yesterday that God would like His work done His way. This means that, if we are going to spend the rest of our lives as followers of Jesus, then we'd better brace ourselves for some unanticipated bends in the road. And perhaps one of the biggest shockers is the news that much of His work is about eternity. Our human tendency is to want everything in the here and now; some of us even dismiss talk of heaven as pie in the sky. I've preached a few times about those Christians who are so heavenly minded they're of no earthly use. Never mind forever, we're tempted to say, let's roll up our sleeves and get on with the business of changing the world today. And we're quite wrong.

The disciples believed in the coming of a messianic figure who would overthrow the hated enemies of Israel and set himself up on a throne in Jerusalem. The notion of a weak, crucified Messiah who would die didn't fit with their thinking at all.

The fact is, there has never been one single Christian in existence who has been too focused on heaven. Those fuelled by the knowledge that there's more to life than what we experience here and now are strengthened to face the darker days, spend themselves for the greatest cause in the universe and look forward to the reward to come (Heb. 10:35)

Most of us forget that we're going to live forever, the bright horizon of the future eclipsed by the ever-present pressures of today. Is life currently especially tough? Remember. There's something far better to come.

There's something far better to come

Prayer: Father, place a sense of eternity in my mind, my priorities and my motives. Amen.

ONE of the more uncomfortable surprises of life is when 'good' people do bad things. There's always something so disappointing when we discover that a loved, trusted Christian leader has been living a long-term double life, an eloquent preacher on Sundays and a profligate on Mondays. I've heard it said: 'I don't understand how they could fall in that way: I could never do that.' Personally, I'd prefer to never say 'Never'. I'd rather stay aware of my weaknesses, and be alert to the potential pitfalls: 'So, if you think you are standing firm, be careful that you don't fall!' (1 Cor. 10:12).

The truth is that good people are capable of doing some very bad things. Peter had just spoken words of revelation, a truth revealed to him by heaven: congratulations, Peter. Now, just minutes or perhaps moments later, he blurts out a notion spawned in hell, and he even rebukes Jesus – a strong word here that Mark normally uses to describe rebuking an evil spirit. The rock had become the stumbling block (Matt. 16:23). And Peter wasn't alone in his misguided ideas; true to his character, he was acting as spokesman for the rest of the disciples. Mark notes that Jesus speaks to Peter, but looks at the whole group, giving the sternest rebuke, 'Get behind me, Satan!' He was effectively commanding Peter and his pals to get back into place – in step, as followers behind Jesus, not bosses who tell Him what to do. We can do great good – or great harm. Peter was, at times, oblivious to his own weaknesses (Luke 22:33). Do you know how and where you might trip up?

The myth of utterly good people

BIG PICTURE:
Mark 8:32–33
Matthew 16:13–20

FOCUS:
'... Peter took him aside and began to rebuke him.' (Mark 8:32)

Prayer: Show me where I am weak, Lord. Deliver me from being one who walks in darkness. Amen.

Against the tide

Once in a while it's good to remember that when we determine to follow Jesus, we're swimming against the tide, marching in precisely the opposite direction of the crowd. Satan offers glory without suffering, and Jesus invites us to see suffering turned into glory. The world invites us to be free-spirited individuals who do their own thing, but Jesus calls us to get in step with Him, whatever the cost. We're surrounded by media messages that encourage grabbing and winning, and He speaks of giving and losing.

Sometimes being a Christian is about sheer obedience. No one feels like volunteering for death row; selecting the pathway of pain doesn't come naturally to us. I'd prefer a couch to a cross. Notice that we're called to deny self – not self-denial, which reeks of asceticism. The cost of discipleship may include giving up something for Lent, but cuts far deeper. Jesus makes the Christian life sound rather tough, and it is. Luke adds that this cross bearing is a decision taken daily (Luke 9:23).

But there is an important detail to remember as we hear this solemn call from Jesus. His is the right way.

Sometimes being a Christian is about sheer obedience

Weekend

PAUSE for a moment. In the episodes that we've scanned in Mark so far, we've seen the magnificence of Jesus, contrasted with the muddling of His disciples. And as we'll see tomorrow, their ham-fisted ineptitude continues: in fact, things go into major meltdown while He is up on the mountain with Peter, James and John.

But as we trudge up the mountain with them, and catch a glimpse of a man in shining white having a little chat with Moses and Elijah, we realise Mark is keen to impress upon us that Jesus wants to build our faith. This whole scene is created to help out those who made up His inner circle. The dazzling white glory, the guest appearances of those two Old Testament superstars, and even the voice of God the Father booming His love and approval from the heavens; the whole event was designed to build faith into His closest followers and friends. The disciples' lack of faith was a great concern to the Lord (Mark 4:40; 6:50–52; 8:17–21).

Jesus doesn't just demand that we believe, but is the One who is willing to help us to grow in faith; faith itself is sometimes a direct gift of the Holy Spirit at work within us (1 Cor. 12:9).

That doesn't mean that He'll perform supernatural stunts in order to impress us. But we can ask Him to expand our faith (Luke 17:5) and lead us through moments and days which will help us in our believing. He did just that for His friends, and as His friends today, we can ask for something similar.

Prayer: Lord, increase my faith, and may I be someone who brings strength and nurture to the faith of others. Amen.

Increase our faith

BIG PICTURE:
Mark 9:2–13
1 Corinthians 2:1–5

FOCUS:
'After six days Jesus took Peter, James and John with him and led them up a high mountain, where they were all alone. There he was transfigured before them.' (Mark 9:2)

An aid to faith

BIG PICTURE:
Mark 9:14–29
Joel 2:12–17

FOCUS:
'After Jesus had gone indoors, his disciples asked him privately, "Why couldn't we drive it out?" He replied, "This kind can come out only by prayer."'
(Mark 9:28–29)

AN OLD story is told of a little boy who prayed for a bike and didn't get one. Finally he slipped into a church, stole a statue of the Virgin Mary, and then prayed again that night: 'Jesus, as you know, I'd like a bike. I suggest that You give me one, if You ever want to see your Mother again …' He obviously thought that prayer was about twisting God's arm.

The blundering brigade that was the nine disciples were unable to work a miracle because they hadn't prayed and, even though it's only in some later manuscripts that fasting is added, it's part of the programme. Fasting isn't my favourite thing. I've got friends who have successfully navigated their way through extended times of fasting, but as of yet, I've only ever managed three days. (OK, it was two and a half.)

But Jesus assumed that His followers would pray, fast, and give (Matt. 6:16–17). Going without food in order to focus on God more diligently is a thoroughly biblical idea. But why? Is the practice of fasting little more than a spiritual hunger strike, something to manipulate a response?

Yesterday we saw that God wants our faith to grow, and today we see one of the ways that it can happen. Faith can be cultivated by prayerful discipline. Like a trip to the gym, fasting strengthens the muscle of faith as we give ourselves to prayer without distraction.

Jesus is not corralled by prayer and fasting, but in the unfolding partnership and adventure that is the life of discipleship, discipline will obviously be vital if we are to know God's power at work through us.

Prayer: Lord, help me to embrace discipline and yet not fall into legalism. Amen.

Faith can be

cultivated by

prayerful

discipline

Nervous around Jesus

BIG PICTURE:
Mark 9:30–32
Hebrews 4:14–16

FOCUS:
'But they did not understand what he meant and were afraid to ask him about it.'
(Mark 9:32)

I DON'T like being around people who surround themselves with eggshells for me to walk on. I'd rather hang out with people that I can relax with and be myself – including God. But sometimes being around God has made me jumpy.

I went through a lengthy period of my Christian life when I was very nervous to be around Jesus. Yesterday we considered the importance of prayer and fasting, and my hesitation about being in God's presence certainly didn't help me develop spiritual disciplines. I thought that the Lord was permanently dissatisfied with me. Whatever my efforts, I felt I could never pray quite enough, read enough chapters of the Bible, or talk enough about Jesus to others. Like a whipped puppy flinching, ready to recoil from yet another beating, I preferred Jesus at a distance. Who knows what He might say if I got too close to Him?

The disciples developed a similar hesitation. This was not a brief season of fear – the Greek text reveals that they lived in this nervous state for a while. Perhaps stung by Jesus rebuking Peter ('Get behind me, Satan!') they worried and battled with their fears, but didn't share them with Him.

So what can inspire confidence in us, to run to God with our little questions, our messes and sins, our questions and fears? We are invited to come with confidence to 'the throne of grace' (Heb. 4:16) where authority mingled with kindness dwells. Don't hold back, even with questions and struggles that seem foolish: He offers to help, providing wisdom without finding fault with us (James 1:5).

Prayer: Teach me to be at home with You God, through the blood of Christ shed for me. Amen.

Real success

BIG PICTURE:
Mark 9:33–37
1 Samuel 18:1–9

FOCUS:
'He took a little child and … said … "Whoever welcomes one of these little children in my name welcomes me; and … the one who sent me."' (Mark 9:36–37)

CHILDREN enjoy a freedom that is gradually eroded by the shackling that so-called maturity brings. They giggle without being self-conscious, sometimes say the first thing that pops into their minds, and will often welcome a newcomer into their circle with the warmth and trust that we sophisticated grown-ups reserve only for our closest friends. They are the greatest. And the disciples didn't realise that fact.

Deception creates further deception. Once you've missed one vital truth, you're likely to meander into other alluring avenues of error and confusion. The disciples were reluctant to let go of their long-cherished notions of a political messiah who would boot out the hated Romans and set up his own hierarchy. Despite all that Jesus had taught them to the contrary, error dies hard. But one bad idea leads to another, and so now they are squabbling between them about who will be the top dog. Perhaps they were a little stung by Jesus only taking His inner cabinet of Peter, James and John to the fluorescent Mount of Transfiguration, and so controversy about greatness erupts.

Endlessly pursuing fame and applause is a waste of life. Our hunger for recognition shows that there's a Grand Canyon sized void in us that will never be filled, no matter how many applaud us: King Saul was a tragic example. And to be a celebrity is not to be successful in life; Jesus shows us, using the example of a child (the word for a young person and servant was used interchangeably) that real success in life is to give yourself for others, with the carefree, untainted motives of a child.

Endlessly pursuing

fame and applause

is a waste of life

Prayer: God, give me the simplicity of a child. Amen.

Envy disguised

BIG PICTURE:
Mark 9:38–41
James 3:13–18

FOCUS:
'"Teacher," said John,
"we saw a man driving
out demons in your
name and we told him to
stop, because he was not
one of us."'(Mark 9:38)

WE DROVE by a sign advertising a massively successful church – huge crowds were flocking to its services. The minister I was with told me that some of his pastoral colleagues were nervous about the fast-growing church. 'They're not sure that the pure gospel is being preached.'

We Christians can be experts at franchising. Most of us nurse the notion that our church is probably the best in town, the translation of the Bible that we use is probably the purest, our programmes and methods are the most effective, and of course, our worship style is the most heartfelt, creative and pleasing to God. When I became a Christian over three decades ago, I found it hard to believe that there were any believers that existed beyond the immediate horizon of our denomination. Thank God, all that has changed for the better but still we can feel discomfort when we find that God is blessing another group who may do things differently from us – especially if He is apparently blessing them more than us.

John, wanting to change the subject from the 'I am the greatest' conversation, told of how he had rebuked a man for exercising a deliverance ministry in Jesus' name. He probably expected a pat on the back from Jesus for 'minding the shop'. And he had conveniently forgotten the disciples' own total inability to bring deliverance to another desperate young man (Mark 9:17). Sometimes we attack those who aren't part of our outfit simply because we don't like the fact that they are more successful than us. It's called jealousy and along with 'selfish ambition' it's the root cause of what the Bible describes as 'disorder and every evil practice' (James 3:16).

Prayer: Father, please help me celebrate when others experience more of You and Your blessing than me. Amen.

Mark 9:42–50
Judges 6:25–27

... take an axe
to what
doesn't belong

Weekend

Take sin seriously

Christianity can turn into a vague habit. What started out as a determined walk with Jesus can turn into a casual stroll, as we amble along, more careless than careful. But there's something very intentional about being a disciple, as Jesus' teaching about our attitude to sin demonstrates. Any of us who have settled into sleepy spirituality must surely hear the wake-up call in all this language about amputation and self-mutilation. As we hear Him command us to lop off our hands and feet, and gouge our own eyes out, we're relieved to know that He is not speaking literally (although one figure in church history, Origen, didn't realise that until after he had castrated himself. Oops).

What is being called for is a no-nonsense attitude towards those enticing 'little' sins that seem to charm their way into our lives. Worn down by the rationalisations, we welcome things that belong in the dustbin. When we tolerate sin, our lives lose the tang that 'salt' brings. Our behaviour means that we are not different and we cease to be useful. Let's not hesitate or procrastinate, but figuratively speaking, take an axe to what doesn't belong. And as we think during this last week about issues that really matter to Jesus, let's make them our priorities too.

RECENTLY I spotted in America one of the most nauseating examples of our modern culture – a drive-through divorce window. Tired of that boring marriage? Now, you don't even have to get out of the car. That relationship can be nuked for a mere $99, sign here please …

Everything seems to be disposable these days – contact lenses, cameras and even relationships. And the problem isn't only in the USA; a friend who lives in a leafy Cotswold village told me just last week that she has many women in her friendship circle who are going through divorce, 'because they just don't love their husbands any more'. She had an insightful response: 'I tell them, what kind of reason is that?'

The Bible's teaching on divorce is complex. I won't risk bruising some of my readers with an over-hasty comment here. But once again we see that Jesus calls us away from an attitude that trashes a marriage (or for that matter, a friendship or a relationship with a church) simply because it would take too much effort to work at it, or we are in the mood for something different. Some rabbis in Jesus' day taught that a man could divorce his wife for burning his food. Jesus called those who followed Him beyond such selfishness and superficiality. He delivered these words in an area governed by Herod (the divorced king who had John the Baptist's head because he spoke up about Herod's relationships). And in speaking these words, Jesus gave far greater status and indeed protection to women.

Don't 'feel' in love today? There aren't easy answers, but the quick fix fixes nothing.

Prayer: Help me to love when I don't 'feel' love, Lord. Thank You for Your faithfulness. Amen.

Relationships matter to God

BIG PICTURE:
Mark 10:1–12
Colossians 4:7–9

FOCUS:
'Therefore what God has joined together, let man not separate.'
(Mark 10:9)

People 'on the margins' matter to God

BIG PICTURE:
Mark 10:13–16
James 2:1–7

FOCUS:
'People were bringing little children to Jesus to have him touch them, but the disciples rebuked them. When Jesus saw this, he was indignant.'
(Mark 10:13–14a)

SOMETIMES I hear Christian leaders talking about the need to develop 'strategic relationships', which I think is a wordy way of describing networking with people who can advance our ministries, churches or organisations. Talk like that makes me nervous. When I get the hint that someone wants to know me because of someone I know, or some door I can open, I'm tempted to run.

When the disciples tried to slap a 'No Entry' sign up in the faces of some parents and their children, they caused an ignition of anger in Jesus – and they made a classic mistake. With their persistent dreams of thrones and greatness, perhaps they thought that Jesus only sought to do business with the movers and shakers of His day, the people who could actually make a difference. What use would children be to His strategic plans? If women had few rights in Jesus' time, children had still less.

We can be guilty of a similar mistake. Surrounded as we are by labour-saving devices that serve our every need, we are tempted to treat our relationships in the same way. In a 'you-scratch-my-back-I'll scratch-yours' world, we need to be careful that we don't edit people out of our days because they serve no purpose in advancing us or our cause.

And the notion that children can do nothing for us is so very wrong, too. With their huge capacity to ask questions, create delight with a giggle, and disrupt our schedules and our sleep patterns, children are surely the most blessed and delightful interruptions on our greyer days. Are you busily, efficiently networking? Lighten up a little.

Lighten up a little

Prayer: Father, help me to see others as You see them, and not through the lens of self interest. Amen.

TODAY I caught myself positively longing for and dreaming about owning a new refrigerator, one of the great big brutes that look like a spaceship, all gleaming stainless steel, with the ice maker and cold water dispenser in the front. There's probably nothing wrong with owning such a thing, but to fantasise about it is a little sad – and short-sighted.

All of which nudges me to remember how things seem to attract our worship. If worship is about making something a priority, being willing to make sacrifices in order to have it and thinking happy thoughts about the object involved, then there are a few refrigerator adorers out there.

Jesus is not teaching a universal principle that the only way to be saved is to sell everything and give it away – this was a specific instruction to one young man, and not to everyone else. The high flier concerned had it all; being rich, young and in a position of authority – and he also had a fairly impressive dose of religion. He was a smooth operator too, calling Jesus 'good' – a description reserved for God alone in Jewish culture, and one that Jesus rejected, seeing as the man had not realised His true identity yet. Sadly, the man with plenty of buying power thought that salvation was also within his budget – which is beyond the reach of all the billionaires that there have ever been.

This affluent young man was in danger of missing the most vital component of life: a true relationship with God. It wasn't just that he had money – money had him. Hummed any worship songs to a fridge – or some other object – lately?

Prayer: Be first, Lord Jesus, in my life, today and always. All I have is Yours. Amen.

Our priorities in life matter to God

BIG PICTURE:
Mark 10:17–31
Galatians 5:19–26

FOCUS:
'At this the man's face fell. He went away sad, because he had great wealth.' (Mark 10:22)

The ordinary matters to God

BIG PICTURE:
Mark 10:32–45
Matthew 25:31–46

FOCUS:
'For even the Son of Man did not come to be served, but to serve, and to give his life as a ransom for many.'
(Mark 10:45)

IN OUR journey so far through Mark, we've encountered an incredible number of signs and wonders, dazzling miracles that light up the dark sky of the human condition and remind us of some rather important news: there is a God and He is alive, active and well. Tomorrow we will end this part of our journey with yet another stunning example of the power of God in action. But let's not limit God to the extraordinary and think that serving Him is only about seeing astonishing power. We've also noticed that smaller acts attract God's attention, such as the welcome of a child, the sharing of a glass of cold water and the willingness to go within the walls of a prison to carry kindness. And, as Jesus sorts His throne-hungry disciples out once more, their desire for greatness and prestige never far from the surface, He reminds them that His entire mission on earth was to serve – the literal translation is 'one who waits on tables'.

Let's be honest – we could use a few more miracles. But there is something truly awe-inspiring about a humble human serving others in a grabbing, go-getting world. We looked at the issue of being servants before – but seeing as it's a subject so close to the heart of Jesus, another reminder is good. Some commentators say that this verse about the 'waiter Saviour' is the keynote verse in Mark's Gospel, written as it was for Romans, for whom status and power were so important.

Next time we're tempted to get a little snooty, let's remember that we are under the orders of a wonderful waiter.

His entire mission on earth was to serve

Prayer: Help me to do the ordinary well, in Your name, and for Your glory. Amen.

I'M COMMITTING myself to pray a specific prayer for every one of my readers this month. It's a prayer for endurance. I know well that there are times when we feel like we're on the mountaintop with a Jesus who helpfully seems to light up our darkness with His glorious splendour. And there are other seasons when we disciples don't feel much like discipline, when faith seems harder than usual, and worship feels like fairly pointless community singing, as we gather together to serenade the ceiling – or so it seems.

As the disciples trudge onward towards Jerusalem, they come across a man who so needs Jesus, he just won't shut up, even when his outbursts bring a rebuke from the embarrassed crowd. In fact, the telling-off he receives only inspires him to yell louder.

May that quality of perseverance be found in us. When believing is a lonely choice, may we be willing to risk the anger of the crowd. When prayer seems to bounce back unheard, may we take heart and pray again. When others tell us that nothing can change, may we realise that we follow the One who has the power to change everything.

And may we be more than those who just 'see' truth. Like the formerly blind Bartimaeus, let's jump up and walk with Jesus. Let this be our ambition: wherever Jesus is headed, that is where we'd like to go too.

Paul's prayer for the Romans (15:5–6) sums it up:

'May the God who gives endurance and encouragement give you a spirit of unity among yourselves as you follow Christ Jesus, so that with one heart and mouth you may glorify the God and Father of our Lord Jesus Christ.'

God bless you.

Perseverance matters to God

BIG PICTURE:
Mark 10:46–52
2 Timothy 2:1–13

FOCUS:
'Many rebuked him and told him to be quiet, but he shouted all the more, "Son of David, have mercy on me!"'
(Mark 10:48)

Singing in the Rain

Singing in the Rain

IT was Gene Kelly who immortalised the song 'Singing in the Rain'. As he celebrated that 'glorious feeling' he created a piece of classic movie history in 1952. But beyond simply a few fancy footsteps and a catchy tune, is it really possible to sing when it's raining? When trials and troubles seem to gang up on us, or we get mugged by another one of life's little surprises, what will happen to our faith?

Have you ever had one of those weeks where everything appeared to be collapsing around you, people whom you thought you could depend upon disappeared and God wasn't in conversational mood – or so it seemed? We all have them – they are guaranteed. But as followers of Jesus, we can learn how to sing in the rain, quite literally, without becoming unreal about our challenges or resorting to a superficial, happy-clappy faith. So let's visit the second half of Mark's Gospel and see how Jesus steered His way through His last seven days on earth. He was very well aware of trouble ahead but trekked across His battlefield of blood, sweat and tears with poise, dignity and passion.

There's encouragement, inspiration and a few surprises in store. Jesus knows how to dance in a downpour and is willing to teach us the steps – and the tune.

So don't lose your song – whatever the weather!

God bless you!

Beyond the horizon of self

When clouds gather in our lives, and we head into a storm, it's shocking when people around us apparently carry on sunbathing. The businessman walks stunned from a bankruptcy court, or a newly-widowed lady leaves the funeral, only to be horrified because people are still chattering in the street and children still giggle in the playground. Don't they know what has happened? How can they act as if nothing of consequence has taken place?

Suffering can shrink our horizon down to just ourselves. We become so consumed with our worries, pains and fears, nothing and nobody else matters. We're tempted to become impatient with the tiny concerns of others, compared to the Goliaths we are wrestling with.

Jesus was just two miles from Jerusalem, where whips would cut Him and nails would pierce Him. He commandeered a donkey – and yet was concerned lest His disciples be accused of theft; so He reminds them to assure anyone with concerns that it would be returned safely.

Are you in a season of pressure? Ask God for grace to help you to look beyond yourself and cut some slack to others who might be guilty of nothing more than getting on with life.

Suffering can shrink our horizon down to just ourselves

Weekend

The Prince of Peace comes

BIG PICTURE:
Mark 11:4–11
1 Peter 4:7

FOCUS:
'When they brought the colt to Jesus and threw their cloaks over it, he sat on it.' (Mark 11:7)

IN THE vintage British television show *Dad's Army*, Corporal Jones rushes around screaming at the top of his voice, 'Don't panic! Don't panic!' – while he himself is frantic agitation on legs. One of my many weaknesses is that I can tend to react quickly rather than responding calmly when the ocean of life gets choppy. My flawed logic is simple: why pray when you can flap?

Emotional turbulence seems to come to me quite naturally. And I like to fix things, now. Just now the telephone rang and details of a situation that is frustrating emerged – and I so want to sort it right away – which is seldom the best idea. Pausing can restore our emotional equilibrium; there is continual encouragement towards self-control in the New Testament, especially in Peter's writings, a man who graduated from Impetuous University (1 Pet. 1:13; 5:8; 2 Pet. 1:5–7).

Jesus rode into the ancient city, a picture of poise and peace, master of an unbroken colt. He knew very well that His riding into town in this way was the action of a returning triumphant warrior (and more importantly, Messiah) that would provoke the religious leaders and would begin His walk to the cross. He also knew that most would misunderstand His actions and would look to promote Him as a political hero. But He is calm; He visits the Temple and sees all the seething corruption there – and then walks away, leaving the second epic cleansing of that place until the next day. Jesus knows well how to do pressure, holding Himself together regardless of what is going on inside.

Jesus knows ...

how to do

pressure

Prayer: Lord, when I am in circumstances beyond my control, give me grace to control myself and walk in peace. Amen.

Temper tantrums?

BIG PICTURE:
Mark 11:12–14
Micah 7:1–6

FOCUS:
'Then he said to the tree, "May no-one ever eat fruit from you again." And his disciples heard him say it.' (Mark 11:14)

THE reality television show *I'm a celebrity, get me out of here* drops a handful of previously pampered famous types into a steaming jungle, where food is rare, sleep is fitful and personalities clash. Tempers often flare like the temperature, because pressure changes us, and scary Jekyll-and-Hyde type transformations take place when stomachs rumble.

Crisis wears my patience thin. I am less willing to suffer fools gladly – or notice that it might be me that's playing the fool – when life is dark. Now, as Jesus prepares Himself for major confrontation in Jerusalem, He is most likely stressed and certainly hungry – the text tells us so.

At first glance, it looks as if Jesus is throwing a petulant strop when He finds that the fig tree is bare – especially as this was not the fruit season. This is the first and only time that Jesus used His supernatural power to destroy something. (The expulsion of the demons into the pigs which then drowned in Mark 5:13 is a possible exception, but it was unleashed demonic power that caused that event.) Was Jesus just having a bad day and an innocent tree got in the way? Or is this some Harry Potter-type magic, attention-grabbing wizardry with little purpose?

Look again: here Jesus is showing His unswerving commitment to His mission, as He exposes the withered barrenness that Israel had fallen into. Far from being a hot-headed reactionary, Jesus wants His disciples to see an enduring prophetic reminder about why He had come.

Jesus was no thoughtless prophet or volcanic hothead. Next time you're exhausted, traffic is thick, and dinner is burned, respond – don't react.

Prayer: Help me to stay on track when the path gets rough; may my character be strong enough for storms. Amen.

Do what's right, even if it costs

BIG PICTURE:
Mark 11:15–19
1 Peter 3:8–22

FOCUS:
'On reaching Jerusalem, Jesus entered the temple area and began driving out those who were buying and selling there.' (Mark 11:15)

NO ONE relishes trouble. We all pick the quiet life rather than the din of tribulation. But there are times when we need to choose to do what is right, even though we know we'll be in hot water as a result. As Jesus bursts into the Temple courts and creates chaos as He cleanses the place, it is not the first time. John records a previous visit there, where He used a whip to drive the gaggle of extortionists from the place (John 2:13–22). Back then His action had understandably stirred up trouble; some challenged His authority for what seemed such an outrageous act (John 2:18). But now He is doing it all again, overturning the tables of the twisters, releasing sacrificial doves in a flurry of feathers and demanding that those who used the courts as little more than a short cut from the Mount of Olives show a bit more respect. Now, as then, what He did would create trouble, only this time it was worse; the religious leaders were 'looking for a way to kill him' (Mark 11:18). But He refused to back off.

The principle was worth the price and Jesus knew without question that He was in the right, as He quoted both Isaiah and Jeremiah in justification for this cleansing. The venue for this striking scene was most likely the court of the Gentiles: the only place where non-Jews could worship had been turned into a marketplace. Sometimes, to use Peter's term, we just have to learn to suffer for doing what is right.

The principle was worth the price

Prayer: Gracious God, give me courage to live by Your Word, even when obedience will create trouble for me. Amen.

Faith and trouble

BIG PICTURE:
Mark 11:20–24
Luke 22:31–34

FOCUS:
'I tell you the truth,
if anyone says to this
mountain, "Go, throw
yourself into the sea,"
and does not doubt in his
heart but believes that
what he says will happen,
it will be done for him.'
(Mark 11:23)

I HAD a real problem with these verses in my early years as a Christian. All this talk of faith being able to move mountains and throw them into the sea made me feel more defeated than encouraged. The thought of commanding a towering peak to pop into the ocean seemed obviously quite impossible, and I wasn't blinded to the fact that such a thing had never, ever been done – even by Jesus. Back then, Adrian Plass famously wrote of his attempts to move a paper clip an inch by using prayer; but neither Everest, nor tiny office accessories were going anywhere as a result of his faith. So what is Jesus teaching us here?

The rabbis used the term 'moving mountains' to describe the ability to overcome huge obstacles and seemingly impossible difficulties (Zech. 4:7). Here Jesus calls us to navigate our way through the tough times with believing prayer; and He also commands us to clear out the clutter of doubt and bitterness too. When the clouds gather in someone's life, concentrate on praying not only for their deliverance but also for their faith. Prophesying all the difficulties and spiritual buffetings that would come to Peter's life, Jesus promised that He would pray for the headstrong fisherman that his faith 'may not fail'. Ironically, it is often trouble that is the fertiliser that grows greater faith; so as we walk through the tough times with a determination to trust and pray, we grow in grace and find God is truly faithful.

Don't try to relocate a hill or nudge a paper clip today. But do trust.

Prayer: Lord, give me a gift of faith, especially when tempted towards unbelief. Help me to navigate with confidence in You. Amen.

The clutter of bitterness

BIG PICTURE:
Mark 11:25–26
Hebrews 12:14–15

FOCUS:
'And when you stand praying, if you hold anything against anyone, forgive him, so that your Father in heaven may forgive you your sins.'
(Mark 11:25–26)

FREDERICK Buechner in his book *Wishful Thinking: A Seeker's ABC*, describes just how 'delicious' anger and bitterness can be. 'Of the Seven Deadly Sins, anger is possibly the most fun. To lick your wounds, to smack your lips over grievances long past, to roll your tongue over the prospect of bitter confrontations still to come, to savour to the last toothsome morsel both the pain you are given and the pain you are giving back – in many ways it is a feast fit for a king. The chief drawback is that what you are wolfing down is yourself. The skeleton at the feast is you.'

When life is tough, we need to ensure that we don't further complicate it by allowing bitterness to take over our hearts. Here Jesus teaches His disciples to combine their praying with forgiveness – but don't miss the context for that teaching session. His command that they offer grace to others comes in the very week when He would be falsely accused, terribly beaten, rejected by the crowds, denied by His friends and ultimately executed on a trumped-up charge. This was the week of the whipping; the day was at hand when that cruel crown of thorns would be jammed roughly onto His head and the spittle would fly with the insults. And yet He would end that epic week with the words, 'Father, forgive them' (Luke 23:34).

Jesus initially carried the burden of His own cross but refused to be bowed down by bitterness. He is a willing prisoner of the Romans and refuses to be incarcerated by rage. So He was the freest captive there has ever been. Bitterness will poison our souls and paralyse our praying.

Prayer: Forgiveness doesn't come easily, Lord. May my journey today not be encumbered by a crushing load of bitterness. Amen.

Hush hush

I am a blabber – ask anyone who knows me. I wear my heart on my sleeve, don't mind telling you everything that is going on and am quick to share my opinions. Put me in a time of trouble and my capacity to be Mr. Motor-Mouth increases alarmingly.

... life doesn't need to be about us telling everybody everything ...

But I'm slowly learning that life doesn't need to be about us telling everybody everything we know and feel.

As Jesus refuses to blurt out an answer to the pressing questions of the religious, He isn't playing games – rather His silence is confronting them with the truth. Much as they wanted to, they couldn't deny the power of John the Baptist's ministry of three years earlier – it would have been politically disastrous to do so, as John was a hero to the people. In this case, silence was used with genius by Jesus to show the religious hypocrites the reality of their rebellion. Jesus didn't need their stamp of approval. Even though they were the highest religious authority in the land, He didn't need to prove Himself to them. Sometimes our gushing words are a sign of a desperate need to be approved of. Are you like me – the talker? Ever wondered why?

Weekend

The power of truth

BIG PICTURE:
Mark 12:1–12
Psalm 119:105–112

FOCUS:
'Your word is a lamp to my feet and a light for my path.' (Psa. 119:105)

HAVE you ever wondered why it's so important to read scripture daily? It's easy, living in the 'quickaholic' culture that we do, to sprint into the day without consciously aligning ourselves with God. In the past I rejected the 'quiet time' as being religious and legalistic but I've learned that a life of discipline and reflection is the only way to live beyond survival.

Jesus teaches the parable of the tenants and exposes a harsh reality. He was about to be rejected by Israel; they had a long history of slamming the door in the faces of all the messengers that God sent. And then He poses the tantalising question, 'Haven't you read this scripture?' (v.10). Perhaps they were ignorant – or perhaps they were trying to ignore the truth.

But then let's turn that around: the fact that Jesus *did* know and understand the scripture enabled Him to see the most troubling week of His life from a divine perspective; all that was unfolding in Jerusalem was more than just hard-hearted behaviour and rejection – something was going on that was 'marvellous in our eyes'. And Jesus recalls the word that the Father had spoken to Him at baptism, as He inserts the tiny – but significant – detail of a beloved Son sent (v.6).

Clothe yourself with what God has said. Don't forget to actually read the scriptures given each day with these daily notes (it's too easy to cheat!). Be equipped by His Word today to face the challenges and opportunities of a new week.

Prayer: Father, help me to read, remember and respond to Your Word, as a vital lamp that lights up my footsteps. Amen.

Wisdom under pressure

BIG PICTURE:
Mark 12:13–17
James 3:13–18

FOCUS:
'Then Jesus said to them,
"Give to Caesar what
is Caesar's and to God
what is God's." And they
were amazed at him.'
(Mark 12:17)

LAST night, as I waited in the baggage claim area at Denver Airport, I found myself pondering the fact that people speak very differently when they are under pressure. We saw last week that tiredness can turn the mildest soul into a volcanic eruption. Last evening, watching the baggage staff at work, it occurred to me how stupid it is to get upset with those people when your luggage goes walkabout. It's not their fault. They didn't lose it. They are trying to help you find it; be nice.

Then my thoughts were interrupted by Kay, who informed me that *our* bags were lost and I'd need to chat with those folks that I had been having such warm thoughts towards moments earlier. I think I did fairly well. As a self-confessed blabber (remember my confession a couple of days ago) I want wise, kind words to emerge from my lips when the heat is on. I'd like to be measured and in control when under pressure.

The religious big guns were firing a variety of bullets at Jesus and He was under pressure – they were looking to trap Him – the word here means 'to ensnare a wild animal'. Firstly, they tried to grease the ground beneath Him with their flattery – which didn't affect Him at all. Then came the roundhouse punch, a clever political trap about taxpaying. A wrong word here might put Him at the head of a rebellion (Acts 5:37) or liable to a charge of treason (Luke 23:2). His measured response, brief but loaded with wisdom, was astonishing. May we be like Him. (And my bags showed up the next day.)

Prayer: May I be wise, not to myself but before You. Fill me with Your Spirit; teach me Your ways. Amen.

... be nice

What's your weakness?

BIG PICTURE:
**Mark 12:18–27
1 Corinthians
10:12–13**

FOCUS:
'Then the Sadducees, who say there is no resurrection, came to him with a question.'
(Mark 12:18)

ACHILLES (he with the famous heel) was the bravest hero in the Trojan War, according to Greek mythology. The legend goes that his mother Thetis tried to make him immortal by dipping him in the river Styx. As she immersed him, she held him by one heel and forgot to dip him a second time so the heel she held could get wet too. So it remained vulnerable. To this day, any weak point is called an Achilles heel. Homer, in the original Iliad, said that Achilles' real weakness was pride. What's yours?

A third wave of attack now descends upon Jesus. The Pharisees and teachers of the law had launched the first skirmish (Mark 11:27–33), trying to undermine His authority. Then they divided into factions, with the second wave of assault coming from a coalition of the Pharisees and the Herodians. They had combined flattery and a political hand grenade – if He picked up what they bowled His way, it would have blown up in His face.

Then came the third wave – and this time it was the Sadducees. They don't believe in the possibility of a resurrection and some come with a complicated question about resurrection!

Step back from this for a moment and see that when it comes to the battle of life, the persistent enemy has a variety of weapons available in his arsenal. We may be strong in one area, with a proverbial Achilles heel in the other. Do we know our weaknesses?

Do we know our weaknesses?

Prayer: Show me, Lord, my vulnerabilities and weaknesses, that I might find strength as I pray, share and watch. Amen.

Loving God

BEAR in mind, once more, that Jesus is in His last week on earth. This is a time for last wills and testaments, for parting words and memorable speeches. The three epic years of training the twelve are ending: a sort of graduation day for them is ahead. And now, a teacher of the law gives Jesus the opportunity to express what the ultimate priority is as he puts the question: which commandment is the most important (v.28)?

In quoting the Shema, (Deut. 6:4–5), the words recited morning and evening by pious Jews, Jesus brings us right back to the heart of everything: loving God. This was what compelled Jesus towards the awfulness and wonder of the cross – His love for the Father motivated Him to set His face like a flint and walk into that storm (John 14:31). Sometimes we focus on the truth that love for *us* took Christ to Calvary, and forget that He went there because of His all-consuming love for God the Father – and His obedience.

When difficulties appear in my life, loving God can slip down on my list of priorities. I give my mind to anxiety, my heart to despair and my strength to fixing whatever is wrong – sometimes with little reference to God. Pressure can turn me into one who wants to be the captain of my own soul; I become independent, distanced from God, rather than an eager worshipper. Trouble can turn me into someone with a Christianity that is more of a hobby than the all-embracing, passionate, prioritised loving of God that true discipleship involves. Love God today.

Prayer: Show me how to love You, Lord. Be first, be everything, be my all. Amen.

BIG PICTURE:
Mark 12:28–30
Deuteronomy 6:1–9

FOCUS:
'Love the Lord your God with all your heart and with all your soul and with all your mind and with all your strength.'
(Mark 12:30)

Keep it simple

BIG PICTURE:
Mark 12:31–33
1 Timothy 1:1–7

FOCUS:
'The second is this: "Love your neighbour as yourself." There is no commandment greater than these.' (Mark 12:31)

THE other day I watched a Bible teacher on television whom some describe as 'deep'. I've found out that this can be Christian jargon: sometimes we call a preacher deep when we have absolutely no idea what he or she is talking about.

This chap was putting forward a theory about intercessory prayer that was so complex and muddled that he lost me altogether. Just when I was thinking of turning the television off, he remarked, 'Of course, some of you, who are not spiritually mature, won't be able to understand this teaching.' I punched the power button off on my remote control with attitude. Sometimes false teaching slips under the radar because it's disguised as being 'deep' (1 Tim. 1:3–4).

I want to go deeper with God (1 Cor. 2:10; 1 Tim. 3:9) and genuinely fear slipping into a superficial, uninformed faith. But I'm nervous of an excessive complicating of the gospel. The message of Christ is for the child as well as the scholar. When I'm walking through one of 'those weeks', I often find myself coming right back to basics. There is a God. He loves me. My life is in His hands.

The religious leaders of Jesus' day had created a religious maze. Distilling the 613 precepts of the Law down into 365 prohibitions and 248 commands, and wrapping it all up in a tangle of additional man-made legislation, they hijacked holiness. There was even a regulation banning spitting on the sand on the Sabbath (you might inadvertently 'plough a furrow') – which was treated with the same importance as 'Love your neighbour'. Let's keep it simple.

Prayer: Lord, give me depth and maturity, but save me from the lure of complexity and 'revelation' that is disguised error. Amen.

Intelligent faith 1

Yesterday I pleaded for simplicity over complexity. But that doesn't mean that we are called to kiss our brains goodbye. Some Christians would apparently rather die than think.

Recently I spoke at a conference where some people got very upset with what I said and stomped out in disgust. There was nothing particularly controversial on the agenda; the conference was about challenging the way we do church. As I suggested that a few sacred cows might make good hamburgers, they refused to debate the issue – and left. Of course, they don't have to agree with me – but what worried me was their inability to listen to something that challenged them, or debate their case. Would they rather walk out than think things through?

Jesus encouraged the questioning scribe because, as one translation says, he 'answered intelligently'. One commentator notes that this word describes someone who has a mind of their own; another says the word means 'to have your wits about you'. The Bereans were commended because they carefully searched the Scriptures (Acts 17:11)

Christianity is not an anti-intellectual fantasy that believers use to escape reality. God has blessed us with brains: let's use them.

God has blessed us with brains: let's use them

Weekend

Intelligent faith 2

BIG PICTURE:
Mark 12:34
1 Thessalonians
5:19–24

FOCUS:
'When Jesus saw that he had answered wisely ...'
(Mark 12:34)

YES, I know. We read about the intelligent scribe yesterday – and now we are again. But the appeal for thoughtful faith is far too important just to mention it. Jesus often posed intricate theological questions to reveal truth to those who would wrestle with the problems He posed. His teaching style makes it clear: we need a thoughtful faith.

Once, I heard a preacher who thoroughly irritated his congregation with an annoying habit: after just about every statement he made, he would pause for dramatic effect and say 'Think about it'. His Sunday morning message must have been punctuated by a hundred 'Think about its'. By the end of the sermon, we were all thinking about assassinating him.

But although his repetitive exhortation was jarring, his encouragement was correct: we do need to think about our faith, and, as we saw last week, love God with our minds (Mark 12:30).

Paul encouraged the believers in Thessalonica to examine all things critically and keep firm possession of that which was genuine (one commentator's paraphrase of 1 Thessalonians 5:21).The Greek word translated 'critically examine' is the word which describes how a metalsmith scrutinises precious metals to make sure they are genuine. So make sure that you occasionally read a Christian book that stretches your mind and doesn't just entertain you. Ask questions and be willing to wrestle with awkward issues. And consider: do you have a tendency to swallow any teaching that comes along, accepting as gold something that might be brass?

Faith built on clichés and slogans won't work when the storms gather.

Prayer: Father, error comes well disguised. Help me to see through its garb and know truth. Amen.

No fear?

I KNOW of a lady who spent most of her life so fearful of cancer she refused to allow the word to be spoken in her presence: it was known simply as 'c'. She died recently – of a cardiac arrest. Heart disease killed her; but fear stalked and robbed her of most of her life.

Jesus' brilliance had stunned His interrogators into nervous silence. He had won the debate hands down, and all potential contenders wisely decided that they would surely suffer defeat if they tried to trip Him up anymore – He had tiptoed His way through all their traps.

All of which could have now left Jesus with a quiet life – or at least an easier day. But He refused to back off, and now takes His place in the Temple courts – the heart of the city – and starts asking a few provocative questions Himself. He is not looking for trouble, but refuses to be sidelined. Matthew tells us that the Pharisees came to Him at this point, having heard of His triumph over the Sadducees (Matt. 22:34). The vultures are gathering and the beginnings of a bloodthirsty gang are evident. I would have been terrified to have been the object of their attention; their eyes most likely narrowed with hatred, their conspiratorial mutterings behind cupped hands and their derisive laughter would have combined to strike fear into me.

Did His heart tremble when He saw the gang forming? Bravery is not the inability to experience fear; Mark Twain wrote that, 'Courage is resistance to fear, mastery of fear – not absence of fear.' Nervous, scared even? You're normal. But don't let fear conquer you.

Prayer: Help me challenge fear with faith today. I pray for those who live with terror. Bring peace; calm them today. Amen.

**BIG PICTURE:
Mark 12:34–37
2 Timothy 1:1–7**

FOCUS:
'And from then on no-one dared ask him any more questions. While Jesus was teaching in the temple courts, he asked … '
(Mark 12:34–35)

Courage is

resistance

to fear …

What really matters

BIG PICTURE:
Mark 12:38–40
Matthew 6:19–21

FOCUS:
'Jesus said, "Watch out
for the teachers of the
law. They like to ... be
greeted in the market-
places, and have the
most important seats ...
and the places of
honour ... "'
(Mark 12:38–39)

ONE of the blessings of suffering is the discovery of what really matters in life. Those who have fought great battles in life don't get bothered by petty troubles; suddenly, it doesn't matter if you can't afford the latest plasma television, if your furniture is a little worn (or worse – out of fashion) or if your car has a big enough engine. When you are forced to sing in the rain, priorities sharpen and focus. Love, friendship, faithfulness, celebration, gratitude and enjoying the moment: all these things suddenly matter a great deal.

Jesus, fearless again, exposes the conniving obsessions of the religious leaders, who undoubtedly were seething as they listened to Him speak. They were preoccupied with being minor celebrities, driven to be always first in line; they were grabbing, greedy men who were little more than bad actors when it came to spirituality. With their long prayers and long robes they were all dressed up with nowhere to go. Supposedly men of God and of eternity, they appeared to be spending their life in the trivial pursuit of empty applause. But they were misguided too, with little understanding of God and therefore no idea of how to please Him.

With just days to live, Jesus knew what mattered and warned the crowd against being impressed by the small men. He would lose His robe to some Roman gamblers, be the object of scorn, not greeting, and would end up nailed to the cross, the ultimate symbol of shame. But His was the noblest, greatest life ever lived. Don't play with trinkets when you can go for treasure. Live for what really counts.

Prayer: Father, save me from squandering my life and energy on trivia. Help me prioritise what really matters – to You. Amen.

Priorities and pain

BIG PICTURE:
Mark 12:41–44
2 Samuel 24:18–25

FOCUS:
'Jesus said, "... this poor widow has put more into the treasury than all the others. They all gave out of their wealth; but she ... put in ... all she had to live on."'
(Mark 12:43–44)

WE SAW yesterday that it's good to know what really matters in life. And when you've got that sorted out, then that cause is worth sacrificing for. Instead of wasting a whole lifetime collecting toys (which are quickly discarded as we pursue bigger and better toys) we determine to live for something that will last forever, even if it costs us dearly.

Jesus settled Himself in the area of the Temple courts where offerings were given, in the Court of the Women. There were thirteen chests placed around the walls; the colonnade under which these chests were placed was called the treasury.

Watching the givers line up, Jesus marvelled at the widow who gave until it hurt. We discover that costly choices made for God will always turn His head. It's been said that until you know what to die for, you can never really begin to live properly.

Perhaps few people find such a cause, and so merely survive but never really live. I have watched another act of sacrifice from a very close vantage point. My daughter Kelly and her husband Ben decided to work for a year in Indonesia, in the area most devastated by the Boxing Day tsunami. Their choice meant disruption, discomfort, and distance from friends and family; searing heat and mosquitoes with hob-nailed boots. Their one decision demanded a thousand more, with all of the reorganisation and planning that was required.

But I noticed something as I watched them struggle with their challenging choice. They'd never looked happier.

Prayer: Lord, I don't pick sacrifice naturally. Help me to follow You, when the cost of that journey is high. Amen.

... until you know what to die for, you can never really begin to live properly

189

Everything *can* change

BIG PICTURE:
Mark 13:1–2
Psalm 65:1–13

FOCUS:
"'Look, Teacher!
What massive stones!
What magnificent
buildings!" "Do you
see all these great
buildings?" replied
Jesus. "Not one stone
here will be left on
another ...'"
(Mark 13:1–2)

I LOVE the grandeur of the big city, whether it is the sleek, shimmering skyscrapers of San Francisco or the austere old beauty of historic London. But there's something overwhelming, intimidating, even, about the city, especially when I think about seeing the gospel making an impact. There are just so many people teeming in the streets. The massive buildings speak of power that will not be moved; a statement that some things might never change, especially for the good. Those edifices were there before I was and will stand strong long after I'm gone. Their thick pillars tell me that I cannot change much in the world. I am an ant on the anthill.

And I'm quite wrong. Everything can change. The Temple was a statement in stone, a monument that spoke of history, tradition and religious power, a symbol of something enduring. Perhaps the disciples, country people from Galilee, felt their own smallness as they gazed at those massive stones (v.1). Some of those stones survive to this day and they are 20 to 40 feet long, weighing 100 tons. The polished white stones of the Temple took up one-sixth of the entire city of Jerusalem.

But Jesus saw that this edifice would be overturned, turned into rubble. And demolished it was, in AD 70, by the Romans.

The gospel is no small, privatised belief, a collection of notions put together to help sad people feel better. Jesus stands astride time, knew the future to come and is bigger than any pillar, any planet, any power. He formed the mighty mountains (Psa. 65:6). Everything, truly, can change.

Prayer: Enlarge my vision of You, Lord, and fill me not only with faith, but also with hope. Amen.

Tell us when

It was over 20 years ago, but I remember being handed a large package of books and cassette tapes like it was yesterday. The labelling announced that the author of the material, purportedly a retired NASA scientist, had figured out 66 reasons for Jesus coming back in 1986. Millions bought the materials, and of course September came and went: no second coming. Undeterred, the scientist announced that he had got his 'calculations' wrong; it was all going to happen in 1987. Cha-ching. More books and tapes sold to the faithful – or the gullible?

... leave the dateline jigsaw puzzle alone

Jesus hasn't arrived, and as far as I know, the second coming speculator hasn't been heard of since. The whole fiasco illustrates the speed at which false ideas can spread: Mark Twain observed that a lie runs around the world while truth is still putting on her shoes. But it also shows the human obsession to know things that God chooses not to reveal: the disciples were hoping that Jesus would give them a date for the coming calamities. But they never got an answer. Don't be gullible. Know that Jesus is coming back. And leave the dateline jigsaw puzzle alone.

Weekend

What you can control

BIG PICTURE:
Mark 13:9–10
John 14:1–4

FOCUS:
'You must be on your guard. You will be handed over ... and flogged in the synagogues. On account of me you will stand before governors and kings as witnesses ...'
(Mark 13:9)

'IT'S completely out of our control,' our pilot said just now. You guessed it; I'm on yet another plane flight. I'm tapping away at my laptop computer while sitting on the runway on Denver Airport, en route to Chicago and then on to London. Unfortunately, the weather patterns in the Midwest mean that we have been parked here for a couple of frustrating hours and there's no sign of 'wheels up' ahead. Most of the passengers are frustrated (I, of course, am a paragon of peacefulness!). But the pilot is right: this is completely out of everybody's control; nothing can be done. I'll just sit here, and chat with you ...

Sometimes the circumstances of life are such that we have no control over them whatsoever; the cancer strikes; the drunk driver destroys; the earth shudders and the giant wave hits; the big earthquake shakes. So it is for the Christian; Jesus speaks of a time of trouble when those who follow Him will feel like pawns in the cruel hands of persecuting authorities. His turn of phrase, 'You will be handed over', speaks of a season when followers of His would feel totally powerless, as they are shunted around like packages. It would all be completely out of their control.

But although we are at times unable to change our circumstances, we can exercise authority over our reactions to them, as we refuse to allow the wet blanket of discouragement and despair to be draped over us. Elsewhere Jesus commands us not to allow our hearts to be troubled (John 14:1–4) – presumably because we have the ability to control our responses.

Prayer: Lord, help me when I feel helpless. Amen.

WE SAW last week that fear has a fantastic imagination. I am really gifted at dreaming up 'What if?' scenarios, usually involving disaster. As a new Christian, I had a whole set of 'What ifs?' that centred on being persecuted as a Christian. Many of our brothers and sisters around the world *are* persecuted for their faith; in fact more Christians are being martyred now than at any other point in history. So *what if* Britain evolved into a state where Christianity was illegal, and I was thrown into prison, tortured and abused, and my family and I had our lives threatened unless we recanted our faith? How would I do under those harrowing circumstances? *What if?*

How about you? Do you sometimes imagine yourself in traumatic circumstances, and worry about how you'd cope? Just this morning I heard of the tears of a dear couple in our church; yesterday they watched their only son die: he had been a picture of health before he was snatched away without warning. And as I pray for them, the faces of my own children form in my mind. *What if?*

Jesus tells us not to worry about the 'What ifs?' If we're placed before a persecuting court, the Holy Spirit will be in the dock with us, and will help us with words to say (v.11). Life will bring some clouds: no one gets through it without some turbulence. But I don't have the grace for tomorrow's hurricanes, only today's mild storm. Take it one day at a time.

Prayer: Lord, help me to leave tomorrow in Your hands, as I live this day today. Amen.

What if?

BIG PICTURE:
Mark 13:11–12
Matthew 6:25–34

FOCUS:
'Whenever you are … brought to trial, do not worry beforehand about what to say. Just say whatever is given you at the time, for it is not you speaking, but the Holy Spirit.' (Mark 13:11)

Take it one day
at a time

God is still God

BIG PICTURE:
Mark 13:13–23
Acts 4:23–31

FOCUS:
'If the Lord had not cut short those days, no-one would survive. But for the sake of the elect, whom he has chosen, he has shortened them.'
(Mark 13:20)

... we live in a

hard, painful

world – but not

one that God has

deserted

NO ONE wants to believe in a world governed by nothing. That's why often even the most faithless will 'thank their lucky stars', welcome the black cat that crosses their path, and stroke the rabbit's foot for good luck. We saw two days ago that, when we're being asked to sing in the rain, a debilitating sense of powerlessness can overwhelm us. Prayer can seem pointless, because life seems out of control, a runaway train without brakes, with no one in the driving-seat. Or so it seems. When the rain comes in our lives, the sound of the downpour seems to drown out God's voice and ours too; can He hear us? Why can't we hear Him? Is He ignoring us, making our misery worse? We feel more like victims than victors, buffeted by the winds of chance, with no higher authority that is interested or powerful enough to intervene. God seems to be smaller than the tumour, overshadowed by the overdraft, intimidated by the redundancy letter. Much more of this and He will disappear forever.

But amid all the promised pain that Jesus prophesies, both around the fall of the Temple in Jerusalem in AD 70 and also during the end times, still we see the sovereign hand of God, overriding it all with His utter authority, placing limits on the level of suffering. Fresh from arrest and threats, Peter, John and their friends celebrate their 'sovereign Lord' (Acts 4:24). Of course, we'd all prefer suffering and evil to be totally banished, as one day it will be. In the meantime, we live in a hard, painful world – but not one that God has deserted.

Prayer: Help me to know that, even in the darkest times, You will never leave me. Amen.

The power and the glory

BIG PICTURE:
Mark 13:24–27
Ephesians 1:15–23

FOCUS:
'At that time men will see
the Son of Man coming
in clouds with great
power and glory.'
(Mark 13:26)

IN THE early hours of this morning, my mobile phone beeped with a text message from a friend, who is battling a tsunami wall of problems. She is clinging to God, but unable to think much, or pray with any energy. I sent a text back which included a simple statement: God is bigger.

We saw yesterday that troubled times can shrink our vision of God. The things that intimidate and overwhelm us can appear to tower over God – He's not big enough to cope. But as Jesus continues to talk about the turbulence of the end times, He reminds us that He is bigger than the biggest things we can contemplate.

The sun, moon and stars were symbols of power in the ancient world; yet here, using poetic language, the light of that blazing orb called the sun turns to shade; moonlight becomes a memory and even the stars take a dive from their solid positions in the sky. This is symbolic language and so we are not always to take it literally (Peter in Acts 2:15–21 applies the prophecy of Joel about the sun and moon to the events on the day of Pentecost). But the real point is that the Son of Man is painted as the one who comes surfing on the clouds, 'with great power and glory', bigger, stronger, greater than them all, 'far above all rule and authority, power and dominion, and every title that can be given, not only in the present age but also in the one to come' (Eph. 1:21). Ask God to renew your vision of Him. It's probably been shrunk by life.

Prayer: With Moses, Lord, I pray, 'Show me Your glory.' Amen.

What must last, will last

BIG PICTURE:
Mark 13:28–31
Hebrews 1:1–3

FOCUS:
'I tell you the truth, this generation will certainly not pass away until all these things have happened.' (Mark 13:30)

THIS week we've seen that the mighty Temple would be reduced to rubble. The sun, symbolically, would turn cold, the moonlight will be switched off and the stars come tumbling out from the proud positions. But 'this generation' – which some commentators believe refers to the nation of Israel, particularly as Jesus uses the imagery of a fig tree, an established symbol of Israel – would not pass away until everything is wrapped up in God's economy.

Israel's story is a miraculous saga of preservation. Most of the ancient peoples now only appear as names in history books and Bibles. Even the mighty Roman Empire is a name from the past, now long dead and turned to dust. There's much debate among Christians about exactly what part the nation of Israel plays in God's purposes today: some say that she remains totally pivotal in the unfolding drama of the end times, while others see the Church taking that key role now as the significant people of God. But whatever our view of the future to come, Israel remains as a prophetic signpost, pointing all of us back to the reality that there is a God, and He continues to oversee the affairs of human history. History really is His story.

Dark forces have conspired to obliterate them. The atrocities of the Holocaust snuffed out six million lives, a quarter of the dead being children. For thousands of years they were scattered throughout the world, with no homeland to call their own. And yet Israel remains, preserved surely by the hand of God. That doesn't mean that everything she does is right and should be given our unqualified support. But this land remains a living witness to the core truth: God rules.

Prayer: Father, in a world of chaos and crisis, thank You for the signs of Your ongoing rule. You reign, forever. Amen.

When you don't know

Faith is ...
trusting in
God anyway

Weekend

Is it possible that Jesus does not know everything? Shocking as that statement may seem, perhaps Jesus taught that truth Himself. Here He says that not even the Son knows the hour of the second coming. Martin Luther believed that this meant that Jesus had not received that information to pass on in His teaching, and that *as a man* Jesus was unaware of that most significant date. But other scholars, including John Calvin, taught that this was a literal statement for all time; that perhaps in the mysterious relationship of deference and co-operation that is the Trinity, the day of the second coming is only known by the Father (Matt. 24:36), because He alone sets appointments for the 'times and seasons' in the prophetic calendar (Acts 1:7).

What is certain is that in His humanity, Jesus did not know that information that everybody then – and many people today – were so hungry for. And there is no hint of angst in His saying that He did not know.

Faith is not about being able to understand everything; at times it is about peering through the fog, being baffled by the complexities of life, and yet trusting in God anyway.

Don't know it all? Join the crowd. It's OK.

There is a God, and He continues to oversee the affairs of human history.

Stay awake

BIG PICTURE:
Mark 13:33–36
Revelation 3:1–6

FOCUS:
'Be on guard! Be alert!'
(Mark 13:33)

JUST a few days before writing this I turned fifty. I hate to admit it, but I am getting older at a rate of knots. Not only is my hairline sprinting up my forehead, but I am developing a capacity for sleeping previously unparalleled in my life; I think I could nap for England. I have recently slumbered during a movie (it was dull), a board meeting (it was long) and a sermon (it was, well, a sermon ...). Slumber just seems to come naturally to me these days. Turn the central heating up, and my snoring will be heard on Pluto.

And I notice that absolutely no effort is required to nod off spiritually. All we are required to do is give ourselves to what caught people napping in the days of Noah – eating, drinking, marrying – the usual stuff of life. It's not that any one of these things is bad – rather it's being absorbed with them, preoccupied with them as a priority that can kick in with the effect of a fast-acting sleeping pill.

Perhaps that's why the idea of retreat – deliberately taking time out to take stock of where we are in our lives – is such a good idea and one that is becoming more popular among all Christians: not just the reflective, more monastic types.

If there's no time to take a few days out, why not find an hour or two soon to take the pulse of your own Christian life. If we don't, we could end up doing little more than sleep-walking at speed.

Prayer: Save me from that gentle, imperceptible drifting into spiritual slumber. May living not lull me: keep me alert in You. Amen.

Alert to what?

HAVE you ever met Christians who seem to be more aware of the devil than they are of God? Every problem they encounter seems laced with significance: if they drop a milk bottle, catch a cold, or run out of petrol on the M1, it is likely to be Satan's fault.

But there are others of us (and I would definitely fall into this category) who are so weary of over-spiritualising everything, we forget that there are evil forces at work. We must live with our eyes wide open, because spiritual warfare is a reality. Whether we are aware of it or not, we Christians camp out on a battlefield. We are at war.

All warfare involves strategy. Satan is a cunning planner. He approached the first Eden couple with cunning (2 Cor. 11:3) and approaches the battlefield with scheming (Eph. 6:11). Don't underestimate our foe. He times his attacks well. Soundly defeated by the resolute Jesus in the wilderness of temptation, the devil retires discreetly to wait 'for a more opportune time'. Sometimes there seems to be brilliant timing in temptation. I'm mugged by it when exhausted, depressed or just after a bruising disappointment has robbed me of hope.

Ultimately, the purpose of temptation is simple: it is to nudge us to abandon God's will for our lives and stoop down into something lesser that will damage and possibly ultimately destroy us.

As Satan moves in for his massive onslaught upon Jesus, he uses every trick up his sleeve. We'll consider some of his tactics this week, not merely out of academic interest but so that we can be on guard ourselves.

Prayer: Father, may I be neither preoccupied by the enemy nor oblivious to his scheming. Help me be awake and alert. Amen.

BIG PICTURE:
Mark 13:37–14:2
Ephesians 6:10–20

FOCUS:
'What I say to you, I say to everyone: "Watch!"'
(Mark 13:37)

We are at war

199

Poison disguised as piety

BIG PICTURE:
Mark 14:3–5
John 12:4–6

FOCUS:
'Some of those present were saying indignantly to one another, "Why this waste of perfume? It could have been sold for more than a year's wages and the money given to the poor."'
(Mark 14:4–5)

SOME years ago Clive Calver caused a ripple when he wrote a book entitled *With a church like this, who needs Satan?* His title was not a cheap jibe but an accurate comment: sometimes we rush to do the devil's work for him.

People of faith are good at pious talk. We are not irritated with each other, we're 'grieved in our spirits'. We don't say that we disagree and so debate an issue, rather we announce that 'God has nudged us to speak' and with that preface, we effectively end meaningful discussion. So it is here.

An outrageous act of sacrificial worship is criticised by the mealy-mouthed who always want to ration devotion: it should be sensible. They protest that the perfume could have been sold to feed the poor: it all sounds so very right. But then John in his Gospel provides another illuminating camera angle on the proceedings, revealing that Judas Iscariot was the principal cheerleader for the protest, and that his mutterings were in fact poison disguised as piety. He had been used to helping himself from the collective purse, so could have lined his own pockets, had the money been given 'to the poor'. This is hypocrisy at its most nauseating.

Just because those who attack us are good at lacing their words with Bible verses and liberal affirmations that they speak on behalf of God, doesn't make them right – or automatically wrong. Let's be careful lest we rush to defend ourselves using the same tactics. Some of the most serious wounds suffered by Christians have come from the clumsy sword-wielding of their brothers and sisters.

Prayer: Lord, help me see beyond words, to the heart, both in the words of others, and in my own words. Amen.

THIS would be a bloody week, when many ugly, spiteful things would be done to Jesus. 'Faithful' companions disappeared in a cloud of dust when He was arrested, nowhere to be seen when the heat was really on. A kiss of betrayal brushed His cheek. He was surrounded by thugs dressed up as priests, brandishing indictments of blasphemy even as they blasphemed Him, their eyebrows highbrow in mock horror. Square-jawed Roman bruisers punched Him, tossing the Best of them all aside while they tumbled dice for His coat. And in the midst of the muck, the blood, the bile, the rank stench of hypocrisy and evil dressed up as good, there was a rose on the rubbish tip, in Mary's expensive offering of anointing oil. Jesus uses a rich phrase to describe what others despised: 'She has done a *beautiful thing* to me.' Apart from the costliness of it all, what made it so beautiful in His eyes?

Surely her offering showed that she understood a hint of all that was to come in the next few days, as she anointed Him for burial. As the scent of that perfume filled the room, she was saying to Jesus, 'I've heard You. I listened when You said You were going to die, even when others protested that it must never be allowed to happen. I don't understand but I believe what You say. Let me help prepare You for the journey ahead.'

When others are going through a death-laden week, give them the gift of listening. Soothe them with your silence; care with the gift of careful attentiveness. It will be a beautiful thing to them.

Prayer: Teach me the art of attentiveness, that those I meet will know that I am truly hearing them. Amen.

Beauty on the battlefield

BIG PICTURE:
Mark 14:6–9
James 1:19

FOCUS:
'"Leave her alone," said Jesus. "Why are you bothering her? She has done a beautiful thing to me."' (Mark 14:6)

... give ... the
gift of listening

Ugliness contrasted with beauty

BIG PICTURE:
Mark 14:10–11
James 3:13–18

FOCUS:
'Then Judas Iscariot, one of the Twelve, went to the chief priests to betray Jesus to them. They were delighted to hear this and promised to give him money.' (Mark 14:10–11)

WHAT a stark contrast is the grabbing Judas with the generous Mary. And if her selfless act blessed Jesus with its simple beauty, how much did Judas's selling-out wound Him? One of the most difficult blows to take is the betrayal of those closest to us – notice that Mark emphasises how Judas was 'one of the Twelve'. That close-knit band who had walked so many dusty roads together, laughed and cried and stared wide-eyed in wonder at all that Jesus said and did – now one of those who had literally shared His life becomes a turncoat. Not every relational betrayal is the direct attack of the enemy, although in Judas's case it was a direct strategic strike against Jesus from the powers of hell – Judas made a choice and that choice resulted in Satan driving him (John 13:27). But the crushing disappointment that comes when we know we have been sold out by those we thought were our friends can be exploited by the enemy with devastating effect.

So why are we all capable of betrayal? One of the tipping points for Judas seems to have been when he saw his cash flow suffering, as Mary anoints Jesus with pricey perfume. It was then that he met and secured the promise of some cash in hand. Selfishness, greed, envy and a hunger for the immediate rather than the commitment to long-term loyalty can all sow seeds of betrayal in us. What precious relationship is about to be shattered for the equivalent of a few pieces of silver? Think again before you make that deal.

Prayer: Lord, show me where selfishness threatens faithfulness today. Amen.

Steady as you go

Cast your mind back: just a few days earlier, when Jesus made His triumphant entry into Jerusalem, He did so having sent two of His disciples ahead to collect a colt (Mark 11:2). These men aren't named in the text but some commentators believe that one of them was Peter, because of the amount of detail that was included and the fact that Mark is considered by some to be Peter's 'eye-witness' account.

... everything was under control then, and it still is now ...

Now it's all happening again; two disciples are sent ahead – Peter and John (Luke 22:8), this time to organise a room for their final meal together. Just as the colt was found, so the man who owned the room was met. Although there's no insistence made here that these were supernatural events – it may simply have been a case of Jesus carefully pre-arranging things – Jesus' eye for detail is wonderful when you consider the pressure that He was under. Perhaps the sending of the two was a gentle reminder – everything was under control then, and it still is now, whatever chaos breaks out.

Has God led you through a storm before? Remember, and be strengthened for any rough weather you may be facing today.

Weekend

Suffering but still loved

BIG PICTURE:
Mark 14:16–26
Psalm 118:1–14

FOCUS:
'I will not drink again of the fruit of the vine until ... I drink it ... in the kingdom of God.'
(Mark 14:25)

HOW would you spend your last night? I've wondered what my priorities would be if I found myself just a few hours away from an appointment with the executioner. Many Christians around the world face that reality: never forget that tens of thousands are martyred every year because of their love for Jesus Christ. So what if they came for us?

Jesus chose to spend His final hours over a meal with His best friends. The conversation over the food was real, gritty and even awkward, with moments of tension and sadness. And there was time to remember what was important, with bread broken and wine sipped.

Then a song was sung; music carries a power to move and strengthen us, to unite and to solidify truths that life has eroded. The hymn chosen would have been the *Hallel*, part of Psalms 115–118. So what words did Jesus use on His last night? We'll pause for a couple of days and consider His worship.

He proclaimed that God is good and that His love is eternally enduring (Psa. 118:1–5). Suffering can whisper a dark accusation about God's character – does He really care? Is He bothered about us? Difficult times carry a double power: not only do we suffer but we wonder. Perhaps we battle sickness but then hurt spiritually as well as physically, tormented by thoughts that God is dead or, worse, alive but uncaring.

Jesus embraced suffering convinced that He was loved by His Father – it was the closing stanza of the hymn, the last words He sang (Psa. 118:29). Whatever else you don't know, know this: God loves you.

Prayer: Help me to know Your love for me, Lord, when my circumstances and feelings suggest that I am unloved. Amen.

I WAS in a Sunday morning church service when it happened. I was due to speak on the somewhat obscure but powerful subject of 'The right hand of blessing'. In Bible times, the right hand was always the hand used to favour and bless someone and it speaks of God's strength and power (Exod. 15:6). So, Jesus is now seated at the 'right hand' of the Father (Mark 14:62) – and Joseph sought the primary blessing of the right hand for his eldest son, Manasseh (Gen. 48:12–20).

No one else knew my subject for the sermon, the worship team was just coming to the end of their final song, and suddenly I noticed one of the leaders of the church heading towards me. She was clutching a bottle of anointing oil in her hand. With a huge smile, she just whispered, 'Jeff, give me your hand – your right hand, please.' I extended it nervously and she poured some oil upon my open palm, prayed briefly, and I returned to my seat. I stood up seconds later to speak on the right hand of God's favour, with my own right hand dripping with oil, the symbol of the Holy Spirit. I was overwhelmed with gratitude: it seemed that God was shouting His love at me that day, and the power of the moment was certainly not lost on the congregation. It was a morning of thankful tears: God is not just *with* us (Psa. 118:7), but *for* us. In Christ, we are the apple of His eye. Remember this when life throws all that it can at you – your value is eternal.

Prayer: Lord, I thank You for Your loving kindness, which is better than life. Amen.

God's right-hand people

BIG PICTURE:
Mark 14:26
Psalm 118:15–24

FOCUS:
'When they had sung a hymn, they went out to the Mount of Olives.'
(Mark 14:26)

In Christ, we are the apple of His eye

Success redefined

BIG PICTURE:
Mark 14:26
Psalm 118:25–29

FOCUS:
'When they had sung a hymn, they went out to the Mount of Olives.'
(Mark 14:26)

AS I write today from Ethiopia, a land that has had its heart ripped out by drought, the AIDS pandemic and government corruption, I have met some of the most magnificent people. In their warmth, hospitality and sacrificial sharing, they truly know how to live. Wandering through the streets today, I spotted a self-help 'dream your way to success' book, written by a famous western success guru who could learn a thing or two himself from these people.

God has a strange definition of what it means to be successful, quite different from the superficial markers by which we measure a person's success. To us, successful people are distinguished by power, affluence, fame and looks. They scurry to the top of the ladders of life; focused, quick and nimble.

A life cut short at 33, with nothing materially to show for yourself except the clothes on your back, would hardly constitute success in most people's eyes. But as Jesus fixes His jaw in the direction of the cross, He prays for success (Psa. 118:25). It's very obvious, but perhaps we need reminding that a life that ends with a full bank balance but an empty heart, a fistful of diamonds but not enough real friends to count on one hand, and a legacy that includes material bounty mingled with regrets and bitterness, is no success at all. The word 'success' that Jesus prayed is sometimes translated 'prosper' – but if prosperity is to be measured superficially, then His mission would be declared a failure. Calvary's hill is a long way from Beverley Hills. But He triumphed, and gained true, real success.

Prayer: Save me from a life spent chasing 'success' that is prized by many, but declared futile and empty by You. Amen.

'I DON'T trust anybody – that way I won't be disappointed.'

So says a friend of mine, who embraces an approach to relationships that I could never share. It's not that he's wrong but that just wouldn't work for me. As an idealist, I am hopeful, always preferring the happy-ever-after endings, and tending to expect that my friends will be marathoners, partners with me for the distance that is life.

That means that I have had plenty of relational disappointments along the way – and I'm sure that I've not always been all that I could have been to my friends. So while I could never adopt my friend's stoic philosophy, I do think that we should approach our relationships with a bit more gritty reality, and shed some of our naivety. We are fallen human beings, saved but still in the process of growth and change.

Jesus was under no illusions about the frailties of those closest to Him; knowing that they depended so much upon His leadership, He realised they would be like lost, lonely sheep on a bleak hillside once He had gone.

And He wasn't swayed by speeches that would ultimately turn out to be hollow aspirations and unfulfilled promises, like Peter's insistence that he would uniquely stay true, prompting a flood of pledges of allegiance from the others that wouldn't survive even one day. Their heady vows would disappear in the dust they made as they fled.

Don't be tormented when those you expect much of disappoint you. They – and we – still haven't graduated from the human condition.

Prayer: Lord, help me hope, without naivety: when I am disappointed, help me to yet hope again. Amen.

Realistic expectations

BIG PICTURE:
Mark 14:27–31
Job 6:14–20

FOCUS:
'"You will all fall away," Jesus told them, "for it is written: 'I will strike the shepherd, and the sheep will be scattered.'"'
(Mark 14:27)

Don't be tormented when those you expect much of disappoint you

The stunning surprise of trouble

BIG PICTURE:
Mark 14:32–34
Hebrews 5:7–8

FOCUS:
'He took Peter, James and John along with him, and he began to be deeply distressed and troubled.' (Mark 14:33)

PAUSE and take a long look at this remarkable scene, as we see Jesus struggling; He is 'deeply distressed and troubled' – the words include a sense of amazement, in the same way that the disciples were astonished (Mark 10:32). Jesus knew well enough that death was coming, and had repeatedly tried to explain what was to come to His slow-witted disciples, but then when He finally came face to face with His painful destiny, He naturally recoiled at the awfulness to come. Even though He knew what He knew, He found himself overwhelmed by horrified surprise. It's one thing to contemplate suffering in the future; it's quite another to find that today is the day of pain.

There's usually an element of surprise in suffering – especially because most of us have little prophetic warning of trouble ahead. Most of us live in the delusion that bad things happen to other people. No one assumes cancer, premature bereavement, or some other tragedy will be part of their lives, and so when they are, we go into shock.

But Jesus is open in His struggle and makes no attempt to hide His anguish from His trusted friends. There's no 'stiff upper lip' here, no stoic attitude that pretends that all is well. Jesus was in the deepest despair. Faith doesn't smile a grin of fixed pretence: it faces the unfortunate surprises of life with reality. If you are facing suffering today, reach out for help. And if those around you are struggling – reach out to them. You can at least make sure whatever they are going through, they don't go through it alone.

Prayer: Lord, help me weep without shame with others when I need to; to know their strong support when life slides downhill. Amen.

Prayer and people

Mark 14:35–42
2 Corinthians
1:3–7

Jesus did not want to go to the cross. He would have been very familiar with this cruel and agonising method of execution used by the Romans and quite naturally recoiled from the pain to come. Understandably, He pleads with the Father, hopeful that there might be some other way. There's tender intimacy here as He addresses the Father using the Aramaic word 'Abba' – this was later used by the Early Church (Rom. 8:15). 'Abba' is the name which every Jewish child still uses within the home to address their father.

We need
prayer and
people both

Jesus spends three specific periods crying out to God but punctuated His prayer times by going back to His disciples. Sadly, they were exhausted and were deep in sleep even while He battled.

But notice that Jesus leaned on *two* resources in this His darkest hour – prayer to His Father, and companionship with His friends. He breaks His times of intense intercession twice to go back and be with them. God comforts us – and often uses human beings as the agents of that comfort (2 Cor. 7:6).

When I'm stranded in one of life's downpours, I need to talk to God and talk with my friends. We need prayer and people both.

Weekend

Unhelpful help

BIG PICTURE:
Mark 14:43–52
Job 16:1–5

FOCUS:
'Then one of those standing near drew his sword and struck the servant of the high priest, cutting off his ear.' (Mark 14:47)

THE huge battle of Gethsemane was over: Jesus knew now that there was just no other way; it was to be the cross for Him. His hour had come and the little gang, led by Judas the turncoat, rushes towards Him.

So Peter (he's not named here, but John fills in the blank in John 18:10) tries to help things out by swinging a sword, resulting in the high priest's servant losing an ear. Only detail-minded Dr Luke recorded that Jesus fixed the problem by healing the ear (Luke 22:51).

Once again, Peter is revealed at his best and worst – ready to die in a sword fight, so desperate was he to protect Jesus, and yet blundering around doing utterly unhelpful things that Jesus had to undo.

It's bad enough going through the rainy seasons but then our sadness and frustration can be compounded when well-meaning people around us clumsily try to help us out – hurting as they do. The person who insists that they 'know how we feel' – when in reality no one really does – or who rushes to suggest that someone must be sick because they don't have enough faith for healing is likely to be guilty of some serious ear amputation.

When we see others hurting, let's resist the temptation just to do something, anything, thoughtlessly. Our intentions may be for the best, but our actions may make things worse. We may end up like Job's well-meaning but unhelpful friends. Do you have the equivalent of a sword in hand? Think before you strike.

Prayer: Lord, let me know when my actions will hurt even though my motives are to help. Amen.

When we see others hurting, let's resist the temptation just to do something, anything …

MOST of the time, I enjoy church services. Like the majority, I am occasionally numbed by 'extended' worship (should singing a song through more than ten times be a crime punishable by stoning?), 'solid' preaching (which sometimes might be sound enough but carries no potential to inspire or encourage), or 'deep' prayer meetings (where everyone is confused, possibly including any passing angels ...). But I remain totally convinced of the value of gathering regularly in a corporate setting to affirm my faith with others.

One of the challenges that we all face, however, is connecting our Sunday mornings to our Monday mornings. The carefully crafted atmosphere of a church service can seem a million miles from the gritty challenges of everyday life. There's always a danger that our teaching and worship can sit in a vacuum, fractured from everyday reality.

Remember that we saw last week that Jesus most likely sang about the 'right hand' of God with His friends at the conclusion of that final meal. Now He takes the core idea of that song into the intimidating chamber where the high priest and his cronies held court, insisting that His future, as the Son of Man, would include Him 'sitting at the right hand of the Mighty One'. What He had sung with friends He rehearsed before His enemies.

The 'service' shouldn't end with the benediction. Let's listen, write down, meditate upon, remember and discuss together the things that we hear on Sundays. That way our Mondays will truly be impacted by God's Word.

Prayer: Save me, Lord, from a compartmentalised life where Your Word fails to direct me. Help me hide Your Word in my heart. Amen.

Remembering that song

BIG PICTURE:
Mark 14:53–65
Psalm 119:11–16

FOCUS:
'"I am," said Jesus. "And you will see the Son of Man sitting at the right hand of the Mighty One and coming on the clouds of heaven."'
(Mark 14:62)

Why deny?

BIG PICTURE:
Mark 14:66–72
Isaiah 40:29–31

FOCUS:
'He began to call down curses on himself, and he swore to them, "I don't know this man you're talking about."'
(Mark 14:71)

THIS tragic episode describes the lowest point of Peter's life, as he infamously denies Jesus, exactly as prophesied, in synch with a nearby crowing rooster even. But just why did he cave in as he did? He was so totally convinced that he would pass the test and stand unwaveringly as a follower of Jesus: now he explodes with rage and calls down curses upon himself, so desperately does he want to distance himself from the newly-arrested prisoner. What has gone wrong?

In the first place, Peter was exhausted – we know that from the disciples' droopy-eyed performance in Gethsemane. Sleep deprivation is dangerous; good people do bad things when their energy levels are seriously depleted. Secondly, he was probably already seriously disappointed in himself, with all that sword swinging, ear removal, and then the desperate scramble from the garden when Jesus was arrested. When we feel the flush of failure, we can lose hope: the flawed logic is simple: I've already made a mess of things, so what does it matter if I wade further into the mire?

And then probably raw fear was the final straw for Peter. 'Below in the courtyard', implies that Jesus was upstairs when the Sanhedrin met. Perhaps Peter could hear the blood-curdling jeering, and the terrible sound of fists pummelling flesh, as the blindfolded prisoner became a helpless punchbag for soldiers and priests.

Fatigue, failure and fear; this was a lethal cocktail that turned a good man into a cursing coward. Thankfully, forgiveness and restoration were available.

Prayer: Keep me strong, hopeful, and courageous, Lord. May my life today express loyalty to You, not denial of You. Amen.

HAVE you ever found yourself accused, because someone has taken something that you said – perhaps out of context – and then twisted it just enough to indict you? As someone who speaks from a lot of platforms, that happened to me recently. I was incensed, desperate to defend myself and put the record straight. And sometimes it's important to do just that – to clarify a misunderstanding. As we'll see, Jesus epitomises supreme self-control as the religious leaders battered Him with fists and falsehoods – but He did insist on clearing up one important matter.

Those little men with loud voices had reached a decision, and the trial stood at a critical point. As a Jewish council, they had only one capital crime to present to Pilate: treason. The accusation was that Jesus had claimed to be a king and, as a dangerous revolutionary, He was a threat to Roman rule. Six times in this chapter Jesus is called 'the king' (vv. 2,9,12,18,26,32). The Jewish leaders knew that a religious charge would not make Pilate indict Jesus, so they trumped up a political charge.

Pilate put the question: 'Are you the king of the Jews?' Mark's account implies that Jesus simply said that He was indeed the King. But then John's Gospel shows us another camera angle, as Jesus explains that He is not claiming kingship in the usual human sense, with an army to resist His arrest, but that His kingdom is 'from another place' (John 18:36). He poses no military threat. Sometimes, it's good to defend ourselves and clarify misunderstandings. But not always, as we'll see …

Prayer: Show me when to speak, and when not, Lord. Deliver me from fear of speaking up and from speaking rashly. Amen.

Setting the record straight …

BIG PICTURE:
Mark 15:1–2
John 18:33–38

FOCUS:
'"Are you the king of the Jews?" asked Pilate. "Yes, it is as you say," Jesus replied.' (Mark 15:2)

Sometimes, it's good to defend ourselves and clarify misunderstandings. But not always …

… and staying silent

BIG PICTURE:
Mark 15:3–5
Isaiah 53:1–7

FOCUS:
'But Jesus still made no reply, and Pilate was amazed.' (Mark 15:5)

THE ancient Jewish writer Philo once said: 'Envy naturally attaches itself to whatever is great.' No wonder the magnificent Jesus provoked envy in the sad men who accused Him (Mark 15:10). Envy is a toxic force, the root cause of all kinds of trouble. Scripture warns us that, 'where you have envy and selfish ambition, there you find disorder and every evil practice' (James 3:16). Like a corrosive acid, envy will eat a hole in our souls. The religious hierarchy, driven to distraction with jealousy, get their fangs into Jesus and the venom of multiple accusations pours out. It's a scene of sheer evil. Matthew Henry astutely remarks that corrupt priests are generally the worst of men. Be wary of some religious, Bible-toting zealots. Driven to do terrible things in the name of God, they are the not-too-distant cousins of those who burned people at the stake in the name of Jesus.

But if the wrath of the priests is shocking, then the silence of Jesus in the face of their insults and false charges is all the more remarkable, as Pilate noticed with some amazement. He steadfastly refused to respond to their baiting. Silence in a Roman law court did not imply guilt.

We need to ask God for wisdom to know when to defend ourselves, but also to know when silence is golden. Certainly there are some occasions when even a million words would never satisfy our critics: perhaps at times like that, we're better to leave our case with the God who is able to vindicate those who truly are innocent.

Prayer: Give me wisdom, grace, and self-control when I am criticised unfairly, Lord. Amen.

Rainy days ...

Sometimes my days are rainy because I get downhearted at the way we Christians act. When a church tears itself apart, we can act with little care for how the local community will perceive our dreadful behaviour. We can forget that we are ambassadors for Christ (2 Cor. 5:20) – and that when we act badly, then we stain *His* reputation.

... remember this: the world is watching

Weekend

So it was with the religious hierarchy, who had met by night (which was totally illegal), had brought a string of unreliable, contradictory 'witnesses' (flagrant corruption) and then went cap in hand to Pilate, the Roman governor, who alone had the authority to pass a death sentence. An intelligent man, Pilate would have seen right through the sanctimonious mutterings of the chief priests and their underlings. In spite of their political corruption, many Roman officials appreciated justice and tried to deal fairly with prisoners. Mark records that Pilate knew that the Jewish leaders were not interested in justice but wanted vengeance (Mark 15:10). But the Jewish leaders were so hungry for blood, they ignored the fact that their behaviour made a mockery of their faith.

When we are men (and women) behaving badly, remember this: the world is watching.

Abused again and again

BIG PICTURE:
Mark 15:16–20
Jude 3–10

FOCUS:
'They began to call out to him, "Hail, king of the Jews!" … they struck him on the head with a staff … Falling on their knees, they paid homage to him.' (Mark 15:18–19)

IT WAS my first day at work in a city bank, and I had determined to read some Scripture during my break. Unfortunately I carried a Bible the size of a minor planet, which created a stir. A loud chap put his sandwiches down and launched into a tirade of abuse: from that day, I was known at work simply as 'God'. Most of the time I smiled, but inwardly I groaned; being the brunt of acerbic humour on a daily basis isn't much fun.

We live in an age where nothing seems to be sacred. People often mock what they don't understand, jeering at what makes them uncomfortable. In that sense the Church will always be an ideal whipping boy for cruel humour: if all else fails, then those who clench their fists against God will try to trivialise what they can't control. So it was with Jesus; the pomp and order of the judicial process gives way to a time of ritual abuse at the hands of a herd of military thugs. But Mark gives us a detail that is easy to miss, as he records that the beatings and the spitting went on 'again and again', reflecting the imperfect tense of the Greek verb: this was malice that kept going.

Having just spent time with some Christians who have experienced imprisonment at the hands of a government that has tried to obliterate the Church, I'm very conscious that most of us know very little about what it means to suffer for the gospel. But if you are the bearing the brunt of others' mockery, know this: you're in excellent company.

Prayer: Strengthen all who suffer for Your name, today, Lord. Give grace to them to stand firm. Amen.

I MENTIONED a few days ago that I have been in Ethiopia, visiting some amazing initiatives to care for children who are in a truly desperate situation. I expected to be shocked and moved by the raw, crushing poverty, and I was. I braced myself for the harrowing experience of sitting at the bedside of a woman who is about to succumb to the ravages of Aids. But I was moved more by the sheer beauty and selflessness of these most stunning people. I have never bumped into such unashamed love or sacrificial welcome, or witnessed community as I have seen it in these last few days, where neighbours rush to adopt Aids orphans (despite their own desperately stretched resources), not even because they have faith but because they simply see it as the right thing to do. I was told the cities were generally safe places day and night and that the crime rate is low, which amazed me. If I had nothing, what measures might I take to feed my own children? Selflessness is always an arresting, breathtaking sight, one to behold and treasure.

As Jesus hung on the cross, the repeated cry from the crowd summed up their expectation of what a man in dire straits would do: save himself. But the cross stands as an eternal reminder that there is another way, a way that will always attract attention in a grabbing, greedy world. It's where we live and die to give, rather than to take; to serve, rather than be served. Want to pull a crowd? Live like a servant.

Prayer: Help me put self second today God, and grant me opportunities to serve. Amen.

Selflessness and selfishness

BIG PICTURE:
Mark 15:21–32
Matthew 20:26–28

FOCUS:
'Those who passed by hurled insults at him … saying, "So! You who are going to destroy the temple and build it in three days, come down from the cross and save yourself!"'
(Mark 15:29–30)

Selflessness is always an arresting, breathtaking sight, one to behold and treasure

Utterly alone

BIG PICTURE:
Mark 15:33–41
Psalm 22:1–31

FOCUS:
'And at the ninth hour
Jesus cried out in a loud
voice, *"Eloi, Eloi, lama
sabachthani?"*– which
means, "My God, my
God, why have you
forsaken me?"'
(Mark 15:34)

MARK doesn't give us a detailed, blow by blow description of the bloody horrors of death by crucifixion: he succinctly affirms, 'And they crucified him' and spares us the gory details (Mark 15:24). The fact is that there was something far more awful than even the most gouging wounds from those cruel whips or the shocking piercing of the nails; that was the sense of abandonment and aloneness that Jesus felt as He took upon Himself the megaton weight of the sins of the world. As we consider Him hanging there, we peer into a mystery, as He plunged into a black hole of being utterly, totally cut off. To be alone in the universe, the pawn of chance or luck, with no God available to help or thank, is no life at all. A poet once spoke with pride at the thought of being the captain of his own soul. I can't think of anything worse; life without God is desolate and meaningless.

Yet today there are still so many who are hauling themselves through life, scrabbling to heal their own wounds, be the answer to their own prayers, and survive as models of self-sufficiency. God, as far as they are concerned, is either non-existent or indifferent.

Jesus tasted that sense of desolation and separation from the Father, so that we might be reunited and partnered with God forever. Are you watching someone you love who is singing in the rain? Pray for strength, for wisdom, for endurance, but most important of all, pray that they may know God himself, up close and personal.

Prayer: For those who do not know You, let me be a light, a servant, a life that points to You. Amen.

Unexpected heroism

BIG PICTURE:
Mark 15:42–47
John 19:38–42

FOCUS:
'Joseph of Arimathea, a prominent member of the Council, who was himself waiting for the kingdom of God, went boldly to Pilate and asked for Jesus' body.'
(Mark 15:43)

LIFE is full of unexpected heroes. This morning, I was praying for my friend, Canon Andrew White. You could pass him in the street and never be aware of the brave heart that is his. I've been with Andrew and watched him at work in the Israeli/Palestinian conflict in Jerusalem. As I write this today, he is away from his family home yet again, desperately trying to help bring some calm to the continual chaos in Baghdad. And as well as all this, Andrew battles huge health problems every day. But massive challenges often serve as the stage upon which unlikely heroes tread.

So it was with Joseph of Arimathea. While the disciples of Jesus were in hiding, it was this good man who attended to the dead body. He was prominent, rich, and a disciple of Jesus (Matt. 27:57) but had been a secret, underground follower because of fear (John 19:38). But now he nails his colours to the mast and, literally in Mark's version, 'becomes bold', goes to Pilate and asks for the body of Jesus. John tells us that Joseph was joined by Nicodemus, who had previously quietly visited Jesus at night time (John 3): now he too openly declares himself as a friend and follower of Christ (John 19:39). Sometimes extreme pressure nudges us to discover strength that we hardly knew we had.

Perhaps you're facing some massive turbulence today. Is it possible that God is inviting you to step into a new phase of courageous faith? Perhaps an unexpected silver lining in your cloud is the discovery of strength that you never felt was in you.

Prayer: Let me be a hero in the ordinary today. Take me to a new level of faith, love, and service. Amen.

Sometimes extreme pressure nudges us to discover strength that we hardly knew we had

Forgetting the resurrection

BIG PICTURE:
Mark 16:1–8
1 Corinthians
15:12–34

FOCUS:
'Very early ... just after sunrise, they were on their way to the tomb and they asked each other, "Who will roll the stone away from the entrance of the tomb?"'
(Mark 16:2–3)

IT SEEMS somewhat bald to put it this way, but here goes: I keep forgetting the resurrection. In the blur of everyday life and ministry, the incredible truth that Jesus is very much alive, right now, can get buried, filed away as a mere theological belief, part of a creed that I say, a conviction that I carry, but little more. I talk about Jesus every day of my life, but sometimes, the avalanche of words sweeps away the core truth: He is risen.

The two Marys and Salome, hurrying to the tomb of Jesus, are certainly to be admired for their devotion. Sadly, they had missed the point about the resurrection too. Even though Jesus had repeatedly said that He would rise on the third day, the truth had not quite landed with them (Mark 9:9–10,31; 10:34).

When you forget the resurrection, you waste a lot of life on things that don't matter – like carrying spices to anoint a body that isn't there. You fret, anxious about apparently insurmountable problems when, actually, these things have been taken care of. Because Jesus is alive, even the biggest stones can become parking spots for passing angels (Matt. 28:2). When you forget the resurrection, you weep rather than witness. Faith is useless and forgiveness a vain hope (1 Cor. 15:14,17).

Of course, it takes practice to accept the really good news. Initially the poor women were terrified into silence. But eventually, thankfully, they got it. He really has risen. Got that?

Prayer: I affirm my faith in You, now, Lord Jesus, the resurrection and the life, my coming King. Amen.

One word

There's a lot of debate among scholars about the authenticity of these verses in Mark – some manuscripts don't include them. But let's still consider them – they are a valuable summary of the beliefs of the Early Church and don't contradict other scripture.

Jesus' appearance to Mary Magdalene is wonderful, especially in a culture where women were denigrated. Jesus sweeps away the prejudices by making Himself known to a woman – and one with such a dark past.

Jesus sweeps away the prejudices ...

But in his Gospel, John paints a more tender portrait of their meeting. Mary's eyes were swollen with tears of despair but then He appears: not in a blinding flash of light, or with a drum roll of fanfare but as someone that you could mistake for the gardener. It's only when He speaks her name that she suddenly realises the truth. It's Jesus!

There were so many things that He could have said at that moment. 'I told you so.' 'Death is finished!' 'Mission accomplished.' 'I've got the keys of death and hell.' But instead, Jesus' priority was to reassure one of His distressed followers.

When it comes to friendship, Jesus really does know how to do it.

Weekend

Patience, that virtue

BIG PICTURE:
Mark 16:12–14
Luke 24:13–35

FOCUS:
'Afterward Jesus appeared in a different form to two of them while they were walking in the country.'
(Mark 16:12)

THE famous Emmaus Road story is told in more detail by Dr Luke. A weary couple of friends are trekking the long road home, exhausted and exasperated, when suddenly Jesus joins them for a stroll. Most sermons that I've heard suggest that the troubled pair were supernaturally prevented by God from recognising Jesus, which may be true, but the text doesn't insist that this was the case. The Greek word, '*krateo*', means that 'their eyes were under arrest or in custody' – it's the same word used to describe the arrest of Jesus. Perhaps tiredness, disappointment, unbelief or a preoccupation with just getting home after that most difficult weekend meant that Jesus was right there with them – and they didn't notice. Certainly something similar often happens to me. I don't expect God to do or say much on my tougher days, and yet sometimes those are the very times when (looking back) I can trace His handiwork.

Notice another fact too: they were heading the wrong way when Jesus walked with them. As soon as they realised the truth, they turned right around and headed back to Jerusalem to share the great news that He was alive. That doesn't in any way give us a licence for rebellion and sin, but I'm glad that Jesus doesn't give up on me when I'm heading up a cul-de-sac; He really does patiently look for lost sheep. Perhaps you love someone who is heading the wrong way: He is able to show up and meet them on that road.

Prayer: Save me from ignoring You, Lord. Be real to me when I'm headed the wrong way. Help me turn around. Amen.

Charming snakes

BIG PICTURE:
Mark 16:15–18
Acts 28:1–6

FOCUS:
'In my name they will
drive out demons ...
they will pick up snakes
with their hands; and
when they drink deadly
poison, it will not hurt
them at all ...'
(Mark 16:17–18)

IN AMERICA, there are some churches (thankfully only a few) that take these verses so literally that they dance with snakes and drink poison as part of their services. Viewing their worship on television is a disturbing experience, as they work themselves into an ecstatic frenzy, and then pass the reptiles around. All of this is supposed to demonstrate faith. Most of the congregation have been bitten, and some have died. Deliberately dicing with venom and poison is not what is being suggested here. Jesus *did* say that we had power over snakes (Luke 10:19) and Paul did escape an encounter with a viper unharmed, but he was building a fire at the time, not deliberately reaching into a basket (Acts 28:3).

And we've already noted that this text is unreliable: I'd like something a little more solid before waltzing with a rattlesnake or taking a sip of cyanide. One commentator notes that a better translation would be 'if they are *compelled* to take up snakes or drink poison' (by a persecutor). These sincere but seriously misled people who provoke serpents are doing little more than tempting God (Matt. 4:5–7) as they deliberately expose themselves to danger.

But some of us do that in more subtle ways. Some in the Early Church specifically sought martyrdom, believing it to be the most glorious death. They brought trouble upon their own heads. Sometimes in our misplaced zeal, our thoughtless words, our clumsy attempts to stand for Christ, we stir up trouble unnecessarily. It's important to be bold enough to suffer for *doing good* (1 Pet. 3:17); it's madness to suffer for being foolish. Trouble will come, that's a promise. But don't go hunting for it.

Prayer: Lord, increase my faith, and save me from fanaticism. Amen.

Sometimes ...

we stir up trouble

unnecessarily

Six incredible weeks

BIG PICTURE:
Mark 16:19
Acts 1:1–11

FOCUS:
'After the Lord Jesus had spoken to them, he was taken up into heaven …'
(Mark 16:19)

WE PRAYED yesterday and asked the Lord to increase our faith – which is no mean feat. It's a fact that's often overlooked but Jesus spent six weeks after His resurrection when He constantly appeared to His disciples and spoke about the kingdom of God (Acts 1:3), with disciples who seemed more interested in discussing the earthly kingdom of Israel (Acts 1:6). Narrow thinking dies hard.

And then Luke makes it clear that He gave 'many convincing proofs to them' that He really was alive. I'm encouraged that Jesus worked so hard to build their faith before finally ascending to be with His Father.

Sometimes I feel so very guilty about my lack of faith: over the years I've seen far more than my fair share of God's activity and supernatural power, so much so that I often feel that He 'spoils' me – and yet I still possess an uncanny ability to worry – and wonder. But I find myself in good company; one might have thought that a couple of hours, or even a day or two, in the private company of the resurrected Jesus would be enough to galvanise the disciples' faith and strengthen them for the challenges ahead – but it took a further crash course that lasted a whole six weeks!

Sometimes we can be tempted to promote the incredible little band that was Jesus' disciples into super-sainthood, but the fact is that they were just like us, with our capacities for greatness and grime, for passion and passivity, and for faith as well as unbelief. He worked with them. He'll work with us too.

Prayer: Train me to believe, Lord. And thank You for enrolling me in the lifelong academy of faith. Amen.

Just as He said

BIG PICTURE:
Mark 16:19–20
Hebrews 1

FOCUS:
' ... and he sat at the
right hand of God.'
(Mark 16:19)

SO THE epic story draws to an end. It's usually here, if I read a book or watch a movie, that I feel a sense of elation (if the ending has been a happy one) followed quickly by a sense of dissatisfaction, as I remember that even the best story is just that – a story. The lights in the cinema come up and reality lands upon me with a crash: my time of escapism has finished.

But this is not so with the story of Jesus. So utterly changed were His disciples, they embark on a life-and-death mission in partnership with the Lord who works with and through them, casting all cares for their own survival aside as they throw themselves into the mission and march, heads down against the torrent of rain that is persecution, to turn the world the right way up.

And all that Jesus said and sang about His own future came true. At that final meal, we remember that He sang about the right hand of God. When He stood before His accusers, He affirmed that the right hand of God was where He was heading. And now, we see that all of this was not bluster or rhetoric but, His work finished yet ever-continuing through His people, He ascends and sits triumphant at that very place.

Sometimes, when the weather of life is at its worst, and we wonder if we'll ever see the sunshine again, it's good to remember: He is safely home. And one day, we will be home safe too.

Prayer: Continue Your mission, in and through me, all the days of my life, until I see You face to face, risen Lord Jesus. Amen.

He is

safely home

Elijah: Prophet at a loss

Elijah: Prophet at a loss

SOMETIMES I've heard great warriors described as people who are fearless. I'm not so sure that it's a helpful description. Surely even the bravest are not without fear – rather they refuse to be conquered by it, and have learned to push through and overcome, despite the huge wave of fear that threatens to overwhelm them at any moment.

Elijah conquered his fears – most of the time. His name means 'The LORD is God' and at first glance it seems the man always lived with that certainty. But a closer peek shows us there were times when Elijah wasn't quite so sure; he went through seasons when he was crippled by self-doubt, lost all perspective and the only prayer he could muster was for death. In short, sometimes Elijah meant 'the Lord is God?', with an emphasis on the question mark. Yet here was a man who took on the most powerful, wicked, determined people ever, who pointed the prophetic finger at kings and queens, who learned not to fear silence, the impossible – or even death itself.

But his case history is not without blemish. He also buckled under pressure, ignored the God who was passing by, and refused to fully put God's radical plans into action.

Let's accompany him on his journey, and learn how to live faithful lives – where today, we lived unbowed by fear.

Holy and human

BIG PICTURE:
James 5:13–20
1 Corinthians 1:26–31

FOCUS:
'Elijah was a man just like us.' (James 5:17)

HIS name immediately conjures up images of a swashbuckling superstar: Elijah, the brave confronter of cowardly kings and wicked queens. The fearless faith warrior who stood atop Mount Carmel, laughed out loud at an intimidating gang of demon-worshippers, and then demanded that flames leap out of nowhere. Elijah, the master of miracles, who raised a dead child to life. In short, not like us at all. I fear that faced with a Cruella DeVille-type like Jezebel, I'd feel led to tell her that she was the fairest of them all. As for flames coming forth at my command, I was the worst Boy Scout in history. My attempts at fire-making produced a feeble campfire that half-cooked some chicken and took half the troop out with food poisoning.

But before we go on what I hope will be an exciting journey with Elijah, let's stop and be encouraged by one vital truth that Scripture is loud and clear about – and that is that Elijah was *exactly* like us. He was just as capable of sin, doubt, compromise, and fear, because he was a real, flesh and blood human – and one with obvious flaws too. I love Elijah, because he could be brave and faith-filled one moment and wondering where God had gone the next. Sounds quite like me. His story is not so much about the extraordinary man, but the life of an ordinary man in the hands of an extraordinary God. There's hope for us all. Even a failed fire starter like me.

Prayer: Father, thank You for the real-life portraits in Your Word. Help me to count myself in for Your purposes. Amen.

There's hope for us all

The good old days

Romans 1:18–32
Hebrews 13:7–8

God was big
enough then –
and He hasn't
changed

Weekend

'It's more difficult to be a Christian these days, because things are definitely getting worse' – so it is often said. We can easily think that if we had just been born at another time, somewhere else, then it would have been easier. But our nostalgia is misguided. I look at the homely black-and-white television pictures of 1950s America, and it all looks so innocent, so appealing. Surely it was simpler to be a follower of Jesus back then? Try telling that to a black person, sitting at the back of the bus and enduring the fearsome sight of burning crosses lit by hooded Ku Klux Klan members, some 'pillars' of their local church. I'm not convinced that things are any worse than they've ever been – perhaps we're just a lot more obvious about our sinning. Human nature is what it is, and has always been, as Paul makes clear in his letter to the Romans.

This week, we'll take a good look at Elijah's world, and see that in some ways, his challenges were similar to our own. But God was big enough then – and He hasn't changed. God is great enough for you, with your life – now.

THE Arctic region experiences months of continuous darkness, with no sunshine in sight. To those that live there, it must seem that the black sky is a suffocating, permanent fixture. Will sunlight ever return?

Sometimes there are situations in our lives that seem unchangeably dark. The cancer is inoperable. The debt is too mountainous – bankruptcy is the only way out. The marriage is 'too far gone'. Hope fades, and the will to make any effort or sacrifice to see change effected dies with it.

Elijah grew up 2,800 years ago in Israel's dark ages. The golden days of David and Solomon were long gone. A series of royal rogues had steered the nation into disaster, with six successively evil kings over a 58-year period. The record of their reigns makes depressing reading. The first two were idolaters, they were followed by a murderer, and then number four was an alcoholic *and* a murderer. The fifth was accused of spiritual treason, and if all of that were not bad enough, the sixth was described as being worse than all the others before him. And now, ruling king number seven, Ahab, was even worse, and he ruled for a 21-year season of death and decay. If you had lived during that period you could have been forgiven for thinking – wrongly – that the nation was set in a permanently downhill direction. Some people were born, lived their whole lives and died in that seemingly never-ending dark night of history.

What is it that you have written off as impossible to change? The impossible remains possible with God.

Prayer: Lord, help me hope again for dark situations where no light has been seen for a long while. Amen.

Nothing can change?

BIG PICTURE:
1 Kings 16:29–34
Mark 9:14–23

FOCUS:
'Everything is possible
for him who believes.'
(Mark 9:23)

Non-conformity and powerlessness

BIG PICTURE:
1 Kings 18:4
Romans 12:1–2

FOCUS:
'Do not conform any longer to the pattern of this world ...'
(Rom. 12:2)

Is it time to

break step

and step out?

IN SOME ways I'm glad that Christendom – the time when the Church largely controlled government and everyday life – is well and truly dead. The corrupting nature of power is easy to prove when we consider the terrible things that were done in the name of Christ, when 'Christian' people held the reins of nations and kingdoms. But it's hard to live in a culture where those that do hold the reins seem so committedly anti-Christian. I saw this firsthand recently in Ethiopia, where the government there appears to discriminate against the Christian Church but favours the Muslim community.

Elijah must have felt something similar, living in Israel under the leadership not only of King Ahab but also his evil wife Jezebel. She was almost evangelical in her love for Baal worship, erected a huge temple in Baal's honour, and had built up a full-time team of 450 prophets and 400 prophets of the goddess Asherah.

What must it have felt like to be a lover of God during this time, when the 'new' religion was sweeping the land – a religion, which, as we will see, was highly appealing to base human nature? Elijah and those like him were called to stand their ground, even though the ground beneath them felt like quicksand. There is a power at work in the world that will always demand that we conform and act like everyone else. But the majority can still be wrong. James Crook put it well: 'The one who wants to lead the orchestra must turn his back on the crowd.' Is it time to break step and step out?

Prayer: God, help me to be faithful, when faithfulness seems like lonely foolishness. Help me today. Amen.

WHAT can fourteen people do in ninety minutes or less? Set plans in motion for the extermination of eleven million people, that's what. In January of 1942, the top Nazi hierarchy met in a pleasant Berlin suburb, to plan the so-called 'Final Solution'. I've read the minutes of their meeting, which took place over a buffet lunch. Committee minutes don't usually stir me – but these make chilling reading. These people conducted their business, not with crazed blood lust, but as calm, calculating and intelligent technocrats, driven by an entirely logical ideology – at least in their eyes. One of the participants noted the atmosphere of the meeting was one of co-operation and agreement. Bad ideas wreak terrible carnage.

So it was in Elijah's days. Ahab and Jezebel's religion called for worshippers to frantically engage with their slow-witted gods through sacrifice, and taught that human life was cheap. That was their theology – which led to horrifying practice.

Now it was deemed spiritual to take a new-born child, still warm from the breast, and hurl it into the flames, as the monotonous drums vainly muffled its screams. Bad theology is indeed a terrible taskmaster.

That's why it's so important to take very seriously what you believe. Read, study, stretch your mind, watch the news, get informed, join a library and engage in discussion. Don't nod your head in placid agreement with every notion that floats by. There's a battle going on to capture our minds. So, with the psalmist, let's learn His righteous laws – and for God's sake – think.

Prayer: Lord, save me from deception, error disguised as truth, falsehood that destroys and distorts. Keep me in Your ways. Amen.

Innocent blood and Baal worship

BIG PICTURE:
2 Kings 17:7–17
Psalm 119:1–8

FOCUS:
'They bowed down to all the starry hosts, and they worshipped Baal. They sacrificed their sons and daughters in the fire.'
(2 Kings 17:16–17)

Faithful, but different

BIG PICTURE:
1 Kings 18:3–4
1 Kings 19:18

FOCUS:
'While Jezebel was killing off the LORD's prophets, Obadiah had taken a hundred prophets and hidden them in two caves, fifty in each, and had supplied them with food and water.'
(1 Kings 18:4)

ELIJAH stood boldly in the face of unspeakable evil – but he did not stand alone. There were others alive at the time that were willing to risk life and limb for God, but they did so in ways quite different from those chosen by Elijah. The prophet would become an open confronter, who would capture the hearts and imagination of a nation; others were called to quiet, even furtive faithfulness.

One of those men was Obadiah, a high-ranking minister of state who was in charge of the royal household. He was the original double agent. Risking certain death if discovered, he set up a rescue programme, hiding a hundred of God's prophets away in caves, and supplying them with the essentials for their survival. He had loved God for many years (1 Kings 18:12), but was never called to take centre-stage in the way that Elijah was. He was another part of God's jigsaw – different but vital nonetheless.

Sometimes great achievers can succumb to being contemptuous of those who don't do things their way. The great William Wilberforce, abolitionist of slavery, was condemned by some Christians in his day because they misunderstood his skill as a political tactician and dismissed him as a compromiser. In reality, Wilberforce did what he believed God was asking him to do – with brilliant and world-changing effect.

Elijah would eventually march to the mountain top, while Obadiah quietly rushed down to the caves, clutching vital supplies for God's prophets in hiding. Both were needed in their day. You are vital – and so are those who are quite unlike you.

Prayer: Lord, give me grace to appreciate those who serve You in different spheres and methods from my own. Amen.

Elijah and home

BIG PICTURE:
1 Kings 17:1
Amos 7:10–15

FOCUS:
'Now Elijah the Tishbite,
from Tishbe in Gilead
…' (1 Kings 17:1)

SOMETIMES people ask me what my most terrifying preaching engagement was – a very easy question to answer. It was when I was privileged to address the National Prayer Breakfast that is held annually in the Great Hall of Westminster. Loaded with history, it was here that King Charles I received his death sentence from the gathered parliament. Helpfully, I fared rather better. The architecture of the Houses of Commons and Lords, with the lavish paintings and statues of the good and great, conspire to create a sense of massive power. As a lad raised in London's East End (with an accent that is definitely not 'posh') I felt like I didn't belong. It was grand and intimidating.

Elijah was a kid from the 'wrong' part of town. Tishbe in Gilead was such an obscure place that archaeologists can't tell us its exact location. Gilead was separated by the Jordan River from the rest of Israel, politically and geographically. It was beautiful, the place where healing spices were made (the 'balm' of Gilead) but the locals were tough, serious shepherds, country folk. Dressed in camel-hair cloaks with thick leather belts, they looked and sounded nothing like the sophisticated crowd in the royal Samaritan court. So pronounced was their accent that in times of war they would ask unidentified soldiers to pronounce one word: 'Shibboleth' (Judg. 12:5–6). The hapless enemy, unable to imitate the local dialect, was found out immediately.

Like Elijah and Amos, sometimes God puts us in places where we don't feel we fit – but there, we might be in the very epicentre of His purposes.

Prayer: Lord, keep my heart at peace when I feel out of place. Teach me to be secure because of Your calling. Amen

… sometimes God puts us in places where we don't feel we fit …

Praying in prayer

I'm not terribly good at prayer. I've written a book on it, preached about it endlessly, and recently discovered a level of freedom as I realised that much of my thinking *is* prayer, and that *good* prayers don't have to be *long* prayers. Some of my best prayers are the 'arrow' type – swift and to the point. But there are times when we need to learn that waiting in prayer is hard work – just as Jesus experienced in Gethsemane. There we see agony, wrestling and struggle. Recently I was in a meeting where we were discussing a prayer 'vigil' – that lasted half an hour. We all wondered whether this was more of a 'McVigil' – fast food intercession.

Elijah 'prayed': the phrase in James 'he prayed earnestly' means 'prayed in prayer'. Perhaps this was an extended prayer symphony of angry tears, whispers and shouts, body pressed hard into the earth, shoulders shaking, fists hammering the ground. James, who wrote those words, apparently believed in prayer. Tradition tells us that he spent so much time in prayer that his knees became calloused. Sometimes my feet ache from too much rushing around: perhaps my knees could do with taking a bit more strain.

... waiting in prayer is hard work ...

Weekend

The word coming alive

PRAYER is not just a religious duty, something Christians do to prove that they are Christian. Prayer puts us before a living God who still speaks. It's a heart-racing, awesome experience to catch a sense that the God who created the universe is talking to *you*. Christians often speak of those times when a particular scripture seems to come alive with meaning, when God makes His eternal word a 'now' word.

Many people abuse the concept of God speaking, justifying everything they do – especially their bizarre and sometimes thoughtless actions – by announcing that 'God told me.' I have heard that phrase enough times to put me off the possibility that God might whisper something in my ear for the rest of my life.

But I'm quite wrong to react like that. The essence of Christianity is relationship; God is still in the business of conversation.

Surely that was the key to Elijah's praying. His request for a divinely commanded drought was not some idea that had popped into his head. As a man who knew the law, he knew that God decreed that idolatry would usher in a drought of judgment. His was biblically inspired logic: Scripture had come alive in his heart, and now he felt confident to ask for what God had promised. He also knew that this would be a slap in the face for Baal, who was supposed to be 'The rider in the clouds', and the sender of rain. When the rains stopped, Baal worshippers believed that their god was dead. This drought would send a clear message about who was in charge.

Feed on God's Word today. He still speaks.

BIG PICTURE:
James 5:17–18
Deuteronomy 11:13–17

FOCUS:
'He prayed earnestly that it would not rain, and it did not rain on the land for three and a half years.' (James 5:17)

Prayer: Bring Your Word to life in my heart, Lord. Speak: I am listening. Amen.

Clearing up confusion

BIG PICTURE:
1 Kings 17:1
Romans 1:8–16

FOCUS:
'Elijah ... said to Ahab,
"As the LORD, the God
of Israel, lives, whom
I serve, there will be
neither dew nor rain
in the next few years
except at my word."'
(1 Kings 17:1)

WE SAW yesterday that a drought would send a clear signal to the worshippers of Baal – no rain, no god. But there was just one problem: their religion taught them that if Baal was dead, it would be at the hands of yet another god – and legend had it that the assassin was Mot, the god of death.

If drought came, Elijah knew that there was a possibility that Israel, from Ahab and Jezebel down, would turn once more to Yahweh. But what if, in their deluded dullness, they just switched allegiance to Mot instead? All of Elijah's prayerful work would be wasted. There was nothing else for it: someone would have to march into that threatening palace and tell them what was what. So Elijah had to take his life in his hands and stand before the fearsome royal couple. He knew that he might get a sword through the heart for his trouble.

In a culture where uncertainty is fashionable, we are called to live clearly for God. Political correctness has gone mad; that means we can feel that it is almost blasphemous to make any absolute truth claims about Jesus in a multi-faith, relativist society. But we are called to be loyal to our God, not the shifting trends of a confused culture. That doesn't excuse Christians who confuse rudeness and ranting for clarity, but still we are called to live – and speak – in such a way that leaves no one in any doubt as to where our loyalties lie.

Elijah calmly stood his ground. God help us do the same.

Prayer: Father, give me clarity untainted by arrogance, boldness to speak, mingled with a willingness to listen. Amen.

TODAY, there is a fabulous opportunity for people to discover what Jesus looks like. All they need do is take a look at us, the people of God.

Sounds like an intimidating or presumptuous comment? Certainly I would never have made that statement in my early years as a Christian. I used to apologise for my own foibles and the inconsistencies of the Church by encouraging people to just 'look up at Jesus'. But how could they do that, what with Him currently being invisible? God has always intended that His people be a lighthouse that shines in the darkness – this was true of the people of Israel (Isa. 42:6) and the Church (Matt. 5:14). That means that the way we live really matters – God's honour and integrity are at stake.

Elijah took more than his life into his hands when he marched resolutely into Ahab's court – the very existence and power of God were laid on the line by his invocation 'As the LORD ... lives ...' This is the language of an oath (cf. Jer. 38:16); people frequently swore by their gods – Jezebel swore by Baal when she later threatened Elijah's life (1 Kings 19:1–2). This was not some vague threat or possibility – Elijah was announcing what he knew was an absolute certainty, and staking the reputation of God on his prediction coming to pass – an action that could have only been taken after some serious prayer and listening to God.

Let's do whatever we do today with excellence: not so that we will look good but so that He will.

Prayer: Help me to live well, not so that I may be noticed, Jesus, but so that You will. Amen.

The honour of God

BIG PICTURE:
1 Kings 17:1
Matthew 5:14–16

FOCUS:
'As the LORD, the God of Israel, lives …'
(1 Kings 17:1)

God has always intended that His people be a lighthouse …

Before two kings

BIG PICTURE:
1 Kings 17:1
1 Corinthians
16:13–14

FOCUS:
'As the LORD, the God
of Israel, lives, whom
I serve, there will be
neither dew nor rain
in the next few years
except at my word.'
(1 Kings 17:1)

HOW on earth do you become brave?

I've often wondered how I'd perform if my faith were put to the test. Around the world today, our brothers and sisters in the persecuted church are suffering because of their love and loyalty for Jesus Christ – there are more Christian martyrs now than there have ever been in Christian history. So, faced with pain or even death, would I quickly deny my faith and scurry away, branding myself forever as a weak coward – or would I be courageous?

Truthfully, I have no idea, and don't even bother to torment myself with the question anymore, seeing as I will only have God's strength and grace for that event if it actually happens. My speculation would be a waste of time. But as I ponder Elijah's standing before the might of Ahab's dark power, fully aware that a snap of the fingers from the king could mean a quick death – or worse, long, agonising torture – I wonder, how do you become that brave?

Perhaps a key is given away by Elijah's prophetic language. He describes the God of Israel as the one 'he serves' – a better translation is 'the one before whom I stand'. So Elijah stands before two kings – not one; however great Ahab's power was, Elijah was aware that the king of Israel was a tiny potentate compared with the might and majesty of his God.

Perhaps we're standing before an intimidating edifice of a problem today, and we feel small in its shadow and powerless before it. Look again: you also stand before a God who is bigger than all.

... you ... stand
before a God who
is bigger than all

Prayer: Keep me conscious that I stand, Lord, before two powers: the challenges I face and You, my forever strong God. Amen.

DAVID, a dear friend of mine, had to walk through a battle with cancer. It was a journey into the shadowy land of uncertainty. There were days of waiting for test results, months of wondering if the treatment would prove a total success, and huge disruption of everyday life (those who struggle with life-threatening diseases still have to negotiate their way through the ordinary, Monday morning stuff).

David loves music, and his favourite song was 'My Glorious' by Delirious. I can remember watching him raise his hands in worship, affirming that God was bigger than both the air we breathe and the world we will soon be abandoning. He needed to affirm the greatness and power of God, bigger than cancer, bigger than even life and death. The greatness of God is something we pondered briefly yesterday in Elijah's life, but we need to pause. Not only did that vision nudge Elijah into bravery, but it also would sustain him during the more difficult days. The great God would protect him, provide for him, and direct his paths.

Jim Packer once remarked that a vision of a 'pygmy God' produces pygmy Christians. Too often my vision of the Lord shrinks down to someone who might help me find a parking space, but who doesn't seem to have too much to do with creating the outer reaches of the universe. Little life looms larger than the expanse of eternity. I need to remind myself of His majesty and might. I'm praying that God will increase my sense of His greatness, and I'm including you in the prayer.

Prayer: Lord, show us Your greatness and glory. Amen.

God *is* bigger

BIG PICTURE:
1 Kings 17:1
Psalm 47:1–9

FOCUS:
'As the LORD, the God of Israel, lives, whom I serve, there will be neither dew nor rain in the next few years except at my word.'
(1 Kings 17:1)

Leaving it to God

God knows, or so the saying goes. But I like it when I know too.

I don't like those movies with ambiguous endings, where you don't know the final outcome. Having invested a couple of hours in watching it, I'd like to know what happened at the finish. And I'm not too thrilled about those cliff-hanger quiz shows where a huge prize hangs in the balance, the contestant has given their answer – but we have to endure a commercial break before we find out if they are to be millionaires or paupers.

It's okay for us ... not to know

Weekend

Elijah dropped his prophetic stun grenade in the palace and walked out – off the stage of Israel's national life for a whole year as God shunted him away to the brook Kerith – a location we'll visit this week. Without waiting for Ahab's response to his message; Elijah's off to enforced obscurity. There was something that was far more important than knowing the outcome of his palace trip – the shaping of Elijah's character, preparing him for the next round of battle with the Baals.

It's okay for us, like Jehoshaphat, not to know. We just have to leave some things with God, who does know.

Obedience

AT FIRST glance, it looks like Elijah did a proverbial 'runner' – rushing into hiding from what was now probably a seething king. The English translation of the text includes the word 'hide'. But we've already seen that others were in hiding; the senior civil servant Obadiah was running a secret refuge for prophets. So if Elijah wanted to hole up for a while, he could have joined them, where the benefits of community would have been his.

Consider as well that when Jezebel later issued a death threat to Elijah, he took matters in his own hands, ran away and hid, and God sent him straight back into that dangerous situation (1 Kings 19:3). Whatever the ultimate motivation here, it seems that at this earlier stage of Elijah's ministry, fear wasn't the dominating force that drove him – obedience was.

Obedience is the heart of discipleship. Sometimes, we don't feel like doing what is right, have a host of better ideas and wonder about the logic of doing things God's way. But obedience must be our daily choice.

So why does God insist that we obey Him? Has He got some ego problem? Is He so despotic He needs always to have His own way? Does He delight in mocking our cherished ambitions? The opposite is true. God is the source of all wisdom, and really does know what is best for the children that He loves so urgently and completely. Let's gladly submit to Him today: ultimately, it's for our own good.

Prayer: Thank You for Your rule and reign of love, not suppression. I gladly yield to You, Father. Amen.

BIG PICTURE:
1 Kings 17:4–5
John 14:15–24

FOCUS:
'So he did what the LORD had told him.'
(1 Kings 17:5)

Silence is golden

BIG PICTURE:
1 Kings 17:2–7
Psalm 131:1–3

FOCUS:
'He went to the Kerith Ravine, east of the Jordan, and stayed there.' (1 Kings 17:5)

TODAY I begin a ten-day writing retreat. Deadlines are looming, my long-suffering editor's legendary patience is wearing thin, so I have holed myself up, away from it all. My wife is 6,000 miles away, my menu possibilities are limited, and my telephone is silent. I am scared, and occasionally find myself staring at the phone, willing it to ring. Two hundred and forty hours of virtual silence yawns before me like the Grand Canyon. I feel an insane urge to rush out, mug a total stranger and engage them in meaningless conversation.

I'd be the first to extol the virtues of community, reject as ridiculous the notion of individualised, privatised Christianity, and insist that, biblically, spirituality is not a solo exercise, but is always done together. God calls a people, not just people. And I've not been that good with 'quiet times'. Some years ago, I threw them overboard in a reckless attack on anything that I considered to be remotely religious or potentially legalistic. I was foolish, and felt a sense of spiritual leanness as a result.

Quietness leaves me alone with, and sometimes at the mercy of, my own thoughts. It insists that I process rather than react, and affords me the luxury of uninterrupted reflection. Prayer is easier, because I have a sense that God, with whom all things are possible, can possibly get a word in edgeways.

Elijah was destined to be parked by a brook in solitary confinement for around a year. Perhaps most of us can't take the luxury of a year, or even ten days – but ten minutes of sheer quiet could change your day.

Prayer: God, give me moments of pause. Save me from turning today into a frantic sprint: walk with me. Amen.

JAMIE Oliver I'm not. So because I'm no culinary genius, my discovery of instant porridge has been a delight. Now, in just 120 seconds, I can whip myself up a delicious concoction of oats with a hint of apples and blackberries. There is but one problem. Just lately, the two-minute wait has seemed so very long. I find myself cheering the microwave on, urging it to cook ever faster, desperate to hear that little chime that announces that my Scottish cuisine is ready for consumption. I like things fast.

I'd like to be a good Christian by this time tomorrow, praying with razor-sharp sensitivity and faith-packed authority. But most of all, I'd like to weigh in as a heavy-weight when it comes to godly character: a significantly holy super-saint. Okay, it's not going to happen overnight. How about by Thursday afternoon?

But character is created in a slow cooker. Look at those verses again. Elijah didn't spend his days in a paradise location; Kerith was an ugly place, a gash in the desert. The weather was hot – often 120°F in the afternoon – and the water would have been coated in thick, green algae. This was no crystal clear mountain stream. But he didn't just go there – he stayed there.

'God's man or woman,' says Kierkegaard, 'is early selected and slowly educated for a job.' Kosuke Koyama writes in *Three Mile an Hour God*[1] that God works at the speed a person walks. Perhaps, like me, you find yourself where you don't want to be, painfully learning a long-term lesson in God's lifelong academy.

Be patient. God is.

Prayer: Lord, I long for the fruit of the Spirit – but forget that fruit takes time to grow. Give me patience with myself – and others. Amen.

Kosuke Koyama, *Three Mile an Hour God* (Maryknoll: Orbis Books, 1980).

Microwavable maturity

BIG PICTURE:
1 Kings 17:1–6
2 Peter 3:18

FOCUS:
'He went to the Kerith Ravine, east of the Jordan, and stayed there.' (1 Kings 17:5)

... character is

created in a slow

cooker

Weird waiters

BIG PICTURE:
1 Kings 17:5–6
Numbers 22:21–41

FOCUS:
'The ravens brought
him bread and meat in
the morning and bread
and meat in the evening,
and he drank from the
brook.' (1 Kings 17:6)

ALFRED Hitchcock's chilling movie *The Birds* is a disturbing work of cinema. The almost silent gathering of those dark-eyed creatures with their razor sharp beaks is a menacing sight – and one not dissimilar to what Elijah experienced twice daily when his stomach growled.

We saw yesterday that the prophet in semi-retirement was parked on the backside of the desert, not ensconced in a luxurious resort. There was a twice-daily food drop helpfully provided by a squadron of divinely navigated ravens. We might picture them showing up in perfect formation, like the Red Arrows, only black, each one dropping tiny pieces of perfectly charbroiled sirloin steak onto a silver platter marked 'X'; Elijah tucks a starched white napkin into his collar and picks up a silver knife and fork …

The birds were rats with wings. Ravens fed on offal, carrion and general rotting matter – they loved to patter around rubbish tips. They were listed in the law of Moses under 'd' for *detestable*. Technically, no law was being broken because Elijah was fed by the birds, and he didn't choose to eat his waiters. But it was an unusual tactic, these visitations from very unclean food servers.

Perhaps, as Elijah watched yet another flock of ravens spitting their offerings at his feet, he was learning that God is ever full of surprises, and is beyond our figuring out. Sometimes what He does comes through those that we would least expect, and He uses methods that we would not anticipate – or even emulate, what with His waiting birds and, in Balaam's experience, talking donkeys. He is totally consistent – but rather unpredictable.

… God is ever full of surprises …

Prayer: Surprise me, today, God. Stretch my thinking; overturn my hidden prejudices, teach me something new. Amen.

IT'S been a year, the ravens have become your friends, and you've learned not to fear silence or solitude. And then you begin to notice that the level of that water hole is going down – it really is drying up.

Let me tell you what my reaction would have been. My first conclusion would be that the waters were running out because I'd sinned: for some reason, whenever something goes wrong, I rush to conclude that I am under some act of judgment and that the natural calamity is my fault. Hard on the heels of this fear comes the thought that God has now abandoned me; that He has become weary of my small-mindedness, my tendency towards the same sinful pathways.

The brook dried up. This was simply the ending of one chapter in Elijah's life, and the beginning of a new, exciting episode; but notice that the brook failed before the word came.

Perhaps you're at that junction now. A door that you thought was going to stay open has suddenly slammed in your face, and you're at a loss to know what to do next. Don't panic, or rush to buy that sackcloth suit – but ask God: what next? If Elijah had lingered at Kerith, he would have missed the greatest adventure of his life, and ultimately, he would have died of thirst. Sometimes it's only in looking back that we can be grateful for the ending of a season. Hold steady – you might be on the brink of the biggest adventure of *your* life.

Prayer: Grant me grace for cul-de-sacs as well as open roads. Give me faith when a door shuts and wisdom to know when another one opens. Amen.

A door closes, another opens

BIG PICTURE:
1 Kings 17:7
2 Corinthians 2:12–17

FOCUS:
'Some time later the brook dried up because there had been no rain in the land.' (1 Kings 17:7)

1 Kings 17:8–9
Psalm 145:1–21

| ... His tactics
and strategies
vary

Weekend

Methods and miracles

Seven hundred times the divine delivery service, the ravens, had swooped over the brook. To see a miracle once is a wonder – to see it repeated must have left an indelible imprint on Elijah. Every time they came, he realised that all of nature is ultimately subject to the commanding word of the Creator. Each visit shouted to the lonely prophet that God could be trusted. But sometimes those who have seen great things develop the belief that God can only work in a specific way, and they begin to hallow the *method* that God uses rather than the *miracle* itself. Now God was calling Elijah to a stretching journey of eighty miles – in the wrong direction, deep in the heart of enemy country, to be the guest of an impoverished widow. The raven delivery service would have been a lot easier.

Our God of unfathomable greatness (Psa. 145:3) remains the same – but His tactics and strategies vary. Don't sneer at that other church because they don't sing your songs or emulate your style. Don't keep doing the same things simply because they've worked until now. Why not pray the risky but vital prayer that invites God to bring change?

I LIKE it when life makes sense, God gives me guidance that is entirely logical, and my questions are answered. When I can understand, faith is an easier walk. Unfortunately, life often doesn't unfold that way, even if you are right in the centre of God's purposes for your life, as Elijah was at this moment.

Put yourself in his sandals. You're tired, hungry, and somewhat bewildered at the thought of showing up at a stranger's house for your first 'normal' meal in a year. You're looking forward to some conversation after months of isolation. But your host is a very confused, undernourished soul on the brink of death. When you ask her for something to eat, she declares that the cupboard is empty of food – and her heart void of hope. This is her last meal for her and her son, and then they would die. But God had promised provision from this poor woman's hands, and so another miracle unfolds.

Have you ever been in a situation when you sensed that God was asking something of you, and then circumstances seemed to pile up, one after the other, to contradict totally what you thought God had said? When that happens, *do* check, with trusted friends and prayerful counsel, that you have heard rightly. Terrible and sometimes tragic things have been done by Christians who insisted that they had heard from God – when it was wishful thinking that turned sour. But if God has spoken and you've taken responsible steps to check with Scripture and other mature Christians, then stand your ground, and don't be afraid.

Prayer: Father, help me trust that Your hand is at work, when circumstances suggest that You are nowhere to be found. Amen.

Living with contradictions

BIG PICTURE:
1 Kings 17:10–12
John 21:1–14

FOCUS:
"'As surely as the LORD your God lives," she replied, "I don't have any bread ... I am gathering a few sticks to take home and make a meal ... that we may eat it – and die.'"
(1 Kings 17:12)

Home matters

BIG PICTURE:
1 Kings 17:13–16
Ephesians 5:22–6:4

FOCUS:
'So there was food every day for Elijah and for the woman and her family.'
(1 Kings 17:15)

I AM currently feeling really quite spiritual. These last few days, prayer has been easier than usual, I've been able to think things through with an abnormal clarity, I sense I am hearing from God and, as far as I know, I've not irritated anyone for a while. You've guessed it. As I mentioned earlier, I'm alone, on a ten-day writing retreat. After an initial period of adjustment, where I had to get used to my own company, I quite like the solitude – at least for a while.

It's easier to be godly when alone. Walking and praying on the lush green South Downs in the South of England, as I've been able to do today, isn't demanding. Trying to love God and other humans when you are awakened by your children's violin practice at 7am (and you fear that a number of animals are being strangled) is not quite so easy. The test of our faith has to be in the hubbub of relationships.

In public, I can fake kindness. But around those nearest and dearest to me, I am the real me. American politician Mark Hatfield confesses: 'The home is the toughest environment of all for leaders. Why is it that the ones we love the most are the ones we are most impatient with? My wife has often said to me, "I wish you were as patient with your children as you are with your constituents."'

Elijah takes his place in a family home – where fresh challenges will come. Zarephath means 'smelting furnace' – and home and relationships will be the refining fire that shows what we really are.

It's easier to be godly when alone

Prayer: Give me faith for the silent times, faith when it is peaceful, when it is busy and when I'm surrounded by noise. Amen.

WE SAW yesterday that it's in our own relationships that much of the refining work of God comes. One of the most difficult trials to walk through is when we are hurt by the very people that we are closest to. If someone distant takes a swipe at me, it smarts, but I'm not mortally wounded. But if a close friend or family member disappoints, then the pain can be excruciating.

Elijah had walked through an ongoing daily miracle with the woman and her son, but when her boy dies, she turns on Elijah and strikes like a rattlesnake. Suddenly, it's Elijah's fault that the boy died (he would have died of starvation months earlier had it not been for the prophet), he has something against the woman (yes, that's why he prayerfully laid on a miracle for her) and he only came to remind her of her sin (now what sin would that be exactly, since no one has mentioned it until now?).

So what turned a happy home into a boxing ring? Notice how quickly the distraught woman links her son's death, Elijah's being in the home and her past sin together. There's a skeleton in the closet and it's making her angry and spiteful.

And so she hits out. Unresolved issues in our relationship with God will affect our relationships with others. When someone is unkind, stop and wonder what might be going on beneath the surface. Who knows what pain lingers behind those acid words? Perhaps the problem is not really with us at all. And how should we react? We'll consider that tomorrow.

Prayer: Help me to see past the surface when others hurt me: give me sensitivity to their pain, and the grace to respond well. Amen.

Rejection comes

BIG PICTURE:
1 Kings 17:17–18
Proverbs 15:1

FOCUS:
'She said to Elijah, "What do you have against me, man of God? Did you come to remind me of my sin and kill my son?"' (1 Kings 17:18)

Kindness expressed through prayer

BIG PICTURE:
1 Kings 17:17–23
Luke 6:27–36

FOCUS:
'She said to Elijah, "What do you have against me, man of God? Did you come to remind me of my sin and kill my son?"' (1 Kings 17:18)

IT'S hard to meet contempt with kindness. It takes real grace to keep serving someone even as they attack you. Who knows, they might interpret your willingness to be gracious as an admission of guilt for the very things that they accuse you of. Now, they insist, you are trying to work off your shame! But Elijah is broken-hearted at the tragedy that has befallen this little family: there's no time for defensive words, or theological discussion about past sin – it was time to pray. We are clearly taught to pray for our enemies and for those who mistreat us. While the woman was not Elijah's enemy, she was acting like one. Surely we are changed as we pray for those who are unkind to us: we see them differently, and feel differently about them.

Elijah opens the floodgates of his heart with his praying – we get a glimpse of that 'praying in prayer' again as he rages at God. And in the unusual act of 'stretching' himself upon the boy three times, as he presses his body against the prone, cold body of that lad, some commentators suggest that he was taking a radical stance: 'my life for his life, let my breath be given for him'. Of course, in praying like this, Elijah touched a corpse – and that would make him ceremonially unclean for seven days (Num. 19:11).

As I contemplate Elijah praying like this, I confess my poverty in this area – I know very little about this kind of intensity and passion in intercession. Perhaps you'd like to join me as I ask God: Lord, teach us how to pray.

Lord, teach us how to pray

Prayer: Teach us to pray with passion, persistence, and love, even for those who bruise us with their words and deeds. Amen.

IMAGINE the atmosphere in that room as Elijah carried the once dead, now living son downstairs to a tearful reunion with his mother. But something more than physical resurrection has taken place here. When Elijah first showed up at this house, the woman spoke to him about the Lord *his* God (1 Kings 17:12). But now both she and her son have seen and experienced enough of the power and love of God, and she exclaims, 'the word of the LORD from your mouth is the truth.' She has come to see the reality about God for herself – and all because God choreographed things so that she would provide a lonely prophet with a home for a while.

It must have been impossible to live with a man like Elijah without bumping into God. I'm reminded of the story of Gordon Maxwell, who went to India as a missionary. So obvious was his faith and his behaviour, that when he asked a local Hindu to teach him the language, the man refused, claiming that if he spent time with Maxwell, he would inevitably become a Christian.

That's something to aspire to, especially as many of us quietly feel that living with us might have the opposite effect. Elijah lived the message in the home, before he took the next mighty step to the hill: onto the platform of confrontation at Mount Carmel.

Prayer: May those closest to me be drawn closer to You, through me. Amen.

Influence is ours

BIG PICTURE:
1 Kings 17:24
Matthew 5:13–16

FOCUS:
'Then the woman said to Elijah, "Now I know that you are a man of God and that the word of the LORD from your mouth is the truth."'
(1 Kings 17:24)

1 Kings 18:1–15
Acts 15:36–41

Be sacrificial,
zealous – and
kind

Weekend

Life

The gentle touch

Elijah is now moving swiftly towards the epic
showdown atop Mount Carmel. All of his life has
been leading up to this nation-shaking contest. On
the way to the palace of Samaria, the fiery prophet
bumps into that Old Testament double agent,
Obadiah. Look at the way Elijah deals with Obadiah
when he stammers out his fearful protest, worrying
that he might lose his own head if he reports that
Elijah is in town and Elijah then disappears. As
Elijah marched resolutely towards Carmel, he could
easily have slipped into believing that everyone
should be as bold and confrontational as him; a trap
that committed people often fall into. They pray
through the night, so why can't everyone else? They
commit their summer holidays to serving in a two-
thirds world situation (a wonderful thing to do) – so
why are the rest of us heading for the Canaries?
Like Paul, who hastily dismissed John Mark, we can
write others off if they aren't as strong as we perceive
ourselves to be.

But Elijah spoke kindly to Obadiah, and swore an
oath that pledged that his appearance at the palace
was certain: Obadiah need not fear.

Be sacrificial, zealous – and kind.

I'VE recently discovered another rather bizarre weakness in my life – one among many. I tend to agree with my critics immediately, rather than thinking through their criticisms. When told that I have done something wrong, I often apologise: which, at first glance seems quite noble. But is it? It's not always very honest (if I haven't done what I'm accused of, and I know it) and it is also linked with a basic desire to please people. If we're not sure that we're guilty of wrong, we'd be better to thank our accusers, and take some time to think and pray about their comments, rather than rushing to hold up our hands in surrender and falsely admit to something, just for the sake of peace.

As Elijah met Ahab, the surly king hurled an abusive, accusatory missile at the prophet, and denounced him as the 'troubler of Israel' – the Hebrew word here is a very strong insult, meaning 'one who brings disaster'. Ahab was convinced that his statement was true – this wasn't just royal name-calling. After all, Elijah had made it clear that it was by *his* word that drought would begin – and end. In a sense, Elijah was the choreographer of judgment. But a moment of reflection – and Elijah's blunt response – shows us that Ahab was also quite wrong, for judgment day had come because of his wickedness. Without hesitation, Elijah set the record straight. And the apostle Paul set the record straight too about his wrongful imprisonment. Be open and humble when someone suggests that you got it wrong – listen, take advice, and be prayerful. But don't plead guilty when you're not.

Prayer: Lord, help me put things right when I'm wrong, but save me from confessing to what I have not done. Amen.

Wrongly accused

BIG PICTURE:
1 Kings 18:16–18
Acts 16:16–40

FOCUS:
"'I have not made trouble for Israel," Elijah replied. "But you and your father's family have. You have abandoned the LORD's commands and have followed the Baals.'" (1 Kings 18:18)

In authority

BIG PICTURE:
1 Kings 18:19–20
Luke 9:1–6

FOCUS:
'Summon the people from all over Israel to meet me on Mount Carmel. And bring the four hundred and fifty prophets of Baal and the four hundred prophets of Asherah ...'
(1 Kings 18:19)

Together, as the people of God, we have authority in Christ's name

AHAB had it all. A beautiful palace in Samaria, sumptuously decorated, no expense spared – artifacts have been found, showing that even the bed ends, table tops and chair backs were ivory clad. He also owned a country house in Jezreel; all this, and incredible power too. His regime was backed up by 2,000 chariots and 10,000 soldiers.

Elijah looked like just another peasant in his crude camel skins, a nobody. But now look again at these two men who hailed from such different worlds – and see that Elijah, not Ahab, was in charge. A four-year programme of drought had been arranged by the prophet – and now it is Elijah who is setting the king's appointments, as he summons royalty, the Baal and Asherah prophets, and the nation of Israel to gather for the showdown at Mount Carmel. Ahab had all the surface trappings: Elijah had all the power and authority in this situation.

As followers of Christ, we've been given spiritual authority – but I'm wondering if I use it. Without getting into an instant guilt trip about prayer, I'm still challenged that I'd probably see more of God's activity if I took more time to pray. Are we so intimidated by the superficial power of others that we forget that we can move heaven and earth in Jesus' name?

Perhaps I'm so nervous of the 'name it and claim it' extremists that turn God into little more than a valet to meet my selfish needs that I've overreacted and don't see answers to prayer, because I don't get around to asking. Together, as the people of God, we have authority in Christ's name.

Prayer: Lord, help me to realise that I have authority in You, to see prayer answered, powers toppled, and Your kingdom come. Amen.

THE Christian life is often compared with running in a race; images of sleek athletes striding down the track come to mind, unless you're me. I run every day, and the word stagger is more appropriate to describe my style of running. At times, an oxygen tent from above would be helpful as I limp my way through the last torturous yards.

In challenging the gathered people of Israel, Elijah uses a term (translated 'waver' here) that means 'to limp'. They have wavered backwards and forwards between Yahweh and Baal, perhaps trying to get the best of both religions. Baal was primarily a weather-god and handy at harvest time. Yahweh, on the other hand, may have been popularly thought of as a god from the desert regions of Sinai (see Hab. 3:3–7). Some thought of Yahweh as 'a god of the hills and not a god of the valleys' (1 Kings 20:28). Baalism certainly came in useful if you wanted some sexual indulgence: you could sin away and still feel spiritual.

Now the people have to make a choice – it's one or the other. You and I face that choice daily: the tempter doesn't usually throw down the gauntlet and demand that we totally abandon our love for God – but subtly invites us to mix up a cocktail, a little compromise here, a dash of self-indulgence there. Perhaps, at the beginning of another day, it would be good to set our sights on decisive living, where we follow God – wholeheartedly. Limping isn't fun; it's painful, looks terrible and, ultimately, will slow your jogging down to a complete stop. Let's choose well.

Prayer: Father, give me grace to say 'Yes' to You, and 'No' to that which draws me away from You. Amen.

You can't have it both ways

BIG PICTURE:
1 Kings 18:20–21
Joshua 24:1–15

FOCUS:
'How long will you waver between two opinions? If the LORD is God, follow him; but if Baal is God, follow him.'
(1 Kings 18:21)

I'd prefer not to

BIG PICTURE:
1 Kings 18:20–21
Jeremiah 13:1–11

FOCUS:
'But the people said nothing.' (1 Kings 18:21)

WE SAW yesterday that 'limping' Christianity will characterise our experience if we fail to be decisive about our choices. But sometimes, like Israel on Mount Carmel, we don't openly refuse God – we just stay in silent rebellion, lips sealed, arms folded.

In Herman Melville's *Bartleby the Scrivener*, Bartleby is a scribe who copies legal documents. The meek and mild Bartleby is liked and appreciated by his employer; but then the boring and previously predictable clerk begins to rebel. Asked to proofread a document, Bartleby refuses, and uses a phrase that becomes the theme of the rest of the book: 'I'd prefer not to.' Soon every request from the employer, no matter how reasonable, is met with the same wooden response: 'I'd prefer not to.' The employer, who could have simply fired Bartleby, desperately and yet patiently tries to win him over and coax him with kindness; but eventually, Bartleby refuses to do any work, and incredibly, makes the office his permanent home, establishing squatter's rights. Once again the employer embodies longsuffering and kindness, and invites Bartleby to vacate the office building and live in his home; amazing grace that is met by the same reply: 'I'd prefer not to.'

Ultimately, selfish Bartleby is hauled off to jail, where he goes on hunger strike. His former employer visits him, pleading with him to take some food: 'I'd prefer not to.' As the book ends, the narrator, pondering the polite but unyielding Bartleby, exclaims, 'Ah, Bartleby! Ah, humanity!'

Silence sometimes isn't golden – just solid rebellion. Are there areas where we're smiling at heaven – but saying, 'I'd prefer not to'?

Prayer: When You speak Lord, I will listen – and answer. Amen.

Desperate dancing

THE prophets of Baal moved into a frenzied, six-hour religious workout, desperate to provoke a fiery response from the heavens. The word that is used to describe their dancing is the same word that we considered a couple of days ago – the one that means 'staggering'.

With his provocative sense of humour, Elijah hovers in the background, making comments about the need to wake Baal up – an inside joke, as Baal was believed to be a vegetation deity who had to be awakened each spring from his winter hibernation. Most modern translators have cleaned up Elijah's other little joke, about Baal 'going travelling' – a term that probably means 'gone aside to relieve oneself'.

But freeze the frame for a moment, and consider these desperate dancers: everything is based on them making their god do something. If they can just leap high enough, scream loud enough, or even spill enough of their own blood (as they resort to cutting themselves) then perhaps their deity will torch their sacrifice. This same notion of the 'pay as you pray' god was behind the unspeakable evil of child sacrifice: blessing, if it was coming, would have to be purchased. Human nature rushes to adopt that spiritual equation. There's no such thing as a free lunch, or for that matter, a free pardon. Whatever I get, I'll settle the bill.

Today, there's nothing we can do to make God love us more, and nothing we can do to make God love us less. Salvation really is the ultimate free gift, the greatest present in history.

BIG PICTURE:
1 Kings 18:22–29
Ephesians 2:1–10

FOCUS:
'Elijah began to taunt them. "Shout louder! ... Surely he is a god! Perhaps he is deep in thought, or busy, or travelling. Maybe he is sleeping and must be awakened."'
(1 Kings 18:27)

Salvation really is the ultimate free gift ...

Prayer: Thank You, Father, for giving me what I could never earn. Help me to pass on news of that gift. Amen.

1 Kings 18:30–38
Luke 4:1–13

Tempting God

As Elijah repairs the old altar of the Lord, lays out the sacrifice, and then splashes buckets of water all over the place, he wanted everyone to be in no doubt – this was going to be a bona-fide miracle: no sleight of hand or trickery here. So wasn't this testing God? Jesus was invited by Satan to do some stunts in the wilderness to prove Himself, but refused the offer. Sometimes I've seen Christians pray prayers that are similar to that testing: 'God, if You want me to continue to follow You, then You'd better answer this one ...' So was Elijah's action legitimate?

The answer is found in his prayer for fire, as he insists, 'I am your servant and have done all these things *at your command*' (1 Kings 18:36, italics mine). Just as fire had fallen on David's sacrifice earlier (1 Chron. 21:26), so now, in a terrifying instant, the sacrifice is consumed from flames that leapt out of the sky. No wonder the people fell on their faces and a new shout echoed around the hillside: the Lord, He is God. The fire test was God's idea, and so God obliged. Let's ask that we fulfil His dreams today – not ours.

Let's ask that we fulfil His dreams today – not ours

Weekend

IT'S one of those terrible scenes that occur in Old Testament history, as the prophets of Baal are executed without delay – or trial. Commentators are divided: some insist that Elijah was just fulfilling the law (Deut. 13:1–5) in ordering the executions. And remember the countless babies that had suffered an agonising death at the hands of these evil occultists.

Faithful – or fanatical?

BIG PICTURE:
1 Kings 18:39–40
2 Corinthians 2:1–11

FOCUS:
'Elijah commanded them, "Seize the prophets of Baal. Don't let anyone get away!" They seized them, and Elijah had them brought down to the Kishon Valley and slaughtered there.' (1 Kings 18:40)

But others wonder if Elijah took a step too far – as we've noted, there was no trial (perhaps the evidence was plain) but the day does end with what seems like a lynching, the mob ruling, even though the mob was under the command of Elijah. One commentator suggests that Elijah had a tendency towards fanaticism. As we'll see in the next few days, the man of miracles certainly didn't always get it right, and occasionally his perception was completely wrong.

Perhaps we should simply heed the warning never to allow passionate faith to become damaging fanaticism. Someone once said 'A fanatic is just someone who is more committed to God than you are' – but though that sounds challenging and noble, it's not helpful. A fanatic is not just someone who flies an aeroplane into a building in the name of their god; they go to extremes to demonstrate their commitment, insisting that everyone does faith their way. They go beyond the demands of God, placing extra rules upon themselves or others. The Corinthians went too far in their discipline of one of their number. Fanaticism can be difficult to judge in others, though, so let's be careful to look out for it in ourselves and reluctant to judge it in others.

Prayer: Lord, show me how to walk in the balance and rhythm of grace. Amen.

Instant rain?

BIG PICTURE:
1 Kings 18:41–45
Exodus 14:1–14

FOCUS:
"'Go and look towards
the sea,' he told his
servant. And he went up
and looked. "There is
nothing there," he said.
Seven times Elijah said,
"Go back."'
(1 Kings 18:43)

I'VE discovered that I quite like cookery books. Yesterday I spent a happy few minutes flipping through the pages of Delia and Jamie. They make it sound so very easy: just follow the recipe. Helpfully, I decided to refrain from attempting to cook anything: a new book, *Cooking with Jeffrey*, is unlikely. Be grateful.

I've noticed that some Christians like recipe-based Christianity. Faith that can be reduced to a series of clear steps with a quantifiable outcome sells well – there's no shortage of books, tapes, videos and conferences that offer *14 Steps to Fortifying Your Faith* or *67 Powerful Principles for Prosperity*. I discovered, however, that the recipes don't turn out so well when I prepare them.

Elijah prayed for fire, and it came instantly. Now, as he ends the day by interceding for rain (having prophesied its coming to King Ahab), the cloudburst is not forthcoming, and his servant has to scan the sky for clouds seven times. Finally a tiny cloud is spotted on the horizon. The floodgates were opened, but slowly.

Faith doesn't work like clockwork: prayer is not a vending machine that automatically dispenses the chocolate bar once the coin has been deposited. Christianity is an intimate relationship, not the application of a series of impersonal cosmic principles which always generate the same result. Israel's exodus is an example: in their first battle, they were told not to fight (Exod. 14:1–14). In their second skirmish, fighting was required (Exod. 17:9). God was the same: His strategy had changed. Elijah's story demonstrates an important principle: what God did this afternoon He might not do this evening.

Prayer: Lord, I want to know more than truths about You. Help me to know You, the unchanging God, amidst change. Amen.

Faith doesn't

work like

clockwork ...

WE HUMANS are quite good at putting each other in categories. People are either winners or losers, famous or nobodies, fat or thin, successful or failures. But these generalities obscure the real truth: today's strong person can be tomorrow's miserable failure: our past history may be a helpful indicator of our future performance, but nothing is guaranteed. As we wonder at Elijah, surging past King Ahab's chariot, he looks like a winner all the way. He caps a day of triumph, where fire and rain fell at his word, with an impressive dash back to Jezreel. He looks invincible – when you've won a battle where the odds were stacked against you (one that didn't look hopeful at the start of the day), you could easily believe that nothing could ever bring you down again, that you are unbeatable. And Elijah was more than a strong character: the text records that 'the power of the LORD came upon Elijah', so fuelling his incredible run.

But Elijah's story shows us that everyone – even those who seem to have more than their fair share of God's power – can fall. Within a very short time, Elijah would be running again – but this time he would be fleeing in sheer terror. The triumphant national hero is about to come crashing down; the victor of Mount Carmel is about to become the fugitive of Mount Sinai. 'So, if you think you are standing firm, be careful that you don't fall!' (1 Cor. 10:12) says the scripture. Let's know where we could be tripped up. Let's ask for grace for our weaknesses and vulnerabilities. And let's know that, even when we're winning today, that tomorrow is another day.

Prayer: Show me my weaknesses, and prevent me from being deluded by my strengths, Lord. Amen.

First past the post?

BIG PICTURE:
1 Kings 18:46
1 Corinthians
10:1–13

FOCUS:
'The power of the LORD came upon Elijah and, tucking his cloak into his belt, he ran ahead of Ahab all the way to Jezreel.' (1 Kings 18:46)

The power of fear

BIG PICTURE:
1 Kings 19:1–3
Psalm 27:1–14

FOCUS:
'So Jezebel sent a
messenger to Elijah to
say, "May the gods deal
with me … if by this time
tomorrow I do not make
your life like that of one
of them."'
(1 Kings 19:2)

I CAN remember spending a whole summer under the cudgel of fear. I'd heard through the grapevine that a large, muscle-bound lad in our neighbourhood was out to get me. He had a terrifying reputation, having put a few other people in hospital, and I awoke every day with the same suffocating dread. Perhaps today would be the day for me to experience hospital food. After six weeks of agonising, I decided to go to his workplace to see if the rumours were true. We met, and he treated me like an old friend: I had thrown a summer away, sacrificed to fear.

It was fear that toppled Elijah. Jezebel was a devilishly clever strategist – she could have had Elijah killed, just as other prophets of God had died at her command. But in the wake of the Carmel contest, that wouldn't have been politically expedient. It could provoke a national uprising if the new hero from Gilead was suddenly executed. She realised that she didn't have to kill him – just tell him that she was planning to do so, and let fear do its devastating, gnawing work in his mind and soul.

Her message is loaded with intimidation: one translation of her words is 'I am Jezebel. You are Elijah.' She reminds him of her royal power, and of his humble background.

Perhaps we're more vulnerable after an emotional and spiritual high. Now the man who had looked Ahab in the eye, who hadn't flinched at a fight with a herd of prophets of Baal, buckles as the messenger departs. The smart weapon of fear had scored a hit, right on target.

Prayer: Father, my imagination can summon many threats. Quieten my heart, and help me trust You when I am afraid. Amen.

Jezebel

BIG PICTURE:
1 Kings 19:1–3
Isaiah 43:1–4

FOCUS:
'So Jezebel sent a
messenger …'
(1 Kings 19:2)

IT'S worth rerunning yesterday's reading, and asking why Jezebel managed to send Elijah into such fear. He had been fearless before so many other challenges. We can only speculate, because the Bible only tells us that he was afraid – but not why.

Elijah had not dealt with the Queen before, only her snivelling, cowardly husband. She was known as the real powerhouse of the palace – so did Elijah nurse a fear of her that he did not have for Ahab? Historians tell us that she dressed to kill. She was famous for her arched eyebrows and the jet black lines that edged her eyelids: a fearsome sight. She is the person that Scripture specifically records as 'killing off the LORD's prophets' (1 Kings 18:4). Elijah's death threat came from a mass murderess, and he knew she meant business.

And then she had ignored his summons to appear on Carmel, and so had her Asherah prophets, despite Elijah's demand that the Asherah cultists 'who eat at Jezebel's table' (1 Kings 18:19) gather for the great contest.

Notice also that it was the execution of the prophets of Baal that particularly enraged Jezebel. If Elijah had been operating on his own zeal rather than the command of God when he ordered that slaughter, did he now fear that he had stepped outside the will of God, and was reaping the consequences?

All of these questions remain unanswered, but they point to the possibility that Elijah was terrified because he was moving into unknown territory. Perhaps that's how you feel today. Take heart: the pathway may be unfamiliar, but the God who is with you hasn't changed.

Prayer: Lord, You know the way that I take, even when I don't. Stay close. Amen.

... the pathway may be unfamiliar, but the God who is with you hasn't changed

Reactions regretted

One of my New Year's resolutions was that I would learn to respond to the challenges of life rather than react to them. Most of the things that I've ever regretted doing have come because I've jumped into a situation with both feet, without stopping to think. It's better to calm down, count to 10 (or maybe 633,110) and then take prayerful, careful action.

Faced with a death threat from the palace, Elijah immediately sprang into action: some translations include the words 'immediately ran'. The Hebrew word used means to stand up, so the sense is 'Elijah got up and ran'. His dash put him out of national life for at least six weeks, when he should have been around to help with a possible nationwide return to Yahweh.

There's no pause for prayer, no consultation with Obadiah, there's no turning to God at all – just an urgent, knee jerk reaction, and this from a man who had sat by a brook for a year, and had waited all day for the prophets of Baal to complete their futile performance on Mount Carmel.

Are you ready to jump into something, or go somewhere – without having thought or prayed it through? Wait.

It's better to calm down, count to 10 ...

Weekend

RECENTLY I got together with a group of friends to be with one of our number who is currently battling with cancer, and for whom the future, humanly speaking, looks bleak. Our time shared together was memorable – there were tears, words of comfort, encouragement, empathy and prayer. It was simply quite beautiful. Friendship, especially during an autumnal season in our lives, gives us the hopeful scent of springtime.

We've already seen, through our visit with Elijah to the Brook Kerith, that there's a time to be alone, to make space for clear thought, reflection, and to learn the lessons that only the classroom of solitude can teach us.

But being on the receiving end of a death threat is not one of those moments. When we're in a panic, it's useful to gain the support and care of trusted friends: this is what we were made for (Gal. 6:2).

Friendship enables us to take our fears out from the labyrinth that is our mind, with all of its shadows and dark corners, and place them under the floodlight of relationship. There, enriched by the insights of fellow travellers, we are able to see our challenges more clearly. But Elijah turned his back on all of this, and allowed fear to do what fear so often does: shunt him into isolation. At His darkest hour, Jesus urgently needed the support and prayers of His very best friends – do we actually think that we are better, or stronger than Him? Come out of isolation. Phone a friend, or someone who looks like they could become one.

Prayer: Help me not to hide from others when fear comes stalking. Remove the self-obsession that blinds me to other people's burdens. Amen.

Phone a friend

BIG PICTURE:
1 Kings 19:3
Matthew 26:36–46

FOCUS:
'When he came to Beersheba in Judah, he left his servant there'
(1 Kings 19:3)

Making things worse

BIG PICTURE:
1 Kings 19:4–5
Luke 22:49–51

FOCUS:
'... while he himself went a day's journey into the desert. He came to a broom tree, sat down under it and prayed that he might die.'
(1 Kings 19:4)

IN COLORADO, where I live, we have a few bears wandering around in the woods – and once in a while, down the high street of our town. In bygone days, a bear trap that slammed shut and locked onto the foot of the bear was used (thankfully it's illegal now). It was particularly cruel: the more the animal struggled, the more terrible damage was done.

Elijah is struggling like a man caught in a trap – and only hurting himself more. One of the results of our reacting rather than responding to crisis, and insisting that we go it alone, is that we end up either working hard but changing nothing or, in some cases, making things worse than they already are. By running as he did, Elijah stayed well in the danger zone, because he fled to Judah, forgetting that Ahab's daughter was reigning there with Jehoram (2 Kings 8:16–18). He travelled more than eighty miles – for nothing.

If that wasn't pointless enough, notice that he ran for his life – and then prayed for death – a somewhat illogical course of action. Moses had prayed this prayer at a time of great discouragement (Num. 11:15), and so had Jonah (Jonah 4:3).

And then, probably already exhausted by the tumultuous events on Mount Carmel, he makes things worse because of the physical demands of the journey, which was 'too much for him'. Burned out, he loses all perspective – about who he was called to be, and what God had done. If you feel trapped today – be careful about action that could make things worse. Don't run like Elijah, or strike out like Peter, who panicked in the Garden of Gethsemane.

Prayer: Lord, steady my nerve when I am under pressure. Let my choices reflect faith, not fear. Amen.

... be careful

about action that

could make

things worse

Angels fail to stir

BIG PICTURE:
1 Kings 19:5–6
Luke 22:39–46

FOCUS:
'All at once an angel
touched him and said,
"Get up and eat."'
(1 Kings 19:5)

SOMETIMES I am tempted to think (wrongly) that God abandons me to my bluer days; that when the fog rolls in, and I can't begin to find even a few scraps of joy, then He is displeased, and retreats. But here, Elijah is at his lowest – and it is then that an angelic waiter arrives. No visible angels were in attendance when Elijah threw down the gauntlet in the palace, or soaked the sacrifices on Carmel: at his zenith moments, they were nowhere to be seen. But now in his darkest hour, they show up, just as the angel strengthened Jesus at His hour of horror in Gethsemane.

Not that Elijah notices. Often, when we are low, we miss whatever God does, no matter how dramatic it is.

One of my favourite cartoons shows a character kneeling to pray, saying to God, 'It's not easy to believe in You, God. We never see You. How come You never show Yourself? How do we know You even exist?'

At this point a flower springs to life next to him and a volcano erupts in the distance. An eclipse of the sun turns the sky black and a star shoots across the stratosphere. A tidal wave crashes over him, lightning cracks, a bush begins to burn, a stone rolls away from the entrance of a tomb. He pulls himself from the mud and mumbles 'Okay, okay … I give up. Every time I bring up this subject, all we get is interruptions.'

Perhaps all you'd like to do is sleep, because being awake is too painful. Whether you see them or not, angels are watching over you.

Prayer: When I least sense that You are there, You are. Help me to notice the miracle of God with me. Amen.

Exhausted

BIG PICTURE:
1 Kings 19:7–9
John 21:1–14

FOCUS:
'The angel of the LORD came back a second time and touched him and said, "Get up and eat, for the journey is too much for you."' (1 Kings 19:7)

I AM rather nervous of those spiritual Christians who don't ever seem to have down days. Perhaps I'm just envious, but although I occasionally camp out in a place called victory, I can't say that I live there. And when I'm tired, or jet-lagged, I've noticed that my capacity to believe in God is sharply diminished. Give me enough sleep deprivation, and I can identify easily with my friend Adrian Plass, who says that there are times when he is an Olympic-level doubter.

Helpfully, God knows and is concerned about these practical details. So the angel of the Lord showed up, not with a thousand friends to tap dance on the clouds and hum the hallelujah chorus, or even to give the worn-out prophet a blinding revelation – but to cook him breakfast, and help him rest. Just like Jesus really: it was an unusual priority for Him, having beaten death and hell, to show up on a beach and cook breakfast for His worn-out disciples – but the fact that He did gives us a glimpse of how utterly marvellous He is.

Sometimes a good breakfast is exactly what we need. God knows that there are moments when what we need is not another ministry assignment, prayer meeting, or Bible study – but a hot meal and a good sleep. I've met too many Christians who will immediately decide that they are under serious spiritual attack, when they don't need to lock horns with the devil but take a nap.

Let's be spiritual and sensible, and endeavour to take care of our work, rest and play: He is interested in all of it.

... work, rest and play: He is interested in all of it

Prayer: Give me wisdom to establish rhythm in my life Lord. And thank You that You sometimes bless – through breakfast. Amen.

IF WE tell ourselves a lie often enough, then we'll start to believe it. Elijah had been nursing a total misconception for a while – it was the notion that he was the only faithful prophet of the Lord left – an idea that was totally untrue. He knew about Obadiah, the double agent. He was well aware of the hundred prophets holed up in the cave. And then there were the seven thousand faithful in Israel who had not bowed to Baal. So why does he blurt out, 'I am the only one left'?

Perhaps Elijah genuinely thought that when it came to *true* faithfulness, he was the only genuine article. Had his exhaustion and disappointment caused him to resent Obadiah, who was still living in that fabulous palace? Had his epic performance on Carmel nudged him into a belief that no one could deliver quite like he could? If that was so, he was carrying a crushing weight on his shoulders. We'll see later that Elijah became hesitant about passing on the baton to others: did he have an inflated view of his own significance? Ironically, his running means that he is now holed in a cave – just like those other one hundred prophets.

You are vital – but not irreplaceable. Perhaps to hand on that responsibility that is killing you will mean that it will not be done as well as you would do it – or worse, not be done in the *way* you would do it. Jesus was willing to send His disciples out, knowing that there would be mistakes and misunderstandings – but He insisted on passing the baton on to them.

Prayer: Lord, save me from the deception that insists that what I do can only be done well by me. Amen.

Nobody does it better

BIG PICTURE:
1 Kings 19:9–10
Mark 6:6–13

FOCUS:
'I have been very zealous for the LORD God Almighty. The Israelites have rejected your covenant ... I am the only one left, and now they are trying to kill me too.'
(1 Kings 19:10)

God asks a question

Look at the conversation between God and Elijah once more. It begins, not with a heavenly command, but with a piercing question to the hunched over, exhausted man in the cave: 'What are you doing here, Elijah?' (1 Kings 19:9).

It's surely the simplest question that could have been asked of the fugitive prophet, and one that was designed to bring him right back on track. God knew the answer to His own question, but wanted Elijah to speak out his pain, so that he would begin to face it and move forward.

And it's a blunt question that we'd do well to face ourselves too. Are there places in our lives where we know we should not go? We should stop wriggling, bring the self-justification to an end, and just face the fact, unpalatable though it may be. Sometimes the Lord can cut through all the fog of our deception with a razor sharp sentence. Saul became the apostle Paul as a result of a similar question. So let's not hide behind a wall of words, or try bluff our way out of the challenge. Where, in our lives, would God say: 'What are you doing here?'

Where ... would God say: 'What are you doing here?'

Weekend

AT LAST, God gives the cave man a command – step outside; initially it seems that Elijah ignores it. Incredible though it seems, the man who had jumped to attention and risked his life to obey the word of the Lord in the past sits resolutely with his arms folded in the present. Yesterday's commitment doesn't guarantee a willing heart today.

And so a hurricane force wind – one that shattered rocks – turned Elijah's little refuge into a wind tunnel. An earthquake shakes the mountain – which could cause the cave to cave in. And then fire, perhaps reminiscent of Carmel, appears before the reluctant prophet. But Scripture notes that God 'was not in' these things – so why did they happen?

Is it possible that God was showing Elijah that the work of God will be done, not only through earth shattering miracles and supernatural tumult, but also through the quiet working of the voice of God whispered in the human heart? It was to that quiet voice that Elijah was about to respond.

I'd love to see more of the power of God, but I'd like to stay faithful when nothing epic is happening. Perhaps Elijah needed to learn that God is not only at work when His activity is loudly advertised – that He can use a vast variety of methods and people to get His kingdom purposes fulfilled. I believe that God still does signs and wonders today. But I'd like to trust Him if He doesn't do those signs and wonders – this day. Let's not limit God to the extraordinary. Let's believe when there *isn't* a sign.

Prayer: Father, may my experience of You yesterday not narrow my expectations of You today. Amen.

Power – but God was not in it

BIG PICTURE:
1 Kings 19:11–12
John 4:43–54

FOCUS:
'Then a ... wind tore the mountains apart ... but the LORD was not in the wind. After the wind there was an earthquake, but the LORD was not in the earthquake.'
(1 Kings 19:11)

The still small voice

BIG PICTURE:
1 Kings 19:12–13
John 10:1–16

FOCUS:
'And after the fire came a gentle whisper.'
(1 Kings 19:12)

IT WAS the gentle voice of God that Elijah heard – some have translated the words here as 'the sound of gentle silence' or 'the silent sound'. God is not talking to him in booming tones, which one perhaps might have anticipated. When faith is low, a firm, unmistakable voice from above would be quite helpful.

But instead, God speaks in a barely perceptible hush, which would have been easy to miss. As this followed the hullabaloo of wind, earthquake and fire – without God – commentators have suggested that perhaps God whispered like this to show that He was now going to use Elijah in a more subtle, less dramatic way. Elijah thought that his ministry was over. In reality, one season was ending and another was beginning. The God of the tumultuous miracles was leading Elijah forward into the next phase: would he obey?

It's always exciting to begin an activity or ministry – but there's an art to sensing that the season is coming to a close, and now fresh challenges beckon. Huge amounts of money and effort are often poured into projects and initiatives that God was in, but now He has moved on. It takes grace to start something up – and grace to close it down.

To Elijah's credit, now at last he stands to his feet and edges closer to the mouth of the cave – which God had commanded him to do earlier. But, as we'll see, he still had some way to go yet before he could be useful again. Be open to the whisper of God today – He might ask you to start something, or perhaps nudge you to end something.

Prayer: Give me ears that hear You, and a heart quick to respond to You, Lord. Amen.

Mind lock

THE verse we're focusing on today sounds familiar, doesn't it? That's because it is. Elijah gives the same speech to God – for the second time. He has moved out of the cave, but not an inch in his thinking.

Fear sustains itself by repetition. A thought forms within our minds, which at first we manage to send packing. But then minutes, hours, or days later, it returns and ultimately is so tenacious, it launches a hostile takeover bid for our brains and we can think of little else. Fear has triumphed and a compulsive pattern of anxiety has been firmly established. Now the enthroned thought will fend off attempts to dislodge it with ferocious energy. Our mind is locked into endless orbiting of that fear. Work and play become difficult, because concentration is ruined and sunny days are spoiled. The term 'nervous wreck' well describes someone who has lived this way for an extended time.

The irritating pain that signals little more than advancing years suddenly becomes a potential cancer; a slow month at work seems to signal redundancy around the corner. Fear loves to turn a bump in the road into a roadblock. Part of the problem is the mixture of true and false perspective – and that makes it all so very plausible. Elijah had been zealous, the Israelites had been faithless, the altars were in disarray, prophets have died, and yes, he was on the run from a murderous witch. But the conclusion that all of those truths presented was false – he was not the only one left.

Perhaps it's time to break out of that terrified thinking today. God can help us.

Prayer: Renew my mind, Father. When my mind is overwhelmed by fear, grant me Your quiet peace, and may I think clearly. Amen.

BIG PICTURE:
1 Kings 19:13–14
Isaiah 26:1–3

FOCUS:
'I have been very zealous for the LORD God Almighty. The Israelites have rejected your covenant ... I am the only one left, and now they are trying to kill me too.'
(1 Kings 19:14)

Fear loves to turn a bump in the road into a roadblock

A radical plan

BIG PICTURE:
1 Kings 19:15–18
Isaiah 55:8–13

FOCUS:
'The LORD said to him,
"Go back the way you
came, and go to the
Desert of Damascus.
When you get there,
anoint Hazael king over
Aram."' (1 Kings 19:15)

FORGET the idea that God only leads His children into safe places. Elijah was called to operate in a strategy that appeared to be suicidal. The Aramites were the enemies of Israel – so why would Elijah anoint a foreign king? They were being called to bring judgment upon Israel – and remove Ahab and Jezebel.

But it got worse. Now Elijah was being told to anoint another king over Israel itself, in readiness to take over – Jehu, a man who would have a heart for revival, and who would ultimately deal with Jezebel. But to anoint another king would send the already incensed Jezebel into a fit of rage.

Then the issue of succession for Elijah was dealt with, in the command to anoint Elisha.

So did Elijah obey? Yes and no. He *did* anoint Elisha. He *didn't* anoint Hazael – Elisha had to do that later. And he didn't anoint Jehu. When Ahab's reign ended, Jehu wasn't waiting in the wings. Ahaziah, Ahab's son, reigned two years, and he was just like his father. Then there was Jehoram, another son of Ahab, who was just a little better, but not much, and his reign was inconsequential. Thirteen years were wasted – and then Elisha, now at the helm, anointed another king – Jehu – the man picked out years earlier!

Jehu wasn't perfect, and drifted back into apostasy himself, but he stamped out the worship of Baal by tricking the god's followers into meeting together and then slaughtering them, also destroying their temple (2 Kings 10:18–28).

Even if God's command is costly, and indeed risky, do what He says. To disobey is to waste precious time.

Forget the idea

that God only

leads His children

into safe places

Prayer: Lord, help me to obey You when I don't understand, and when what You call me to looks precarious. Amen.

After Sinai: Elisha

BIG PICTURE:
1 Kings 19:19–21
Psalm 145:1–21

FOCUS:
'Elisha ... took his yoke
of oxen and slaughtered
them. He burned the
ploughing equipment to
cook the meat and gave it
to the people ... Then he
set out to follow Elijah ...'
(1 Kings 19:21)

TODAY I heard of the death of a dear man who, years ago, spent hours with me when I was a brand-new Christian. He was a minister who had been struck down by multiple sclerosis. Housebound, and unable to function in church leadership, he refused to waste his life, but instead poured his failing energy into young Christians like me. He never mocked my questions, or rejected me when I failed. I will be forever grateful for him.

Elijah's influence faded after Sinai – perhaps because he didn't follow through on the instructions that he had received there. In a period of between ten and fifteen years, he only ministered twice publicly, as well as sending a prophetic word through the postal system. These were turbulent years, but years when Elijah was mostly silent. But he did raise up and invest in a worthy successor.

At a recent conference I heard Jim Partridge, a young man who has a passion to see the young people of Britain reached for Jesus. Jim called for a church that is 'filled with youth workers', where we don't just rely upon the youth leader or full-time youth worker for the discipleship of their young people, but where everybody takes responsibility to be one generation telling the story of God to another.

Investing in others takes time and patience. We will be disappointed by some drifting away – especially some of those that showed great promise. We will need to answer endless questions that seem obvious, allow our busy schedules to be interrupted. But the call to disciple is a command, not an option.

Prayer: Lord, grant me grace not only to look for blessing, but to become a blessing, and leave a legacy. Amen.

Naboth

It was five or six years after Carmel, and Ahab hadn't changed – he was still a petulant, self-obsessed fool, sulking like a child; he'd had his eyes on a field, wanting it for a vegetable patch, but Naboth, its owner, wasn't interested in selling. Ahab demonstrates his petulant immaturity (1 Kings 21:4) and Jezebel shows her consistent evil by drawing up a plan to frame Naboth. The poor man was stoned – prompting Elijah to step up to the plate again with fiery words of judgment. But the end of the chapter is remarkable. Bear in mind all the years of Ahab's arrogance, greed, and his stubbornness towards the God who proved Himself on Carmel. Now, as he shows repentance for the first time, God rushes to him with grace, and promises that judgment will be delayed.

Have we begun to scratch the surface of God's truly amazing grace? He quickly forgives those who have mocked Him, throws parties for prodigals still carrying the stench of the piggery, and blesses us even though so often we are indifferent to Him. To the human heart, so thoroughly trained to believe that nothing good is free, grace comes as a stunning revelation. Rest in that grace today.

Have we begun to scratch the surface of God's truly amazing grace?

Weekend

I'M FIFTY (kindly gasp if you would, and not because you thought I was older) and I find myself thinking more about pensions and retirement these days. It's important to prepare for the future; what seemed like a distant horizon is marching towards some of us at speed. But not only should we think about the logistics of how we'll live, surely we should also consider what kind of people we will be in the future.

Elijah's ministry is now drawing to an end. Four years after the Naboth incident, Ahaziah, the king who consulted 'Baal-Zephon' – the lord of the flies – had taken a tumble, wants to know if his injuries are terminal, and gets a straightforward sentence of death from Elijah. What follows makes for uncomfortable but illuminating reading. Two bands of soldiers who were dispatched to arrest Elijah were torched by the fire of God. Elijah is still a man of God: still walking in faith, still able to pray, still sensitive to the whispers of angels. And not only this, but the lessons that he'd learned in the past, back at the now distant Carmel, were applied as he became a discipler in his twilight years.

What will I be when I am older? The reality is, probably much the same as I am today, unless I make positive choices towards excellence, or negative choices that are disastrous, the trend that I am living in today will most likely extend itself in my later years. You can't be an irritating, complaining, faithless man or woman in your middle years and then suddenly turn into a faith-filled, kindly soul later on. Today is the bridge to tomorrow.

Prayer: Lord, help me to establish good patterns in my life today, that I may be a person of God in the future. Amen.

Ahaziah: what will we be?

BIG PICTURE:
2 Kings 1:1–18
Titus 2:1–5

FOCUS:
'"If I am a man of God," Elijah replied, "may fire come down from heaven and consume you and your fifty men!" Then the fire of God fell from heaven ...' (2 Kings 1:12)

Transfiguration

BIG PICTURE:
2 Kings 2:1–18
2 Chronicles 21:4–20

FOCUS:
'Jehoram ... reigned in Jerusalem for eight years. He passed away, to no-one's regret, and was buried in the City of David, but not in the tombs of the kings.'
(2 Chron. 21: 20)

IT WAS time for goodbyes, and it seems that many people had caught the hint that Elijah was ending his life on earth – the chariot was going to swing low to carry him home. After ten years of being together, Elisha hears repeatedly that the time has come.

Look at the contrast between the departure of Jehoram of Judah, to whom Elijah wrote, and the prophet. When Jehoram died, no one mourned: good riddance. But Elijah's being taken up to heaven is both forewarned and grieved, as Elisha cries out and laments: '"My father! My father!" ... Then he took hold of his own clothes and tore them apart.'

We saw when we began this study that Elijah wasn't perfect – a human just like us. He had shadowy days of despair, and resisted some of the radical commands of God. But his going was a huge loss, because his was a life that truly made an impact. No wonder that he 'encores' at the transfiguration of Jesus, alongside Moses. Who knows what the three of them discussed that day, as Jesus prepared to walk the dangerous road to Jerusalem (Mark 9:4). Perhaps Elijah encouraged Jesus to go all the way, and not compromise. And Moses, who was stopped just short of the promised land: did he urge Jesus on too? One day we might know.

The chariot swept Elijah away, and Elisha knew: it was his turn. Time to put into practice the lessons learned and the inspiration gained from ten years with Elijah. Empowered by God's Spirit, Elisha completed some of Elijah's unfinished tasks.

Frail as we are, with God's help available, it's our turn.

Prayer: Lord, fill me with Your Spirit, that I might finish well. Help me to take my turn. Amen.

... it's our turn

Seven – Those deadly sins

Seven – Those deadly sins

SOME years ago I picked up a copy of Tony Campolo's *Seven Deadly Sins* – a book that's now out of print – and found it disturbingly challenging and deeply helpful. We're now going to look at a biblical truth that the world would often like us to forget – the reality of sin.

The seven deadly sins don't appear as a specific list in the Bible. Greek monastic theologian Evagrius of Pontus first drew up a list of eight 'offences and wicked human passions'. In the late sixth century, Pope Gregory the Great reduced the list to seven items. The list was compiled so that the faithful would know clearly what was sin: we can be so easily seduced and deceived and so it's good (especially in a culture which frequently mocks the notion of right and wrong) to allow truth to search our hearts and show us if and where we are drifting.

God wants to show us our sin. He doesn't do it to mock us but because, as a loving Father, He invites us to step up in the nobility and joy of holy living. So let's allow the mirror of God's Word to show us some uncomfortable – but ultimately liberating – truths about ourselves.

Thank you for taking what will be a provocative and at times uncomfortable journey with me.

And God bless you!

I'D JUST bought my London Underground ticket when a loud, pushy evangelist marched up to me. 'The wages of sin is death,' he exclaimed, jabbing at me with a bony finger. 'Are you going to hell?' I replied that I was actually on my way to Westminster. He was not amused and marched off, a portrait of the kind of holiness that I'd like to avoid like the plague. But as he and I parted, I mused over that word 'sin', a term that is so unpopular these days. We live in a culture where tolerance is the order of the day – Mark Greene says that we now live in an atmosphere of 'totalitolerance' where the only sin is to say that something is wrong. In 1993 MTV aired a special entitled *The Seven Deadly Sins* – and the almost universal conclusion from those that appeared was that there is no such thing as sin. The show implied that sin, if it exists, is merely a problem of psychology – we've just been conditioned to believe that certain acts are wrong.

Kurt Loder, the presenter, said, 'The seven deadly sins are not evil acts, but, rather, universal human compulsions that can be troubling and highly enjoyable.'

But he and other cultural experts who appeared on the show are wrong. The Bible makes it clear – repeatedly – that sin is a very real issue and that sin is dangerous and leads to enslavement, destruction and ultimately spiritual death. Don't be fooled by our softly-softly culture: sin is bad for us.

Prayer: Lord, teach me to understand the true depths of sin – and what You have saved me from. Amen.

Sin – a real problem

BIG PICTURE:
Romans 6:1–23
Colossians 2:13–15

FOCUS:
'For the wages of sin is death, but the gift of God is eternal life in Christ Jesus our Lord.'
(Rom. 6:23)

Don't be fooled

... sin is bad

for us

Sin – it's *our* problem

BIG PICTURE:
Romans 3:9–24
Luke 18:9–14

FOCUS:
'As it is written: "There is no-one righteous, not even one ..."' (Rom. 3:10)

PERHAPS most of us like to think that we're not too bad at heart. We may occasionally dip our toe into a grimy puddle, but we're not like those who dive headfirst into the sewer that is sin. There's a temptation to look at the drug dealers, the serial killers and the architects of genocide who roam our planet and congratulate ourselves that we're nothing like them. The Pharisee who gave thanks for the fact that he was 'not like other men' probably believed that he spoke the truth. Peter was surprised by his own capacity to fail, convinced that he alone would stay faithful even if everybody else deserted Jesus. And did Judas, protesting with the others that he was not the guilty one, actually convince himself that he spoke truthfully?

I've mentioned before that, in writing this series of *Life Every Day*, I've had some uncomfortable moments where I've discovered that I have a few more weaknesses and sins than I thought. Adrian Plass has wryly remarked that a Christian leader is someone whose difficulties and sins are always in the past tense. So why aren't some of us who are in leadership a bit more honest about our struggles?

Perhaps we worry that to admit failure is to suggest compromise or even disqualify ourselves from leadership. But to confess one's struggles is not to suggest that sin doesn't matter – rather it is to insist that we are heading in a redemptive direction: we sometimes sin along the way, but that's where we're headed. Leaders – let's get more real. And followers – be gracious when your leaders act like human beings and fail.

Prayer: Father, may I be merciful to others when they act like I do – and let You down. Amen.

... let's get

more real

Jesus' resurrection power

BIG PICTURE:
Ephesians 1:18–23
2 Corinthians 4:4–11

FOCUS:
'… his incomparably great power for us who believe. That power is like the working of his mighty strength, which he exerted in Christ when he raised him from the dead …'
(Eph. 1:19–20)

WHY is it that every Easter yet another rumour goes around to suggest that Jesus Christ was never raised from the dead? Recently there was a fuss about the so-called Judas Fragment; then there was the time that BBC television ran a series because a stone casket was found bearing the name of Jesus (which is like saying that a coffin was found in Birmingham with the name 'John' on it, so therefore the John that you know who lived there must be dead). Why is the world so desperate to keep Jesus dead?

Part of the reason is that the resurrection is the ground of all hope in this world – hope for us to change, hope for the Church to make an impact, hope for a decaying planet to see outbreaks of the kingdom (or reign and rule) of God break out in the midst of our chaos. The resurrection of Jesus was the most significant moment since creation day and not only because it dramatically affects life after death. It also has something dynamic to tell us about our Monday mornings and specifically our struggles with sin. Christianity is not a mere moral code created by a God who watches to see how we will do – rather it is an invitation to us to walk with a God who invites us into the dignity of holiness and then fills us with His resurrection life, by His Holy Spirit, to enable us to see change and the power of sin broken in our lives. Through the risen Christ, we will live forever – and can also live His way today.

Prayer: Lord, thank You for the hope that has come from Your resurrection. Amen.

Romans 1:24–27
Romans 6:1–14

Health warning: sin is bad

It seems that those government 'health warnings' that are printed on cigarette packets are becoming blunter. What began as a quiet whisper: 'Smoking can damage your health' has become an urgent shout: 'Smoking can kill you!' And I am glad for the unsubtle wake-up call – tobacco is such a proven killer, so the more dire the warning the better.

Will we believe the Bible's warning about sin?

I wish that something similar was available to warn us about sin, which so often is presented to us as an attractive fashionable choice in life, instead of the devastating force that it really is. Paul pulls no punches as he writes in Romans about sin and its power to degrade us, strip us of all dignity and ultimately master us. As I read his sobering words, I think of the confession of Soren Kierkegaard, who lived out a long-standing sexual fantasy by visiting a brothel. Later that night, he wrote in his diary, 'Tonight I paid a woman in order to experience my own despicableness.' The temporary high of sexual satisfaction was quickly followed by a plummeting trip into a valley of despair. Will we believe the Bible's warning about sin? I wonder. After all, people still smoke.

Weekend

ONE of the most terrifying moments of my life came when, as a young child, I got trapped on a beach where the tide was coming in fast and the only way to avoid drowning was to climb a steep cliff. My dad was with me, but it was still a heart-stopping climb. As we desperately tried to inch our way up to safety, the chalky cliff kept crumbling in our hands. We would climb a couple of metres, only to slide back down again. My fear was that we would get into an unstoppable slide and end up in the sea.

Sin is a cliff, not a plateau. Once we get into a dark habit, the chances are that moral deterioration will take hold of our lives and the rock of our resolve will crumble away until we find ourselves doing things we never felt capable of. David's tragic and well-known sin with Bathsheba began as a furtive look – and then rolled into adultery and ultimately conspiracy to murder, as he desperately sought to kill Uriah, her honourable husband. The film *La Dolce Vita* tells the story of a man living in the sophisticated circles of Roman society who slides into sexual depravity and the occult; he constantly looks for new depths of sensuality, as what he has experienced before no longer thrills him. Finally he ends up totally controlled by his lust, in a pit of filth and degradation. Sin causes heart disease – the hardening of the heart, a condition that prevents us from hearing God, seeing sense and turning away from the slope of sin. Beware that cliff.

Prayer: Lord, thank You that You have given us new lives and new hearts – may I take care of mine. Amen.

Downhill slide

BIG PICTURE:
2 Samuel 11:1–17
Hebrews 3:7–19

FOCUS:
'But encourage one another daily, as long as it is called Today, so that none of you may be hardened by sin's deceitfulness.'
(Heb. 3:13)

Radical choices required

BIG PICTURE:
Hebrews 12:1–13
Matthew 18:8–9

FOCUS:
'Therefore, since we are surrounded by such a great cloud of witnesses, let us throw off everything that hinders and the sin that so easily entangles ...' (Heb. 12:1)

I CURRENTLY have a hole in my leg and it's not going to get better. The little dent was caused by my being bitten by a black widow spider, which had hidden itself in the log pile outside our house in the USA. The flesh-eating creepy-crawly attached itself to me when I was scurrying around in the dark for wood to feed our fire. It must have snacked away for quite a time – but I didn't notice that it was there. Only the next morning did I discover that I'd been a meal for an unwelcome visitor. If I'd spotted it, I'd have taken swift action, which would have led to a Christian burial for the hungry little predator. Only a fool would allow something so dangerous to park unchallenged on his leg. I was fortunate not to end up in hospital.

Do we sometimes take a careless attitude to sin, knowing full well that we are drifting into habits and behavioural patterns that are displeasing to God and could well bring chaos and destruction into our lives? Over the last couple of days, we've paused to look at the dangerous and downhill effects of sin. And today we hear the urgent metaphor that Jesus used about gouging out eyes and cutting off hands – a metaphor only, but one that screams His message loud and clear. Don't give sin the time of day, never mind the times of your life. What is it that we need to throw off, gouge out or amputate?

Do we sometimes take a careless attitude to sin ...?

Prayer: Father, may I never be careless about sin. If there is anything You want to say to me, I'm listening. Amen.

HERE'S a question that is worth thinking about today: how well do we know ourselves? What have we learned as a result of living inside our own skin for all these years? Self-knowledge is an important part of life, but so often we can limit it to knowing what we are good at: most of us know where our gifts and talents lie. But when it comes to sin, it is vital that we know our weaknesses, our blind spots: being aware of a potential area of failure might prevent us from moments of madness in the future. We all know the heat of temptation – but taking note of the nature of those temptations and being prayerfully aware of where our greatest struggles are will surely equip us for future battles.

Blaise Pascal once said, 'One must know oneself. Even if that does not help in finding truth, at least it helps in running one's life ...'

Peter was someone who evidently was not very self-aware. He had an over-confidence about his own faithfulness, convinced that he alone would stay true to Jesus, even if everyone else ran. He also consistently fell into the trap of speaking and taking action before thinking, offering to launch a building project on the Mount of Transfiguration (Matt. 17:4), and jumping to cut off someone's ear in Gethsemane (John 18:10). Sometimes Peter's genuine love for Jesus (don't forget that it was Peter who walked on the water) meant that he jumped to the wrong conclusions. But, as we'll see tomorrow, he learned about himself and gradually changed and matured. Do we know ourselves?

Prayer: Lord, give me the self-knowledge I need to see the planks in my own eyes. Amen.

Do we know ourselves?

BIG PICTURE:
John 13:31–38
Romans 12:3

FOCUS:
'Do not think of yourself more highly than you ought, but rather think of yourself with sober judgment, in accordance with the measure of faith God has given you.'
(Rom. 12:3)

Peter learned about himself

BIG PICTURE:
John 21:15–25
Matthew 16:13–23

FOCUS:
'When they had finished eating, Jesus said to Simon Peter, "Simon son of John, do you truly love me more than these?"'
(John 21:15)

Let's be real

about our

strengths and

weaknesses

YESTERDAY we saw that Peter spent a lot of his life unaware of his own weaknesses and fragilities. But failure is a swift schoolteacher and the tragedy of his vehement denial of Christ brought him down to earth with a solid bump. Now Jesus had been raised and Peter had met Him (most commentators say that there is a resurrection appearance by Jesus to Peter in between the empty tomb event of John 20 and the fishy breakfast of John 21) but Peter was still smarting from his sad betrayal of Christ. So now, when Jesus sits down with Peter and asks if Peter loves Him, the verbose fisherman is careful with his response. When Jesus asks, 'Do you love me?', He uses the Greek word agape – *agape* is the highest form of sacrificial love. Peter affirms that he does love Jesus, but with *phileo* love – a lesser love, the deep affection of close friends. A second time the question is put, with the same answer – Peter won't budge from truthfulness – and then Jesus accepts Peter's answer when, in the third asking, He switches the word 'love' from *agape* to *phileo*.

While some commentators believe that we should not place too much store on this change of words, because John uses them interchangeably in his Gospel, perhaps they indicate that Peter is at last getting real and is more careful in his assessment of himself.

Perhaps Jesus would like to ask us some questions. He won't be put off by honest answers. Let's be real about our strengths and weaknesses.

Prayer: Father, show me today where I am weak – and where I am strong. Amen.

WE LIVE in a world of special effects, where we can no longer believe what we see with our own eyes. Film-makers can make a giant gorilla stomp through New York or portray a city in nuclear meltdown – but it's a high-tech sham.

So was the temptation of Christ real? When Jesus was tempted, was there ever any possibility that He would have sinned? Theologians have wrestled with that hugely important question for centuries – and it's not just an issue for the experts, but sits at the very heart of our faith. If Jesus was ever capable of sin, they say, then it means that God has the potential for moral inconsistency and is not ultimately trustworthy – and Jesus was fully human and fully divine. But if sin was never really a possibility for Jesus, then the temptations He faced were meaningless, His triumph over them was hollow. He offers no real example to us as we struggle with our sins.

When Jesus faced the huge challenge in the wilderness, He did so without the use of His divine power, but in His humanity alone. His victory was won as a man, not as God. He relied on the Father and the Spirit to take Him through – just as we should. And He won the battle: '... in him is no sin' (1 John 3:5).

As we begin our look at the seven specific 'deadly' sins tomorrow, let's remember that triumph does not come as we grit our teeth and try to do better, but as we follow Jesus and walk in the energy and life of the Spirit of God each day.

Prayer: Lord, may I hand my life over to You today – and every day. Live in me. Amen.

Jesus our example and helper

BIG PICTURE:
Luke 4:1–13
Hebrews 4:14–16

FOCUS:
'For we do not have a high priest who is unable to sympathise with our weaknesses, but ... one who has been tempted in every way ... yet was without sin.' (Heb. 4:15)

Luke 18:10–13
Ephesians 2:1–10

Pride

C.S. Lewis calls pride 'the great sin' and devotes a whole chapter to the subject in his classic *Mere Christianity*. Sometimes the sin of pride appears in unusual guises.

A friend was describing a difficult plane journey. 'I spent the whole of the flight wrestling with anger and bitterness. If the plane had gone down in flames, I'd have gone straight to hell …'

... we are absolutely unable to save ourselves

I was both stunned by her theology and alarmed by the notion that while we are saved by grace, we will make it to eternity eventually because of our works. Her insecurity veiled a perverse pride, which all humans share: the notion that we can navigate through life – and death – without God. Pride convinces us that God is quite unnecessary and therefore we see no need to seek Him (Psa. 10:4). But the cross of Christ is a stake driven into the heart of our human self-sufficiency, declaring that we are absolutely unable to save ourselves.

God hates pride (Prov. 8:13): it blinds us to our need of Him and prevents us from living life with the Lord.

The old adage, 'Stand on your own two feet' reeks of pride and isn't biblical. But the truth from Jesus 'apart from me you can do nothing' (John 15:5) certainly is.

Weekend

Offended and proud with it

BIG PICTURE:
Luke 20:46–47
Proverbs 16:18

FOCUS:
'Pride goes before destruction, a haughty spirit before a fall.'
(Prov. 16:18)

SOME people seem to have a special gift of being offended; their demeanour is so frosty that all encounters with them involve a walk on proverbial eggshells. These tetchy folk apparently have been annoyed since birth and got upset with the midwife for slapping them. Don't imagine that they can ever be pleased. They would probably be upset if the dead were raised, because the service took ten minutes longer while the empty coffins were removed.

But is their capacity to be offended a form of pride? Pride causes me to take myself very seriously indeed and to be incensed if anyone gently laughs at my foibles or disagrees with my hallowed opinions. Masquerading under a disguise of sensitivity, the hyper-offended jump if anyone treats them with anything less than the absolute respect which they surely deserve.

But some of our capacity to be upset is nothing less than haughty – and God lists haughtiness as one of the attitudes He most despises (Prov. 6:16–17). Pomposity characterised many of the Pharisees of Jesus' day and their smug aloofness blinded them to the true Light. Pride compelled them to a posturing spirituality, but also convinced them that they were always in the right.

It was Sir Thomas More who spoke of Satan's proud demand of respect: 'The Devil, the proud spirit, cannot endure to be mocked.' Martin Luther visited the same theme, remarking 'The best way to drive out the devil, if he will not yield to the texts of Scripture, is to jeer and flount him, for he cannot bear scorn.' Humility enables us to listen – and laugh at ourselves.

Prayer: Father, if You are speaking through those I would rather not listen to, help me to hear You. Amen.

Pride doesn't have to be terminal

BIG PICTURE:
2 Kings 19:1–37
Daniel 4:28–37

FOCUS:
'Who is it you
have insulted and
blasphemed? Against
whom have you raised
your voice and lifted
your eyes in pride?
Against the Holy One of
Israel!' (2 Kings 19:22)

CONSIDER a tale of two kings. The first is Sennacherib, an Assyrian king who lived 2,700 years ago. He determined, because of pride, to mock God and His people. He threatened Judah with attack, prompting Hezekiah, the godly king of Judah, to cry out to God, and Isaiah the prophet to proclaim that the Lord would intervene on behalf of Judah. But archaeology shows that the subsequent death of 185,000 of Sennacherib's troops was a humiliating embarrassment to the egotistical warrior. Two inscriptions have been found celebrating his victories, but not mentioning his defeat or failure to capture Jerusalem. He died at the hands of his sons: the pride in his heart was terminal. Some people go to their deaths with a lingering but false conviction that they did well: pride blinds.

The story of King Nebuchadnezzar shows that while pride is a difficult attitude to deal with, nevertheless, change is possible. But the 'college' to cure pride is a tough place to be, because human pride is so stubborn. Nebuchadnezzar tottered on the brink of madness until at last he once again raised his 'eyes towards heaven' (Dan. 4:34).

Let's ask God to show us where pride has corrupted our thinking and twisted our views of ourselves and others. And then, let's humble ourselves (1 Pet. 5:6) before the God who is Lord over all and recognise that there is only One who is always right; He is the sovereign, mighty God. His greatness, compared with our insignificance, makes all of our posturing pathetic. Are you ensnared in a conflict where you absolutely refuse to consider that you may be wrong? Think again.

Prayer: Lord, give me grace to see the other person's point of view – today and every day. Amen.

... pride blinds

Pride is exhausting

BIG PICTURE:
2 Timothy 2:14–26
Galatians 1:10

FOCUS:
'Am I now trying to win the approval of men, or of God? ... If I were still trying to please men, I would not be a servant of Christ.' (Gal. 1:10)

WE HAVE friends who live in an area where the local children are tested when they are 11 and the outcome of that exam determines which school they will attend. Some parents live in abject fear waiting for the results, terrified lest their offspring fail to make it to the 'best' schools ...

Of course we want our children to succeed and receive the best education possible – but we should also stop and check our motives when we feel so panicky and driven. Are we just concerned for their well-being – or are we guilty of a subtle pride where we feel that the reputation of our family – and our abilities as parents – is under question if they don't do so well? That kind of pride creates a huge pressure that we absolutely must not place upon the shoulders of our children.

And then pride drives us always to look successful. Erving Goffman, a sociologist, suggests that all human relationships are motivated by the need that we have to appear accomplished and successful. Pride, says Goffman, turns us all into con artists. But all of this striving and 'keeping up appearances' is demanding and exhausting. Like Willy Lowman in Arthur Miller's *Death of a Salesman*, we end up hiding from everyone, even those closest to us.

Ironically, most of the time we have no idea what others think about us – whatever their opinions, they usually keep them hidden. And if we did know – what would it matter? The approval of fellow humans creates a nice feeling, but how much better to know that we live lives approved by God (2 Tim. 2:15), whose opinion really matters.

Prayer: Father, show me how to live a life that meets with Your approval. Amen.

Notice me

BIG PICTURE:
Mark 10:46–52
James 3:13–18

FOCUS:
'Jesus stopped and said,
"Call him."'
(Mark 10:49)

TIMBERLINE Church in Colorado is a large, growing congregation – around 15,000 attended our most recent Easter gathering. It is now my home church. In order to accommodate the large numbers who come every weekend, we have a large, pleasantly functional building – and the person who took a long time to be convinced that we needed the place was the Senior Pastor, Dary Northrop. The building was justifiable ten years ago, but Dary approached the project with extreme caution. How refreshing this was to watch; too many churches get a growth spurt and almost immediately a new facility is under construction.

Tony Campolo challenges this 'rush to build' syndrome, asking whether some leaders suffer from 'edifice complex' – the need to erect a monument to their successful leadership. It's an expensive way to get ourselves noticed and it's 'selfish ambition' (James 3:14). Dary's reluctance to build is a testimony to his character: as a close friend, I've noticed that he has been unspoiled by success.

And Dary has taught his team a simple principle about humble, caring leadership. He remarks that when most leaders walk into a room, their attitude is 'Here *I* am' – and thus they work hard to impress, to make an impact and to be noticed. Dary encourages us to throw away 'Here *I* am' and replace it with 'There *you* are' – a simple but revolutionary shift of thinking that could just transform our days and our lives.

Jesus was a 'There you are' person, picking out and including people that others usually ignored. What's it to be today: 'Here I am' – or 'There you are'?

Jesus was a

'There you are'

person ...

Prayer: Father, make me a 'There you are' person, whoever I am with. Amen.

'I AM the greatest'; so said the most celebrated boxer and big talker of all time, Muhammad Ali. Recently, Ali sold some of the rights to use his name for a cool 50 million dollars. But Ali now lives with a major disability that some say has been caused by Parkinson's disease. Other members of the medical community have asked if his difficulties may have been caused by repeated blows to the head – literally, he is punch drunk. His doctor remarked that as far back as 1981, CAT scans were showing brain damage – but still he fought on. It is so painful to watch him struggling now, the former magnificent athlete with dancing feet now shuffling around like a man in a stupor, his speech slurred. His proud claim was, tragically, short lived.

The One who is truly the greatest never made that claim; instead, He chose a towel to wash the accumulated grime from the toes of His friends and enemy. He resisted a king's crown, often fled from clamouring crowds and preferred the company of societal 'low lifers' to the courts and company of the well-heeled and the privileged. And this came as a result of His clear choices – He 'made himself nothing' (Phil. 2:7) and was not humbled, but 'humbled himself' (Phil. 2:8). The greatest, according to Him, are not the famed, the rich or those who tightly grip the reins of power. Now it is the servants (Matt. 23:11), the children (Matt. 18:4) and the least (Luke 22:26) who are counted great. What do we choose today – big talk – or bigger lives expressed by loving service?

Prayer: Lord, give me grace to value people as You do. Amen.

The Servant King

BIG PICTURE:
John 13:1–17
Philippians 2:1–11

FOCUS:
'Your attitude should be the same as that of Christ ... Who ... did not consider equality with God something to be grasped, but made himself nothing, taking the ... nature of a servant ...' (Phil. 2:5–7)

Genesis 4:1–16
Proverbs 14:30

Will envy taint
our today?

Weekend

Envy: I want your stuff

I was delighted and grateful. I had been dreading
the long flight, but at check-in I was told that I
had been upgraded from cramped Economy to
ultra-comfortable Business Class. Now on board, I
savoured my surroundings. The flight attendants
smiled, there was room to stretch out and the food
was identifiable as food – it was delicious. I felt like
I'd been invited to a nine-hour-long party. And
then, halfway through the flight, I noticed that there
was another cabin ahead – First Class. The seats
were bigger and the passengers served from silver
platters, with even nicer food than ours. For a little
while, until I realised my own madness, I didn't
want to be in Business Class any more.

Envy – or covetousness – is a huge troublemaker.
The first murder recorded in biblical history was
because of envy. Today, wars are fought because
nations jealously eye the land or natural resources of
their neighbours; churches that operate in the same
cities refuse to co-operate and even question and
denigrate each other's success, because of envy.

And envy will spoil even our Business Class days
if we let it, because whatever we have, it won't be
enough. Will envy taint our today?

I KNOW of a young minister who almost lost his job – because he was too successful. He was working as an assistant to an older, more experienced leader. The senior leader took a sabbatical break for three months, leaving his junior in charge. During that time, attendance at the church increased, as did the finances: the usual summer financial malaise was reversed. The assistant preached a sermon series that was popular and a number of people became Christians.

When the senior leader returned from his sabbatical, he was very concerned. Didn't the church need him any more? Was the young man trying to oust him, with his 'new' methods that had created 'superficial' growth? What could have been a hugely significant working relationship began to disintegrate, because of envy, coupled with personal insecurity.

So it was with King Saul and David. The young shepherd boy had become Saul's most successful warrior. At first, Saul recognised the younger man's brilliance, promoting him through the ranks, which was a very popular decision with the general public. But then David's growing cult status unnerved Saul. Pop songs were dedicated to David (with Saul getting just a mention) and even Saul's family joined the fan club, with Jonathan becoming David's best friend. Then Saul's daughter Michal became his bride in an arranged marriage that was designed to trip David up – but she fell in love with him. David and Saul could have enjoyed a fruitful, strategic partnership – but envy destroyed all that. Are there people that you don't like simply because they look so good, they make you look bad in comparison?

Prayer: Father, show me my heart – and help me to change. Amen.

A virus that destroys relationships

BIG PICTURE:
1 Samuel 18:5–30
Galatians 5:16–26

FOCUS:
'And from that time on Saul kept a jealous eye on David.' (1 Sam. 18:9)

Unhappiness with who we are

BIG PICTURE:
Acts 8:9–25
1 Corinthians 3:1–23

FOCUS:

'When Simon saw that the Spirit was given at the laying on of the apostles' hands, he offered them money and said, "Give me also this ability ..."' (Acts 8:18–19)

The Church is not immune to the corrupting force of envy

SOMETIMES envy can creep into the hearts of those who genuinely want to make a huge impact for God with their lives: their ambition, which began as a godly force, is corrupted by jealousy of those that they view as more effective. So it was with Simon, the former sorcerer, who was genuinely converted and baptised, but who struggled with a lingering longing for the 'greatness' that he had enjoyed in his former life. He was willing to part with cash for just a little of the spiritual power that Peter enjoyed.

The Academy Award-winning film *Amadeus* is the story of a good man, Antonio Salieri, a royal court musician, who was destroyed by his envy of the teenaged genius, Wolfgang Amadeus Mozart, who had dazzling talent but poor character. Salieri had wanted to create music that would glorify God for generations to come, but he had to face up to the reality that his talent was mediocre at best: he could entertain, but never inspire. He plotted Mozart's downfall, was driven insane by envy and ultimately cursed God for denying him the talent that his competitor took for granted. What started off as noble ambition was twisted by envy into something spiteful and destructive.

The Church is not immune to the corrupting force of envy. I have watched preachers spend years in the wilderness of jealousy and disappointment because they longed for a platform that would perhaps never be theirs. Let's ask God for faith to know what we can do – and wisdom to know what we can't. And then let's pray for grace to bless those whose gifts are greater than our own.

Prayer: Lord, You give gifts as You see fit – may I not challenge Your decisions! Amen.

IT'S wonderful to share our successes, but we should do so with thoughtfulness – avoiding the temptation to boast. Even our closest friends can only stomach so much of us telling the details of how blessed we are. We can be guilty of provoking others to envy when we talk too much about that trip of a lifetime, that unexpected financial windfall or how spectacularly our genius children are doing in their education.

Thorstein Veblen, one of America's most brilliant economic theorists, claims that much of our spending is driven by a need to make others feel a longing to have what we have. Hence the status symbol car, which may not be desirable because it is safer or higher tech, but simply because it is known to be incredibly expensive. Do we long to drive it so that others will see a sign of our buying power and want what we have? Thus we desire to be envied. Is the rush to possess the very latest all-singing, all-dancing mobile phone a part of that need to be ahead of the pack and be envied?

Sometimes we create a situation of envy and jealousy by making one of our children the obvious favourite, as with Jacob, Joseph – and his brothers, who watched their young sibling being showered with affection. Ultimately God redeemed the situation and turned it around for a nation's good, but Joseph had to endure the pit and prison; and it all began with insane jealousy. Let's be wise about how we share, why we spend and when we favour one person over another. Envy awaits, ready to ruin.

Prayer: Father, may I never be the cause of someone else feeling jealous. Help me guard what I say. Amen.

Tempting others to envy

BIG PICTURE:
Genesis 37:1–11
Romans 1:29–32

FOCUS:
'They are gossips, slanderers, God-haters, insolent, arrogant and boastful'
(Rom. 1: 29–30)

Envy, launching pad of evil

BIG PICTURE:
James 3:13–18
1 Corinthians 13:1–4

FOCUS:
'For where you have envy and selfish ambition, there you find disorder and every evil practice.'
(James 3:16)

ACCORDING to biblical tradition, Satan fell because of envy: in his case, envy of God Himself. Think about the gnarled figure that stands behind every atrocity in world history and reflect that it all began with jealousy. So it is that James in his epistle views envy as being the rot that will spread and, if we don't deal with it, open the way for a host of other sins to take residence in our lives: 'there you find ... every evil practice'.

A man envies his friend because of his beautiful wife; jealousy leads to adultery. Intimidated by the success of that church across town, a leader spreads a rumour and gossip begins its quiet assassination. Seduced by relentless advertising, a man blows thousands on a car he neither needs nor can afford, placing his family in financial jeopardy. All because he wants to look more accomplished and sees the motorised metal appendage as a sign of that success. A woman is suckered by daytime television romances and longs for the elusive on-screen passion, causing her to despise her once beloved, but now paunchy, middle-aged husband. Envy gnaws at her love.

Ultimately, envy is a sign of self-worship – it's a symptom that shows that not only would we like to have what others have, but to take what they have away from them as part of the bargain, so that we can be the head of the pack. Envy is self-love; hence Paul in his celebrated words to the Corinthians puts it bluntly: 'love ... does not envy'.

... envy is a sign of self-worship ...

Prayer: Lord, teach me to be content with all that I am and have – only seeking those changes You want. Amen.

IT MAY be a myth generated to thrill and scare tourists, but the Israeli driver was emphatic. We had stopped in the desert (for a camel ride, actually) but he warned us to look out for the 'seven second' snakes. Apparently, a nibble from one of these blighters and one has but seven seconds to live: not a happy thought, there apparently being no antidote.

Helpfully, the venom of envy does not have to paralyse our hearts, rot our relationships and spoil even our sunniest days. A decision to be grateful – the popular Bible word is thanksgiving – provides an effective antidote to clutching, narrow-eyed jealousy. Giving thanks is not just something we should reserve for mealtimes (or Sundays, or when Christian friends come round for dinner …). Thankfulness is a lifestyle, an insistence that this very moment is worth living for, a gratitude that acknowledges God as our faithful Source and a discernment that sees through the mythical lies of the marketeers and laughs at their ludicrous claims. We need to see that it's a pointless exercise trying to keep up with the Joneses, as they are likely killing themselves keeping up with the Smiths …

And this persistent thankfulness enables us, unlike the elder brother of prodigal parable fame, not to protest when we see the glorious unfairness of another being blessed way beyond what they deserve, because that's true of all of us sinners anyway. Today, the band is striking up and the fattened calf, now barbecued, smells delicious. Let's join the party.

Prayer: 'Stamp out the serpent envy that stings love with poison and kills all joy' (Thomas Merton).

Envy's antidote: thanksgiving

BIG PICTURE:
Psalm 100:1–5
Luke 15:11–32

FOCUS:
'But when this son of yours who has squandered your property with prostitutes comes home, you kill the fattened calf for him!'
(Luke 15:30)

Proverbs 31:10–31
Psalm 139:23–24

Have you allowed any ... self-deceptions to take root in your life?

Weekend

Sloth: laziness

I am lazy. It pains me to write it and seeing as I have worked a 16-hour day today and it is now 1am as I tap these thoughts into my computer, my laziness seems improbable. My family and friends insist that I work too hard. Most days for me look like an overloaded sandwich, since I try to cram as much in as possible. I spend the first few days of a holiday twitching nervously, wanting just to relax, but tormented with a need to do something, visit somewhere or see someone. Yet writing about the seven deadly sins has brought the uncomfortable and surprising revelation: I have a tendency towards laziness.

I'm too lazy sometimes to refuse an invitation, so I rush to do things that I should have turned down. I like to do things that I enjoy and neglect what I think is tedious, which explains the 700 unanswered emails currently cramming my inbox. I'm easily distracted; I tend to work right up against my deadlines and sometimes lack discipline. And laziness is the last sin that I would have felt guilty of. Until now. Have you allowed any similar self-deceptions to take root in your life?

IT'S obvious that a house that is neglected will eventually fall into disrepair and ultimate ruin, which is why the tradesmen section of our *Yellow Pages* is well worn. My family knows that any and all of my attempts to fix anything will lead to disaster and may cause the entire house to fall down. It takes effort and expertise to maintain a home.

But the same is true of human relationships. Love is not so much a feeling, but rather a choice. Isn't the epidemic level of divorce these days due in part to an unwillingness to do the hard work of loving when the feelings wane or disappear altogether? All generalisations are dangerous and it may be that you are in the middle of a marital breakdown right now that has nothing to do with your choices or willingness to take another course, so please don't be hurt by my words. Nonetheless, a lazy culture treats marriage as disposable. Why do the hard work of repair when you can enjoy the thrill of shopping for a new person? Parenting takes work: sometimes it's harder to insist that the bedroom that looks like a bombsite is cleaned – it can actually be laziness on our part when we clean it ourselves, because we can't be bothered with the possible conflict. Church life is often sheer hard work – the Bible only tells us to 'forbear with one another' because the reality is that sometimes putting up with each other's foibles is all we can do. In Hollywood, people fall in love. In the Bible, we are called to walk in love. And the difference is ... work.

Prayer: Lord, teach me to understand when I am being merciful and when I am just being lazy. Amen.

Slothful about life

BIG PICTURE:
Ephesians 5:22–33
Ecclesiastes 10:18

FOCUS:
'If a man is lazy, the rafters sag; if his hands are idle, the house leaks.'
(Eccl. 10:18)

Still working at it

BIG PICTURE:
2 Timothy 4:1–8
Philippians 2:12–18

FOCUS:
' ... continue to work out
your salvation with fear
and trembling.'
(Phil. 2:12)

THE Bible is emphatic – not one of us is saved by works. Our only hope of being right with God comes through the totally complete work of the crucified and risen Christ. But that doesn't mean that hard work isn't part of the deal of being a follower of Christ – it just assures us that efforts are not what saves us. So Paul was able to write to the Church and declare 'I have worked harder than any of you' (see 1 Cor. 15:10). And the mental, spiritual and emotional effort required to give ourselves fully each day as disciples of Jesus is what is being called for as we 'work out [our] salvation'.

The question is – will we continue to labour? So many Christians begin well – and then trail off as life unfolds. I usually run five miles each day, but yesterday I was so exhausted I stopped halfway through the course, laid down and took a 15-minute nap – not an ideal way to get the most cardiovascular benefit from the exercise …

All of which brings me back to my confession of laziness last weekend. I've noticed that I have a tendency to begin projects, but not to complete them. My initial excitement is not sustained, hence the trail of ideas behind me that were born with a sense of hope but came to nothing.

Let's ask God to give us a willingness to 'work' today – and not only to finish life well, but to take those responsibilities and projects all the way to their natural conclusion. Note to self: don't leave things unfini

Let's ask God to

give us a

willingness to

'work' today ...

Prayer: Father, thank You for what Jesus has accomplished – and give me grace to do what I must do. Amen.

WE HAVE friends who have highly musical children. Their son is an accomplished drummer and guitarist and their daughter is fast becoming rather good at the flute and piano. A recent visit to their home saw me trying my hand – or more specifically, my lips – at the flute. Try as I may, I couldn't get a single note out of the thing; it sounded like an animal in pain. Nearby dogs howled in sympathy. I gave up trying.

Young Christians often grow quickly in the faith. Thrilled by the fantastic good news, they have a voracious appetite for learning, are unafraid to ask dozens of questions and are willing to take risks, step out of their comfort zones and be clearly identified as followers of Jesus. That sometimes means that early attempts at sharing faith are clumsy and even aggressive, but the mistakes are part of the learning experience. They are often hard workers too: the first to volunteer, willing to help with the most mundane tasks.

But then, all too often, the growth spurt comes to an end. Armed and confident with a basic biblical knowledge, they settle for faith that is more a vague amble than a passionate pursuit.

The writer to the Hebrews links growth – or lack of it – with laziness. So many people have a vision for personal growth – they want to get fit, lose weight, or learn a language – but ultimately the development of any of those skills takes hard work and discipline. Perhaps you're ambling along – or have been settled for years. It takes work to become mature and go beyond the basics.

Prayer: Lord, if I have settled down, shake me out of my comfort zone. Amen.

It takes effort to become

BIG PICTURE:
Hebrews 6:1–12
1 Corinthians 9:24–27

FOCUS:
'Therefore let us leave the elementary teachings about Christ and go on to maturity …' (Heb. 6:1)

Diligence versus sloth

BIG PICTURE:
Joshua 24:1–15
Proverbs 10:4–5

FOCUS:
'Lazy hands make a man poor, but diligent hands bring wealth.'
(Prov. 10:4)

KAY and I recently got ourselves shiny new mobile phones, which was a nightmare. It seems that the cell-phone market has countless options. All I want is to be able to talk on the phone, but I had to decide whether I wanted to text instead of talk, send video shots of my holidays to friends, have minutes that expire or roll over and limit most of my urgent conversations to between the hours of 6pm and 7am. But the cleverest little ruse of all is the rebate scheme. The phone company is going to give me nearly £200 back this year – but only if I remember to send the fourth, seventh and tenth phone bills back to them. They won't be reminding me – I've got to remember. No wonder the majority of rebates go unclaimed: we are too apathetic to be diligent. Some of us have absolutely no idea what we have in our bank accounts, because reconciling them at the end of every month is work: it's easier just to flash the credit card and hope for the best. No wonder Proverbs reminds us that 'The plans of the diligent lead to profit as surely as haste leads to poverty' (Prov. 21:5).

Successful living demands that we make good and godly decisions – but choosing takes effort. Good choices come as a result of taking counsel, thoughtful reflection and ongoing prayerfulness. Alternatively, we can procrastinate and never seize the proverbial day – or thoughtlessly stumble from one bad choice to another, because careful, wise choosing was just too much effort. Let's work hard to choose well.

Let's work hard
to choose well

Prayer: Father, be in my decision-making today – that my decisions may be Yours. Amen.

Body building – for faith

BIG PICTURE:
Jude 17–25
2 Timothy 3:10–17

FOCUS:
'But you, dear friends,
build yourselves up in
your most holy faith and
pray in the Holy Spirit.'
(Jude 20)

EARLIER in the week I mentioned my taking a nap halfway through my morning run. Now, thanks to *Men's Health* magazine, which sports photos of chaps with washboard abdominals and muscles in places where I don't have places, I know what my problem was: I was totally dehydrated. Failure to drink enough water can cause a massive energy loss during exercise. I learned my lesson and just now managed to complete my morning jog on the South Downs without snuggling up to my electric blanket halfway through.

Laziness means that just as I sometimes forget to eat and drink properly (and have been stranded on the roadside a few times because putting petrol in my car seemed like too much effort) so sometimes I don't 'fuel' my Christian life. As I give myself to the nourishment of Scripture, the replenishment of prayer and the energy boost that comes from worshipping together with God's people, so I have strength for another day. Alternatively, I can litter my life with what American writer Annie Dillard calls the 'artificial touches' of caffeine, television, telephone and computers, which leave me listless and lethargic. Just recently, I watched some daytime television, which is surely the government's secret method to get people back to work. A regular diet of that would leave anyone in hopeless despair and emotional exhaustion. Of course, we can get into a lazy cycle – laziness creates lethargy, which in turn means we can't be bothered to plan for positive, sustaining input into our lives. If that's where we are, let's break that cycle today.

Prayer: Lord, help me today to take in that which is good for me. Amen.

**Proverbs 7:1–27
1 Thessalonians
4:1–8**

Lust is a deadly
business

Weekend

Lust: the great con

Lust is big business. Billions are made annually from the sale of videos, magazines, revenue from sex phone-in lines – and any Internet user knows that the web is a precarious place. It used to be that pornography users had to go to a seedy shop in the wrong part of town. Now a quick trip to the top shelf in the local newsagents, or easier still, the furtive login online will enable any of us to surf in seconds to websites that will offer a huge variety of porn – at a price. Tragically, the price of lust is higher than the credit card bill that arrives. The grinning models have been stripped of far more than their clothing: they have become objects to leer at, rather than humans to cherish. And the viewer is a literal loser too: promised so much, the thrill quickly fades to a numbing disappointment. Shame seeps into our souls and a gradual addiction takes a firm grip. Those who are married might feel a sense of dissatisfaction – their spouse is not the firm (airbrushed) specimen from that website. Lust is a deadly business.

LUST is a sin – but sex is not. Perhaps that's obvious, but we still suffer mildly from a historic hangover when the Church had a negative view of sex. Christians were taught that the Holy Spirit left the marital bedroom when a couple had sexual intercourse and returned when the act was completed. I know of ministers who got themselves into deep trouble because they insisted on teaching appropriately about human sexuality in their churches – they were being faithful to Scripture, which has a lot to say about sex.

God made sex, which says something to us about His nature. He has created parts of the human body for the sole purposes of pleasure. Human intimacy could have been reduced to a hug or a handshake: the procreation of children accomplished by a colder procedure than sexual intimacy. But God has created the playful, giving, joyous (and sometimes vaguely bizarre) act that is sexual intercourse. There's a whole book in the Bible – the Song of Songs – that most believe is an unbridled celebration of erotic love. And so to thoroughly enjoy sex – and take an adventurous, creative approach to it – is not lust. To admire and notice the body and beauty of another is not lust. To struggle with feelings of pent-up sexual energy if you are single or, if you are married, to know frustration because distance or circumstances have interrupted your sex life, is not lust. God has made us sexual beings by design; but for our protection, has provided context for the expression of that powerful element of our humanity.

Prayer: Lord, thank You for one of Your greatest gifts – human intimacy. Amen.

What lust is not

BIG PICTURE:
Genesis 2:18–25
Song of Songs 1:1–4

FOCUS:
'The man and his wife were both naked, and they felt no shame.'
(Gen. 2:25)

What lust is

BIG PICTURE:
Matthew 5:27–30
1 Corinthians 6:12–20

FOCUS:
'But I tell you that anyone who looks at a woman lustfully has already committed adultery with her in his heart.' (Matt. 5:28)

God calls us

away from the

snare of lust ...

IT'S often been said that the main sexual organ of the body is the brain, and Jesus' teaching affirms that to be true. Lust is not just about sexual expression: it's about the mental cultivation of images, fantasies, that we dwell upon, not as an expression of love for another but for our selfish pleasure. Jesus is not teaching that mental adultery is the same as actual physical adultery – but rather showing us the root of lust, which takes shape in our minds. That's why it's important to look after our mental health, by being careful about what we fill our minds with (Phil. 4:8). But notice too that it is both the eyes and the hands that we must keep under control; we all know the times when an admiring look has turned into a lingering leer – and although it's good to express our love and affection for each other as Christians, it's not prudish to remind ourselves that everything that is good can become twisted. Beware the person who only ever hugs the same attractive soul – and that for an extended time – on Sunday mornings!

God calls us away from the snare of lust, not because He is a cosmic killjoy, but because our bodies belong to Him and thus we are to treat them honourably. Paul pointed out that our bodies are part of the Body of Christ and thus, if we sleep with prostitutes, so does Jesus – this shocking analogy should wake us up to the realities of lust.

Prayer: Lord, help me to live a life that reflects Your holiness – in all areas. Amen.

Lust as immaturity

BIG PICTURE:
Judges 16:1–22
Ephesians 4:17–19

FOCUS:
'Having lost all
sensitivity, they have
given themselves over
to sensuality so as to
indulge in every kind
of impurity, with a
continual lust for more.'
(Eph. 4:19)

TONY Campolo tells a story of a middle-aged married man who was trying to chat up an attractive colleague at an office party. There was much giggling and nudging as people watched him desperately trying to prove that he 'still had what it took'. Finally, the young woman, irritated by his attention, gave him truth with both barrels: 'Bill, why don't you just grow up and go home to your wife?'

Lust is immature. It is like play-acting, as we pretend that we're something that we're not. Some have suggested that lust is a denial of death, that we frantically try to retain the charms that we might have had in our youth because we refuse to believe that we're getting older – and heading towards the grave. Lust in married people is childish selfishness; like a toddler who already has a delightful toy but searches for another, we seek another conquest. It is insecurity screaming, as we look for assurance that we're not as unattractive as we feel. Perhaps the mirror is wrong.

The infamous Samson was a baby dressed up as a warrior. This sex addict – who, as Paul says, had 'a continual lust for more', stood no chance against Delilah, the Philistine-planted seductress all undressed to kill. Finally, Delilah's relentless insistence – coupled with her bizarre rope games – wore him down and he revealed the secret of his strength. But as he lost his hair, he lost his identity too, as a flawed man who nonetheless was set apart for God's purposes. Let's be who God has called us to be. And let's grow up.

Prayer: Father, I need to grow up in You. Show me what holds me back. Amen.

Run from lust

BIG PICTURE:
Genesis 39:1–23
2 Timothy 2:22

FOCUS:
'Flee the evil desires
of youth, and pursue
righteousness, faith, love
and peace, along with
those who call on the
Lord out of a pure heart.'
(2 Tim. 2:22)

JOSEPH was quite the hunk, as they say, and his boss's wife had noticed. There was nothing subtle about her come-on, as she pleaded with him to bed her. Many men would have failed where Joseph succeeded, because the Egyptian culture was rife with sexual immorality ('everyone is doing it'), Potiphar's wife wouldn't take no for an answer ('she seduced me') and on the day when she literally grabbed Joseph, the house was empty except for the two of them ('nobody else will know').

So how did Joseph triumph where most men would have tripped? He ran. There was no time for discussion: he knew he had to get out of there, not only because he couldn't trust her but because he refused to trust himself. He refused to break the trust of his employer, who had believed in him: fulfilled lust spits in the face of those who have chosen to believe that we will stay true. Will we disappoint them and shatter their hopes? Joseph was right to sprint.

He shines in marked contrast to Potiphar's wife, whose corrupt behaviour continues even after the failed seduction. She alleges attempted rape, ruins his reputation, gets him fired and has him sent to prison. Joseph would have been just another conquest. Joseph lost his cloak, his job and his freedom – but kept his character intact.

Lust is a persuasive force. It will rationalise, justify itself, plead and scream. Perhaps you're in the furnace of desire and opportunity right now. Think again. Who will weep with disappointment? How many wonderful, priceless relationships will be shattered? Where will it all end? Don't bother to find out. Run like mad.

Think again ...

Run like mad

Prayer: Lord, forgive me when I don't run away from sin. May I do so today. Amen.

STRUGGLING against sin isn't an attractive idea that makes much sense in a 'just do it' world. Giving in, or delaying the day of good moral choices, is more attractive; it was St Augustine who famously prayed, 'Lord, deliver me from lust – but not yet.'

In reality, not only will we need to be decisive about lust, but we must face the fact that the battle will be long and, at times, the struggle will be intense. We are not alone in the battle, as God empowers us by His Spirit, but that does not mean that there won't be some real difficulty along the way. 'I was made that way and I can't help it' is a deception.

Job took lust seriously in his vow to not look with lust at women (Job 31:1). Our choices are important. Paul tells the Colossians to rid themselves of their old habits (Col. 3:8) and 'Put to death … whatever belongs to your earthly nature' – the word here means 'mortify' or 'treat as dead'. To reach a place where we execute something demands daily decisiveness – a vague, respectable Christianity will not do. Let's live shared lives, where others around us know our struggles, have permission to believe the worst of us and to ask the awkward questions.

Let's see through the tarted-up sin that is lust. Lust is an iced cake to a hungry stomach. It looks wonderful, promises much, but one bite reveals the writhing morass of maggots within. Too many fine men and women have messed up their lives as they snacked on a meal that was rotten to the core. Will we join them?

Prayer: Father, may I never use the words 'I can't help it' as an excuse to sin. Amen.

It will be a struggle

BIG PICTURE:
Colossians 3:1–8
Hebrews 12:1–4

FOCUS:
'Put to death, therefore, whatever belongs to your earthly nature: sexual immorality, impurity, lust, evil desires and greed, which is idolatry.'
(Col. 3:5)

James 1:19–21
Proverbs 15:1

Anger

Today I took a long train journey and saw firsthand that our culture is angry. I listened to people snapping at each other on mobile phones. I watched and winced as a few lads ranted, too many empty lager cans on the table before them. It's a familiar sight. Walk around any British city on a Saturday night and you'll see the fearsome unleashing of pent-up anger that too much booze brings, as some hunt for violence just because they enjoy fighting.

But I had the misfortune of sitting next to a toilet that was not working, so the door was locked. As people hammered on the door, I was the deliverer of the bad news to many. Despite the fact that I was not wearing a railway worker's uniform and the lack of facilities had nothing to do with me, one or two more frustrated folks got a little irate with me, the hapless guardian of the loo.

That's the problem with anger: as we'll see tomorrow, anger itself is not wrong – in fact we could do with more of it. It's just that we get upset about the wrong things and at the wrong people.

... our culture
is angry

Weekend

AT FIRST glance, we have a problem. Jesus, the sinless One, was angry. And then Paul exhorts his friends in Colosse to get rid of anger. How come? The Greek words for anger are the same in Mark and Colossians – at times translated 'wrath'. There's no nuance in the words that solve our problem of Jesus exhibiting an attitude that Paul tells Christians to get rid of. How do we solve an apparent riddle?

The answer is surely found in the context of the words. Paul speaks of 'anger, rage, malice, slander and filthy language' – the negative expressions of anger that were never found in Jesus. He was truly the One who was angry but without sin – a reality that is possible for us too – Paul encourages the Ephesians: 'In your anger do not sin' (Eph. 4:26).

Anger that rants, that strikes out, that causes us to spiral out of control – this is the kind of anger that we must rid ourselves of. But we are right to be angry when we hear of children violated, people dying of easily curable diseases around the world, Christian leaders who bruise and abuse people and Christian followers who habitually attack their leaders. Too many Christians are depressed because they are angry, but habitually repress it.

If we're in any doubt about the validity of righteous anger, let's remind ourselves that God, because He loves, is often angry – because anger is the opposite of indifference. What you deeply care about carries the potential to frustrate you. Are you angry? It might be an appropriate anger for a righteous cause, but be careful what you do with that passion.

Prayer: Father, give me the wisdom to see the difference between righteous and unrighteous anger. Amen.

Anger is not always sinful

BIG PICTURE:
Mark 3:1–6
Colossians 3:8

FOCUS:
'[Jesus] looked around at them in anger and, deeply distressed at their stubborn hearts, said to the man, "Stretch out your hand" ...'
(Mark 3:5)

Anger: thoughtless reaction

BIG PICTURE:
John 7:14–24
Psalm 145:8

FOCUS:
'... why are you angry
with me for healing
the whole man on the
Sabbath? Stop judging by
mere appearances, and
make a right judgment.'
(John 7:23–24)

IT'S an amazing but true story. Two brothers serving in the American military exploded a small bomb inside a McDonalds because they were angry over a bad milkshake. They put the bomb on the table and left before it exploded. Thankfully no one was hurt and damage was minor, but the episode proves that, with some people, it doesn't take much to put a light to their blue touch paper.

Anyone who has been around churches knows how true this is. I've seen people enraged because the chairs or pews have been moved (a major cause of contention in many congregations), because the music was a trifle loud or not to their taste or because the version of the Bible used was not their personal choice.

Jesus encouraged His critics to make a 'right judgment'. How many people are languishing in prison cells today, because they snapped and did something they will forever regret? How many churches, friendships and marriages have been destroyed by explosive milkshake madness? A few moments of sanity and reflection could have prevented such unnecessary carnage. My wife insists that I never answer a nasty email immediately – a 24-hour wait is so much better than hasty typing followed by my punching 'Send'.

God is repeatedly described in Scripture as being 'slow to anger'. We'd do well to emulate Him. Are you upset? Think about it.

God is ... 'slow to anger'

Prayer: Father, may I have patience when provoked. Amen.

HAVE you ever met one of those people who aren't happy unless they are unhappy? They are 'quarrelsome' – they relish conflict, thrill at the possibility of making a complaint and relish an outburst with the unseemly joy of a boxer who can hardly wait to pummel his opponent into submission. Such people are a nightmare in any family or community – and especially wreak havoc in church life.

Be careful of these types: they won't easily be placated. When you solve one of their issues, only to have them present a string of other complaints for you to resolve, there's a hint that there might be a deeper problem beneath the presenting issue.

And if you're one of those people who snack on conflict like a delicacy, know that anger, when it's not properly managed, is bad for you. The stress of living just below boiling point will ultimately take its toll on your mental, physical and emotional well-being. As I've quoted before, Frederick Buechner in his book, *Wishful Thinking: A Seeker's ABC*, writes: 'Of the Seven Deadly Sins, anger is possibly the most fun. To lick your wounds, to smack your lips over grievances long past, to roll your tongue over the prospect of bitter confrontations still to come, to savour to the last toothsome morsel both the pain you are given and the pain you are giving back – in many ways it is a feast fit for a king. The chief drawback is that what you are wolfing down is yourself. The skeleton at the feast is you.'

Like a high fat diet, continual rage might taste good – but it might be killing you and those around you.

Prayer: Lord, give me grace to let go all of my cherished resentments. Amen.

Luxurious but toxic anger

BIG PICTURE:
1 Timothy 6:3–5
Proverbs 26:21

FOCUS:
'As charcoal to embers and as wood to fire, so is a quarrelsome man for kindling strife.'
(Prov. 26:21)

Why so angry?

BIG PICTURE:
1 Kings 21:1–29
James 3:3–12

FOCUS:
'Ahab went home, sullen and angry because Naboth the Jezreelite had said, "I will not give you the inheritance of my fathers." He lay on his bed sulking ...'
(1 Kings 21:4)

Our outbursts are just immature screaming ...

HARRY Enfield, the comedian, has created a monstrously angry creature in his character Kevin. This belligerent adolescent screams whenever he doesn't get his own way; his hand forever extended for money, he yells, 'I hate you!' when his long-suffering parents don't instantly cater to his every whim. A disposition like that is difficult in a young adult – it's disastrous in a king.

Ahab, one of the worst rulers of Israel, had almost everything a human being could want: fabulous riches, a beautiful wife and a palace in Samaria that was decadent in the extreme. But he didn't enjoy a scrap of maturity. Whenever he heard something he didn't like (such as a pronunciation of the judgment of God), he would throw himself into a 'strop', get angry and retire to his bedroom to sulk. When the royal juvenile couldn't get his hands on Naboth's field, he was incensed, not only because he couldn't get his own way, but he was probably shamed by Naboth's bravery and his sense of respect for his family heritage.

Sometimes we try to dress our anger up as something noble, when it fact it's not that we are people of passion and principle, but that we feel that our preferences have been ignored. Our outbursts are just immature screaming and we become like petulant, spoiled brats. So what is it that you are so animated about right now? Are you really on a mission from God (and respond to that thoughtfully, because most of us assume that we are reflecting God's opinion!) or is it that things aren't going your way?

Prayer: Father, thank You that You want us to be mature – and are committed to making us so. Amen.

Drawing the lines

BIG PICTURE:
1 Samuel 19:1–6
1 Corinthians 13:4–7

FOCUS:
'Why then would you
do wrong to an innocent
man like David by
killing him for no
reason?' (1 Sam. 19:5)

THE other day I chatted with a lady who is terrified of her husband. She trembles whenever she talks to him, so traumatised is she by his violent, explosive behaviour. So far, he hasn't abused her physically, but as she said, 'His tongue does more damage than any punch.'

As a young pastor, I remember a man in our church who disliked me intensely, and his behaviour became very sinful and destructive. When I preached, he made it as obvious as possible that he despised me; rolling his eyes, sneering at any humour and occasionally even turning his chair to face the wall when I spoke! And when, at the end of the service, I shook his hand at the door, he would inject me with a barbed comment that hurt like a scorpion sting.

One morning, wearied by his overt hatred and stabbed by a nasty comment even as he shook my hand goodbye, I found tears welling up and fought the urge to cry. And then I just decided to let it all out. Standing there, his hand locked in mine, I wept uncontrollably as the confused congregation waited to get out. He watched my grief and immediately apologised: 'I'm so sorry, I didn't know …' He was never unkind again.

You don't have to be on the receiving end of spiritual, verbal or physical abuse. Don't put up with it, or rationalise it. Jonathan challenged his father Saul's irrational rage. Jesus doesn't want you to be a punchbag for some angry person to vent their spleen on. Is that what you have become? Talk to someone you trust. Find help – today.

Prayer: Lord, show me if I am hurting others – and give me grace to challenge those who hurt me. Amen.

Greed

It was one of the most exciting days of my young life. Playing by a bridge near our home, my friend and I peered down into the water at a bag which bulged open – and even from a distance, we could see the glitter of jewellery inside the bag. We had found real treasure! We climbed down into the water, retrieved our priceless haul and rushed home to alert our parents and call the police. Perhaps there would be a reward, or we might even be able to keep our find. How disappointed we were when, a couple of days later, the police told us that our 'crown jewels' were in fact worthless.

There is a T-shirt that boasts: 'He who dies with the most toys wins.' But it's a lie. 'Stuff' can make our lives easier and bring us some fun. But devoting one's life to the accumulation of trinkets is hollow. Have we heeded the biblical warning about the dangers of greed, or have we allowed the advertisers to persuade us that having more equals achieving a better life? How tragic it would be to spend our whole lives in pursuit of what is ultimately just a fake.

... devoting one's life to the accumulation of trinkets is hollow

Weekend

GREED is attractive; so much so, that some Christian leaders have sanctified it rather than warned against its perils. The so-called 'health and wealth' gospel, which teaches that the accumulation of money and possessions is a sign of great faith and God's approval, is a message that is still popular with millions – and no wonder. Undeniably, some of those who teach this message are incredibly generous givers and would argue that they are only seeking to be blessed so that they in turn can be a blessing – so surely it's not so bad after all?

I believe that the 'prosperity gospel' (as it's sometimes called) is actually highly dangerous teaching. For a start, it doesn't work. A recent visit to Ethiopia, where most people are forced to live on a few pence a day – and where I also met some of the most beautiful, faith-filled souls – is testimony to the truth that if 'theology' doesn't work internationally, then it's not worth having. And then this teaching buys into the myth of status – the suggestion that God's smile is expressed by us having a designer brand car. Is God really that superficial – can heaven too be suckered by the myth of image? There's nothing wrong with having a well-engineered, cost-effective car – but the notion that your driving one is a sign of great faith is ludicrous.

Remember the teaching of Jesus that we considered yesterday – that life does not consist in the abundance of possessions? If that is true, why would God reward us with such a hollow prize? Beware the health and wealth fad – it's a deception.

Prayer: Lord, give me a right understanding of Your view of wealth – and faith. Amen.

Sanctifying greed

BIG PICTURE:
1 Thessalonians 2:1–5
Luke 12:15

FOCUS:
'Then he said to them, "Watch out! Be on your guard against all kinds of greed; a man's life does not consist in the abundance of his possessions."'
(Luke 12:15)

Greed and worship

BIG PICTURE:
Luke 16:1–15
Exodus 23:20–33

FOCUS:
'No servant can serve two masters ... he will hate the one and love the other ... You cannot serve both God and Money.' (Luke 16:13)

MONEY should be our servant. But, as Jesus teaches, all too often the servant wants to start a gradual revolution and become our master, pushing God Himself aside. Before we know it, we are effectively worshipping cash. We dream about having more. Our minds are filled with calculations about what we have and what we think we need. We cherish money and fiercely protect our supply of it, refusing to give and leaving generosity to others. Surely there's nothing more unattractive than being around people who so love their money that they are desperate to manipulate all their friends to part with theirs.

But then other serious symptoms of money worship begin to appear in our lives. We work longer hours than is reasonable, desperate to earn more. Our friendships and family suffer: our health deteriorates. We begin to make irresponsible decisions in our 'Buy now, pay later' culture; interest rates compound our indebtedness and before we know it, we're in a hole that we can find no way out of.

Jesus spoke these words to the Pharisees, who were not unlike the health and wealth teachers that I mentioned yesterday, because they equated happiness and holiness with material prosperity. But their piety was a cover-up for greed (Matt. 23:14, see NIV footnote; Titus 1:11).

It's no sin to be wealthy – David and Abraham both were – or to enjoy the benefits of wealth (1 Tim. 6:17). But don't bow your knee, or your heart, to greed. It's a false dead god that won't satisfy, and yet will always demand your fervent homage.

... don't bow your knee ... to greed

Prayer: Lord, help me to value what You value and to be content with what I have. Amen.

I ONCE knew a man who felt that God had told him not to work, because the Lord would just provide for him. I gently pointed out Scripture is rather blunt on the connection between honest labour and food in the stomach. The writer of Proverbs holds up the industrious ant as an example of solid, hard work. I'm sad to report that my friend went bankrupt, and then lost his marriage because of the ensuing financial chaos.

But there is another important side to this story. Greed is an expression of faith and trust – placed in the wrong direction. As we feverishly feather our nests and surround ourselves with 'stuff' that we hope might save us on a day of calamity, we can stray into trying to become the captains of our own souls. The dreadful natural disasters of the last few years have demonstrated well that there are some situations that are just too big for humans to deal with by themselves. Some of our frantic accumulating is actually a misplaced faith that is driven by fear. As we peer nervously into the future, and wish we had prophetic insight about inflation, interest rates, house prices and the weather, our worrying could nudge us towards an ungodly scurrying. In our nervousness, let's affirm that we serve a God who loves us perfectly, and who knows our needs (1 John 4:18).

So let's work hard, buy that insurance policy and take sensible decisions. But let's realise that ultimately, God is our source – and not allow greed to push us into fear.

Prayer: Lord, only You can keep us safe throughout whatever life throws at us. Thank You. Amen.

Misplaced faith

BIG PICTURE:
**2 Thessalonians
3:6–15**
Proverbs 6:6–11

FOCUS:
'If a man will not work,
he shall not eat.'
(2 Thess. 3:10)

Greed and the environment

BIG PICTURE:
Genesis 2:4–15
Psalm 24:1–2

FOCUS:
'The earth is the LORD's, and everything in it, the world, and all who live in it; for he founded it upon the seas and established it upon the waters.'
(Psa. 24:1–2)

Our planet is

being

systematically

destroyed by ...

greed ...

I ONCE lived in a community in Southern Oregon that was almost totally ruined by an extreme environmentalist agenda. It was rumoured that a particular type of owl might have been seen in the nearby forests, which were then deemed totally off-limits to a logging programme that had a very healthy approach to reforestation. Families were destroyed because of that elusive owl. But the sad reality is that we Christians have often surrendered the vital issue of our care for the environment and, in some cases, have left the agenda to people who tend to worship the creation rather than the Creator – so we shouldn't be surprised if extremism results.

Our planet is being systematically destroyed by the greed of our plundering habits, and the need for us to live responsibly is right at the heart of the gospel message. As Christians, we find the beginning of our stories in Genesis 1, where God the Creator entrusted humankind with the heavy responsibility of the stewardship and care of the planet. We don't own the earth but are just temporary tenants. It is vital to recycle, to use water carefully as a precious commodity (just turning off the tap while cleaning your teeth will save a whole swimming pool of water annually), and to find a host of other ways that enable us to live as thoughtful tenants rather than thoughtless consumers.

Greed is self-obsessed and doesn't stop to consider the effects on those from whom we take. Let's play our part in reversing the trend of relentless greed and care for this beautiful earth that God has lent to us for a while.

Prayer: Father, forgive us for our carelessness with Your creation. Amen.

WHEN do we cross over the border between greed and taking appropriate financial responsibility?

Obviously prudent planning, taking time to balance the cheque book and being sure that we are not over-using credit (an epidemic in today's buy-now-pay-later culture) is responsible stewardship – and all of that takes time and thought. One of the greatest problems today is the sad reality that too many of us are careless when it comes to money. Waving a plastic card seems like such a painless activity, but it's not – it's just that the sharp stabbing pain is delayed for 30 days until we open the credit card bill. We could all do with a pause for thought before making that purchase. Creating a budget – and living within it – is vital.

But we can begin to develop a habit where figures and budgets fill our heads more than anything else: where money becomes our waking obsession. Perhaps that's one of the greatest perils of excessive debt – the worry and stress that it creates overshadows our days, and robs us of sleep, joy and the ability to reflect on things that really matter the most.

So let's ask the question – what is utmost in our thoughts? Surely continuous fantasy and daydreaming about accumulation is tantamount to worship, and so edges us into idolatry. It also draws us into a postponed existence (Paul Tournier once said that most people spend their whole lives indefinitely preparing to live) where we are so busy dreaming about what might be, that we fail to enjoy what is. Let's embrace prudence, but reject obsession.

Greed and responsibility

BIG PICTURE:
Matthew 6:25–34
Philippians 4:5–7

FOCUS:
'Do not worry about your life, what you will eat or drink; or about your body, what you will wear.' (Matt. 6:25)

Prayer: Help me to stay in balance about money, Lord, rejecting carelessness, anxiety and greed-fuelled fantasy. Amen.

Gluttony

Oliver Twist famously pleaded, 'Please sir, I want some more.' He was a painfully deprived child in a workhouse. Our 'want more' culture generally is not so deprived, but still we can be fooled into thinking that more is better, as we quite literally eat and drink ourselves to death.

Worldwide, the diet industry is worth multiple billions as we desperately struggle to contain our expanding waistlines and, more importantly, avoid the devastating effects to our health that excess brings. Binge drinking creates a violent threat in most cities as night falls. Gluttony is an old problem – the Israelites insisted on gathering more manna than they needed – with smelly results.

... as we move into Christmas, the danger is more acute ...

Weekend

And, as we move into Christmas, the danger is more acute, as many of us cram our refrigerators with goodies in preparation for the next few days of feasting. And having referred to one Dickensian character, I'm not going to encourage us to emulate another – Ebenezer Scrooge. But let's celebrate without doing violence to our credit cards with unnecessary overspending, and let's eat and drink without creating an agonising hangover headache, or painfully overloading our stomachs with junk. A party today with horrendous results tomorrow is no real fun.

Don't miss the point

BIG PICTURE:
Ecclesiastes 2:1–11
Luke 2:1–20

FOCUS:
'Yet when I surveyed all
that my hands had done
and what I had toiled to
achieve, everything was
meaningless, a chasing
after the wind; nothing
was gained under the
sun.' (Eccl. 2:11)

IT'S here. We've braved the hustle and bustle of the high street shops, we've agonised over our gift selection, the turkey is ready for the roasting and perhaps friends and relatives are gathering. You've just taken two minutes out this morning before the great rush begins. It might be that a double portion of stress is also on the menu today; families gather for seasonal celebrations with high expectations of a perfect day, forgetting that this might be the one time of the year when people who don't normally socialise much are forced together. Or perhaps you are alone this Christmas morning, and this dawn brings a very tangible sense of sadness and loneliness as you remember better days.

Whatever our circumstances, let's not forget what this day is really all about – light coming into our darkness, and God plummeting down from the throne of heaven to the poverty of a borrowed hovel. Christmas reminds us that we are not abandoned and left to our own devices. It glitters, not with the superficial sparkle of fairy lights, but with the authentic wonder that God loves us so intensely that He broke through the barriers of space and time to come to our rescue. And the manner of His coming brings comfort, as angels greet sleep-deprived shepherds on night shift, and as destiny tumbles into the lives of a confused Mary who carried the Saviour, but couldn't find a hotel room to give birth in.

Whatever Christmas gifts you may unwrap – wonderful presents, tired socks that are the wrong colour, or maybe no gift at all, don't miss the opportunity to be grateful for the greatest present of all: Christ, born among us. Without Him, Christmas – and life – really is meaningless.

Prayer: You are the God who comes. You do not wait and watch my helplessness, but You came, as a helpless babe, and became my strong Rescuer. Amen.

Swift to judge

BIG PICTURE:
John 8:1–11
Matthew 18:15

FOCUS:
'The teachers of the law and the Pharisees brought in a woman caught in adultery. They made her stand before the group ...' (John 8:3)

I WAS thinking recently about which sermon, in the thousands I've preached over the years, was my very worst. There are quite a few blundering addresses that could qualify for my all-time worst prize, but perhaps the one that stands out was an early message about how Christians should approach problem areas of their lives. The three stunning points were: (a) Christians sometimes have difficulties (amazing revelation!); (b) when we face difficulties we should pray about them (the only point in the message actually worth making); and (c) if our problems are not immediately shifted by prayer, then we are really not very good Christians. I flush with embarrassment as I recall that Sunday morning.

Tony Campolo says that his most regretted sermon was on the subject of gluttony. Knowing that the Bible clearly warns us against excess, he decided to expose overweight people in the congregation, forgetting the variety of issues that sit behind obesity, and the very real pain that some people who struggle with a weight problem experience. But Tony's main regret was over the way he publicly humiliated some people, because their problem, unlike the person who struggles with lust or pride, is so very obvious.

While overeating is a very real problem that we must be clear about, let's be careful lest, with unkind humour or barbed comments, we shame people and make them 'exhibit A' for our prosecuting attitudes. The religious zealots of Jesus' day lost sight of a woman and made a spectacle of her, for the leering delight of a crowd. Let's run from their horrendous example.

Prayer: Lord, may I never hurt others with thoughtlessness, unkind humour or a heart that rushes to judge. Guard my lips and heart today. Amen.

... let's be careful lest ... we shame people and make them 'exhibit A' for our prosecuting attitudes

Think about it

BIG PICTURE:
1 Corinthians 8:1–13;
10:14–22

FOCUS:
'Therefore, if what I eat
causes my brother to fall
into sin, I will never eat
meat again, so that I will
not cause him to fall.'
(1 Cor. 8:13)

WHAT is a diet? Surely a diet regime is little more than a conscious approach to eating, based on carefully thinking through and planning our intake of food, in order to balance calories, fat and carbohydrates. The problem with most diets (especially the radical so-called 'crash' types) is that we endure them for a while, but then we begin to drift into a less thoughtful approach to the food we consume. The chocolate bar calls us, the fish and chips look and smell so very delicious and we do not so much meander into bad choices, but suspend our decisiveness in order to enjoy the experience. That's why I approach menus and ordering in restaurants with great care – I know that if I can stay focused during that critical two-minute period when I'm making my selection, then I will invariably end up eating something more nourishing and beneficial for my health.

Surely all sin flourishes when we suspend our critical faculties and drift into the temporary madness that overcomes us when we're tempted. If we would just stop and think about the consequences of our actions, we would be less likely to stumble into the folly of sin.

The controversy of food that was offered to idols, dealt with by Paul in his letter written to the church in Corinth, is not an issue that is a contemporary problem for most of us today. But Paul urges a thoughtful approach to eating food that God has provided for our enjoyment, calling us to consider the implications of our eating, as well as savouring the food itself. Let's engage our brain whenever we pick up a knife and fork and open our mouths.

Prayer: Lord, grant me a clear mind and a decisive will to make wise and solid choices in all areas of my life today. Amen.

Glorifying God

BIG PICTURE:
1 Corinthians 10:23–33
Colossians 3:12–17

FOCUS:
'So whether you eat or drink or whatever you do, do it all for the glory of God.' (1 Cor. 10:31)

WHEN it comes to gluttony, or indeed any of the seven deadly sins, one of the reasons that we often trip and fall is because we insist on dividing our lives up into little 'sacred' and 'secular' boxes. God, we think, is interested when we sing hymns or worship songs, teach Sunday school classes and tell others about Christ, but He is at best a passive spectator when we work, laugh and have fun with friends or go out to eat – these being less 'spiritual' activities, which are low on the list of God's priorities.

This absurd notion is similar to the pagan philosophies of Paul's day where it was determined that God was only interested in matters of 'eternal significance'. But Paul makes it clear that God is as interested and entwined in our Monday nights as our Sunday mornings. As we consider the wonder that we can live the whole of life – our eating, drinking, thinking, playing, loving – before Him, all an offering of worship and thanksgiving, so we can see that by the way we approach food and drink we can 'glorify God'.

Glorifying God means putting Him, not my appetites or pangs, first. It means that I am willing to consciously place every single element of my living under His control, and do it well for Him, whether humans notice my choices or not. Ultimately, if we want to get our eating habits sorted, we must reject the lie that we make good choices because we must look better, or become more attractive to others. Primarily, we want to choose well because we have decided to be disciples of Christ, and we live for an audience of One.

... God is as interested ... in our Monday nights as our Sunday mornings

Prayer: Lord, look at me as I live today, and may I be aware of Your gracious, caring gaze. Amen.

It's my body

BIG PICTURE:
1 Corinthians
3:16–23; 6:12–20

FOCUS:
'You are not your own;
you were bought at a
price. Therefore honour
God with your body.'
(1 Cor. 6:19–20)

OCCASIONALLY I've had the misfortune of lending precious, valuable items to friends – homes, cars, books – only to find that, if I am fortunate enough to get them back, they have been treated without care and are very much the worse for wear. It's disappointing. The item itself doesn't matter much; *things* can be replaced. But the borrowers' lack of concern shows me that our relationship is not as important to them as I had hoped. Treat another's stuff carelessly, and you probably don't care much about the one who owns it.

I recently watched a harrowing television programme which featured a horrendously overweight man who was so morbidly obese, he was unable to get out of bed, and had been confined to his bedroom for many years. Unable to lie flat (which would have killed him), his massive bulk took up the whole of a double bed. Doctors warned him that he was just days from death, but still he insisted on eating an endless supply of chocolate and other unhealthy foods, which tasted sweet but were acting like poison to his system. His wife helped him, smuggling a stash of 'treats' into his hospital ward. It was a sorry sight, and, as predicted, within days he was dead. But his insistence to the end was simple. It's my body. I'll do what I want with it.

As Christians, we remember that our bodies are not our property at all. Like the planet where we dwell, which is only lent to us temporarily by the Creator, so our bodies are owned by God, and we should therefore treat them with respect. What we think is so personally ours is only on loan.

Prayer: Lord, all that I have, and all that I am, is Yours. Help me to remember that, and treat well what You have lent to me. Amen.

Resolve and resolutions

James 1:19–27
John 14:15–21

Our consideration of the deadly seven is at an end. Like me, did you discover that that there were some sins in your life that you hadn't noticed? And now a bright new year stretches ahead of us. Perhaps you resist the habit of making New Year's resolutions, nervous that they will not last beyond a day or two. But as we pause with a new horizon ahead of us, why not take some moments and review the journey that we've been sharing these last couple of months. How tragic it would be to have seen some uncomfortable truths about ourselves, only to walk away and shrug off that disturbing vision, forgetting what we have learned. True worship is not just something we sing, or pious prayers carefully woven together, but a life of loving obedience.

> True worship is … a life of loving obedience

And while we're at it, why don't we ask the Lord to make this coming year a season of real growth and effectiveness for our lives and churches, a year when the way that we live becomes like a lighthouse for many others who still need to find their way home to God?

Weekend

Day and Residential Courses
Counselling Training
Leadership Development
Biblical Study Courses
Regional Seminars
Ministry to Women
Daily Devotionals
Books and Videos
Conference Centre

Trusted all Over the World

CWR HAS GAINED A WORLDWIDE reputation as a centre of excellence for Bible-based training and resources. From our headquarters at Waverley Abbey House, Farnham, England, we have been serving God's people for over 40 years with a vision to help apply God's Word to everyday life and relationships. The daily devotional *Every Day with Jesus* is read by nearly a million readers an issue in more than 150 countries, and our unique courses in biblical studies and pastoral care are respected all over the world. Waverley Abbey House provides a conference centre in a tranquil setting.

For free brochures on our seminars and courses, conference facilities, or a catalogue of CWR resources, please contact us at the following address:
CWR, Waverley Abbey House, Waverley Lane, Farnham, Surrey GU9 8EP, UK

Telephone: +44 (0)1252 784700
Email: mail@cwr.org.uk
Website: www.cwr.org.uk

CWR Applying God's Word
to everyday life and relationships

Wise words for a wild world

Lucas on Life Every Day brings you challenging Bible-application notes by Spring Harvest speaker and well-known author, Jeff Lucas.

Published bimonthly, these probing and encouraging notes will help you apply the Bible to your life every day with Jeff's distinctive blend of passion, humour and insight.

ISSN: 1744-0122
£2.49 each (plus p&p)
£13.80 UK annual subscription (six issues)

To see our complete range of Jeff Lucas DVDs, Bible-reading notes and books, visit www.cwr.org.uk/lucas